MASTERING MANDARIN
YOUR PATH TO PROFICIENCY

ALLEN S.C. CHOI

Copyright © 2023 by Allen S.C. Choi

All rights reserved.

No portion of this book may be reproduced in any form without written permission from the publisher or author, except as permitted by U.S. copyright law.

Published by PicoBlu LLC
848 N. Rainbow Blvd. #3519
Las Vegas, NV 89107
www.picoblu.com

ISBN: 979-8-9902139-0-6

PREFACE

The system presented in this book was developed to assist English speaking people to learn Chinese. It was designed to be user friendly and efficient, while interesting and easy to follow. It is also business oriented.

Unique Features of this book include:

- **A Modular System:** 300 characters in 20 modules
- **Block-Building Method:** To build vocabulary, 1 block of characters at a time
- **Cultural Context:** A comprehensive understanding of the Chinese Language through 500 bilingual sample sentences with contextual explanations.

    Includes:

    Characters; vocabulary and expressions

    Idioms, sentences and composition

    Chinese and English

    Character writing and phonetics

    Concept of Tones and Mandarin Romanized Chinese

    Radicals and Chinese character structure

    Traditional and Simplified Chinese characters

    Grammar and sentence structure comparison

    Mandarin, dialects & Minority languages

    Chinese computer typing and word processing

Content and Methodology designed to benefit a broad base of readers:

- For **corporate training** in Chinese language as a short course (50-hours)
- For **college students** as a textbook or as a supplementary study
- For **teachers** and **instructors** who would love to have a handy reference
- For **self-taught** learners seeking foundational understanding

Learning Chinese can be made easy

READER'S GUIDE

(1) This book is arranged in a Modular System:

Learn 300 Chinese characters in 20 modules. By using a block building technique, every sub-module of five (5) new characters is reviewed and practiced with all the characters learned in the previous modules. The most efficient way to use this book is to follow the sequential order of these modules. Focus on the characters: read and write until you recognize them.

(2) It is highly recommended to refer to PART 1 Section 7 when completing learning modules:

Use the "Latin Alphabet Phonetic Transcription of Chinese Characters" to get an idea of pronunciation. To pronounce correctly and read aloud smoothly, it is very helpful to have an instructor or partner to speak with. Today there are many software programs for typing and speaking Chinese. One commonly used input method is the Romanized phonetic transcription, which is provided in this book. This book is intended to provide a foundational knowledge, and background of the Chinese Language.

(3) Refer to the sample sentences and practice as much as you can.

PART 1: Chinese Language background knowledge
presented in summary

PART 2: Modules and Lessons
More than 1,000 words and phrases
More than 500 bilingual sample sentences
Plenty of resources for exercise

PART 3: Vocabulary and Expressions
1,800+ in vocabulary
300+ idioms and expressions
More resources for practice

Chinese Language Foundation: background knowledge presented in summary.

TABLE OF CONTENTS

PREFACE	iii
READER'S GUIDE	iv
TABLE OF CONTENTS	v

PART. 1 — BACKGROUND KNOWLEDGE OF THE CHINESE LANGUAGE

1. Spoken Language; Mandarin / Dialects — 2
2. Written Language; Vernacular Style / Classical Style — 5
3. Radicals -- Structure of Chinese Characters — 8
4. Traditional Characters and Simplified Characters — 18
5. Names in Chinese Language — 14
6. Languages of Chinese Minority — 17
7. Phonetics: Latin Alphabet in Phonetic Transcription of Chinese Characters; The Concept of Tones — 18
8. Computer Chinese Typing and Word Processing — 26

PART. 2 — THE MODULES:

Module 1	- Part 1 : First Group of Five (5) New Characters.	30
	- Part 2 : Second Group of Five (5) New Characters.	33
	- Part 3 : Third Group of Five (5) New Characters.	37
Module 2	- Part 1 : First Group of Five (5) New Characters.	40
	- Part 2 : Second Group of Five (5) New Characters.	42
	- Part 3 : Third Group of Five (5) New Characters.	44
Module 3	- Part 1 : First Group of Five (5) New Characters.	46
	- Part 2 : Second Group of Five (5) New Characters.	49
	- Part 3 : Third Group of Five (5) New Characters.	51
Module 4	- Part 1 : First Group of Five (5) New Characters.	53
	- Part 2 : Second Group of Five (5) New Characters.	56
	- Part 3 : Third Group of Five (5) New Characters.	58
Module 5	- Part 1 : First Group of Five (5) New Characters.	61
	- Part 2 : Second Group of Five (5) New Characters.	65
	- Part 3 : Third Group of Five (5) New Characters.	69
Module 6	- Part 1 : First Group of Five (5) New Characters.	72
	- Part 2 : Second Group of Five (5) New Characters.	75
	- Part 3 : Third Group of Five (5) New Characters.	80

TABLE OF CONTENTS

Module 7 - Part 1 : First Group of Five (5) New Characters. 85
          - Part 2 : Second Group of Five (5) New Characters. 89
          - Part 3 : Third Group of Five (5) New Characters. 92
Module 8 - Part 1 : First Group of Five (5) New Characters. 98
          - Part 2 : Second Group of Five (5) New Characters. 101
          - Part 3 : Third Group of Five (5) New Characters. 104
Module 9 - Part 1 : First Group of Five (5) New Characters. 107
          - Part 2 : Second Group of Five (5) New Characters. 111
          - Part 3 : Third Group of Five (5) New Characters. 115
Module 10 - Part 1 : First Group of Five (5) New Characters. 120
          - Part 2 : Second Group of Five (5) New Characters. 124
          - Part 3 : Third Group of Five (5) New Characters. 127
Module 11 - Part 1 : First Group of Five (5) New Characters. 130
          - Part 2 : Second Group of Five (5) New Characters. 135
          - Part 3 : Third Group of Five (5) New Characters. 140
Module 12 - Part 1 : First Group of Five (5) New Characters. 144
          - Part 2 : Second Group of Five (5) New Characters. 148
          - Part 3 : Third Group of Five (5) New Characters. 153
Module 13 - Part 1 : First Group of Five (5) New Characters. 158
          - Part 2 : Second Group of Five (5) New Characters. 162
          - Part 3 : Third Group of Five (5) New Characters. 166
Module 14 - Part 1 : First Group of Five (5) New Characters. 170
          - Part 2 : Second Group of Five (5) New Characters. 175
          - Part 3 : Third Group of Five (5) New Characters. 179
Module 15 - Part 1 : First Group of Five (5) New Characters. 182
          - Part 2 : Second Group of Five (5) New Characters. 186
          - Part 3 : Third Group of Five (5) New Characters. 189
Module 16 - Part 1 : First Group of Five (5) New Characters. 194
          - Part 2 : Second Group of Five (5) New Characters. 196
          - Part 3 : Third Group of Five (5) New Characters. 203
Module 17 - Part 1 : First Group of Five (5) New Characters. 209
          - Part 2 : Second Group of Five (5) New Characters. 212
          - Part 3 : Third Group of Five (5) New Characters. 215

TABLE OF CONTENTS

Module 18 - Part 1 : First Group of Five (5) New Characters.	220
- Part 2 : Second Group of Five (5) New Characters.	224
- Part 3 : Third Group of Five (5) New Characters.	228
Module 19 - Part 1 : First Group of Five (5) New Characters.	232
- Part 2 : Second Group of Five (5) New Characters.	235
- Part 3 : Third Group of Five (5) New Characters.	238
Module 20- Part 1 : First Group of Five (5) New Characters.	242
- Part 2 : Second Group of Five (5) New Characters.	246
- Part 3 : Third Group of Five (5) New Characters.	249

PART 3. VOCABULARY AND EXPRESSIONS

- Vocabulary: 1800+   254
- Idioms and Common Expressions: 300+.

APPENDICES:

A. Table of 300 Characters: Traditional Print	378
B. Table of 300 Characters: Simplified Print	379
C. Table of 84 Characters: Traditional vs. Simplified	381

ABOUT THE AUTHOR   383

INDEX:

300 Chinese Characters in Alphabetical Order   387

PART 1
BACKGROUND KNOWLEDGE OF THE CHINESE LANGUAGE

1. Spoken Language: Mandarin
   Dialects
2. Written Language: Vernacular Style
   Classical Style
3. Radicals: Structure of Chinese Characters
4. Traditional & Simplified Chinese Characters
5. Names in Chinese Language
6. Languages of Chinese Minority
7. Phonetics:
   A. Latin Alphabet in Phonetic Transcription of Chinese Characters;
   B. The Concept of Tones of Characters
8. Computer Chinese Typing and Word Processing
   A. Input Method
   B. Input Based on Romanized Chinese
   C. Chinese Character Codes
   D. Computer Windows Environment

1. SPOKEN CHINESE LANGUAGE

MANDARIN is the official spoken Chinese in China mainland and Taiwan and is recognized by the United Nations. In Chinese language, Mandarin is known by two different names:

| 普通話 | PU₃ TONG₁ HUA₄ | Common Speech |
| 國語 | GUO₂ YU₃ | National Speech |

Mandarin is based on the spoken language in Beijing. The vast area north of Beijing, Northeast China, basically speak Mandarin. There are dialects within that area but people can communicate without difficulty.

There are many other different dialects in the rest of China. They are so different from one another that people cannot communicate with each other. The further to the south of China, the more diversified it is in speech. The major cities such as Shanghai, Guangzhou (formerly Canton), Wuhan, Kunming and many others, all have their own dialect(s). Examples:

他們 (they) / 不是 (no) / 哪裡? (where?)

In reading the characters, different dialects are
close in sound (phonetics):

Mandarin:	TA MEN	/ BU SHI	/ NA LI?
Cantonese:	TA MOON	/ BUD XI	/ NA LUI?
Chiuchow:	TA MOONG	/ BOOK XI	/ NA LI?
Hakka:	TA MOON	/ BOO SI	/ NA LI?

However, in speech, in daily speaking, they are very different except Mandarin:

Mandarin:	TA MEN	/ BU SHI	/ NA LI?
Cantonese:	KUI DEI	/ NGUM HAI	/ BIN DOE?
Chiuchow:	EE NUNG	/ NGUM XI	/ DI GOR?
Hakka:	GEE DENG YIN	/ NGUM HEI	/ NGAI DI?

(There is no appropriate spelling per Pinyin for the 3 dialects, English equivalent is used. NGUM is a nasal sound. G in GEE is a hard G.)

Just the names of the dialects, when expressed in English, can cause confusion.

Cantonese (廣州話) — The name is based on the city name Canton in the 19th Century named by early Westerners to China.

Diejiu (潮州話) — Based on the sound in that dialect (first 2 characters).

Chiuchow — Based on the sound in Cantonese.

Chaozhou — Based on the sound in Mandarin.

Karkah (客家話) — Based on that dialect.

Hakka —— Based on Cantonese.

Kejia —— Based on Mandarin.

Since Cantonese is the Chinese speech known to early foreigners (Westerners), in some dictionaries Hakka and Chiuchow are the names used. However, in Southeast Asia, the name Diejiu is known instead. Cantonese is spoken in Guangzhou (Canton), Hong Kong and Singapore. Diejiu or Chiuchow is spoken in Thailand, Cambodia and Vietnam among communities of Chinese descent. It is also spoken in Malaysia. Karkah or Hakka is spoken in Indonesian communities of Chinese descent.

Cantonese, Diejiu and Karkah are the three major dialects within one province, namely, Guangdong Province, Southern China. There are other dialects within Guangdong Province, such as Toisan (台山) (Per Mandarin, it is TAI$_2$SHAN$_1$), spoken by early Chinese immigrants to the U.S., close to Cantonese but is in fact a different dialect.

Mandarin as a mother tongue accounts for about 20% of the entire population in China. Since 1950, Mandarin has become mandatory from elementary school education all over China. Therefore, to the majority of the Chinese population, Mandarin is, as a matter of fact, their second spoken language, not native tongue.

There are variations in Chinese expressions, too.

今天 = 今日   謝謝 = 多謝   多少件? = 幾件?
(today)   (thank you)   (How many pieces?)

The first expression tends to be northern style while the second one being southern. People can understand without difficulty.

Another example:

你到哪裡去? = 你上哪兒? = 你去哪裡?
(Where are you going? / Where do you go?)

The first expression is standard Mandarin while the second (NI$_3$ SHANG$_4$ NA$_3$ ER$_1$) is Mandarin dialect, spoken in Beijing in particular and the third one is southern expression.

Beijing Mandarin is considered the standard Mandarin as London English is the King's English. However, Beijing has a lot of its own dialectal expressions. The focus of this book is on Mandarin and written Chinese in general usage as a foundation. Dialects and dialectal expressions are often mentioned for awareness in real life encounter.

2. WRITTEN CHINESE LANGUAGE:

Chinese Characters:

Written Chinese is universal all over China and other parts of the world where Chinese language is written. There are variations in expressions, but people can understand without difficulty. There are special characters created for a certain dialect; these are, however, not in general use. This book is based on general expressions in Chinese: some expression variations are explained to help under- stand the language in real life encounter.

Chinese written language has a long history of more than four thousand years with record. In terms of number of characters, a dictionary can contain more than six thousand with vocabulary over fifty thousand entries. A pocket dictionary for students contains four thousand characters. For daily use, if you master two thousand commonly used characters and know how to use them, you can get around with Chinese people pretty well. This book contains only three hundred characters. However, if you put in your effort, you can build a very solid foundation for your further studies.

Chinese Writing Styles:

Traditionally there are two writing styles of written Chinese language:

白話文   BAI$_2$ HUA$_4$ WEN$_2$ Vernacular Style
          Primarily practiced nowadays; and

文言文   WEN$_2$ YAN$_2$ WEN$_2$ Classical Style
          Primarily practiced in the old days, and academic studies today.

The *Vernacular Style* reflects in words what people actually speak so that people can understand with minimum knowledge of the written words. It has a history of less than a century: practiced in the twentieth Century.

The *Classical Style* was the major writing style before the use of Vernacular Style. In ancient days, the writing was so concise that even today only scholars can really understand and interpret correctly in vernacular expression.

The Vernacular Style is lengthy in writing as compared to the Classical Style, which is always very concise. However, due to the long tradition and history of the Chinese language, the influence of Classical Style writing still exists. Many people in business writing and other applications today still prefer to write in concise expressions close to the Classical Style writing. The large resource of idioms is another example. People like to use classical idioms because a short phrase can express in a concise and precise way. The use of idioms also reflects the language skill as well as education of the person who uses them.

The following example can demonstrate the mighty power of idioms.

Idiom:

    習非成是   XI$_2$ FEI$_1$ CHENG$_2$ SHI$_4$

    Accepting what is wrong as right as people get accustomed to it.

Vernacular Expression:

    習慣了,把錯的也當成是對的。

    XI$_2$ GUAN$_4$ LE, BA$_3$ CUO$_4$ DE YE$_3$ DANG$_4$ CHENG$_2$ SHI$_4$ DUI$_4$ DE.

The four characters of the idiom can express the meaning of the 12 characters in the Vernacular Style writing. This shows how mighty and lively an idiom can be. There is nothing wrong at all with writing in Vernacular Style. However, when an idiom is used appropriately, people would certainly be impressed when they read or hear it, especially when it is written or spoken by a person whose Chinese is his/her foreign language.

Some other examples of idioms:

Idiom:

    自以為是   ZI$_4$ YI$_3$ WEI$_2$ SHI$_4$

    Consider oneself always correct.

Vernacular Expression:

    自己以為自己一定是對的。

    ZI$_4$ JI$_3$ YI$_3$ WEI$_2$ ZI$_4$ JI$_3$ YI$_1$ DING$_4$ SHI$_4$ DUI$_4$ DE.

Idiom:

視而不見　　SHI₄ ER₂ BU₄ JIAN₄

Look but see not. (Turn a blind eye to.)

Vernacular Expression:

看到了也不管，當作看不見。

KAN₄ DAO₄ LE YE₃ BU₄ GUAN₃, DANG₄ ZUO₄ KAN₄ BU₄ JIAN₄.

Chinese Writing/Printing Pattern:

Historically Chinese was written from top down in a vertical line and then line by line from right to left. Nowadays most people write from left to right horizontally and then line by line from top down, similar to writing English. Books are also printed this way. Some newspapers are printed in different patterns: vertical and horizontal lines both exist; and for horizontal lines, from left to right and from top down.

3. RADICALS – THE STRUCTURE OF CHINESE CHARACTERS

Similar to the root, prefix and suffix in English words, there are parts of a Chinese character, known as Radicals, in composing a character. There are 4 categories of Radicals in Chinese characters;

Left Radical:	Attaches to the left of a root;
Right Radical;	Attaches to the right of a root;
Top Radical:	Attaches to the top of a root;
Bottom Radical:	Attaches to the bottom of a root.

There are two rules of thumb in understanding the radicals:

(1) In terms of frequency of occurrence, they are in this descending order:

Left —> Right —> Top —> Bottom

(2) If there are two or more radicals in one character, look for the major one: the one that occupies the left, the right, the top or the bottom portion of the entire character within the rectangular block.

Let's examine some examples from the 300 characters to be learned.

Left Radical: The characters in each of the following groups have the common left radical;

L1. 作 做 你 他 們 便 使 個 候 信 件 但 傳 假

The above left radical is derived from the character 人 REN$_2$ (person), This left radical is known as *Standing-Person Radical* in Chinese.

L2. 很 行 後 得 從

The above left radical is derived from the character 人 (person) and in Chinese it is known as Double-Standing-Person Radical.

L3. 提 投 搞 把 握 打 拼

The above left radical is derived from the character 手 SHOU$_3$ (hand) but modified to express that it is often related to the hand in actions or objects. It is known as *Hand-Tick Radical*.

L4. 請 說 謝 記 該 談 話 講 語 謂 誤

The above left radical is derived from the character 言 YAN$_2$ (speech) which conveys the meaning of words or actions related to speech. It is known as *Speech Radical*.

L5. 慣 懂 快 情 怕 忙

The above left radical is derived from the character 心 XIN₁ (heart) and modified and in Chinese it is known as *Standing-Heart Radical*.

L6. 沒 清 況 決 注

The above left radical symbolizes three drops of water and is known as *Three-Water-Drop Radical*.

L7. 錯 錢

The above left radical is derived from the character 金 JIN₁ (gold) and is known as Character Gold Radical. It is often used to mean anything related to metal. The character 錯 means wrong or error; but it is also used to mean 'filing'. The character 錢 QIAN₂ (money) has a Character Gold Radical because in ancient days copper coins were used as money in circulation.

Right Radical: The characters in each of the

following groups have the common right radical:

R1. 那 哪 都 (除: same radical used on left)

The above right radical can also be used as a left radical as the character in parenthesis. It is known as *Cattle-Ear Radical*.

R2. 到 利 則 別

The above Right Radical is derived from the Character 刀 DAO₁ (knife) but modified and is known as *Knife Radical*.

Top Radical: The characters on each of the

following groups have the common top radical.

T1. 常 當 光

The above top radical is known as *Three-dot-Head Radical*.

T2. 等 管

The above top radical is derived from the character 竹 ZHU₂ (bamboo) and is known as Bamboo Head Radical.

Bottom Radical: The characters in each of the following groups have the common bottom radical.

Radicals -- Structure of Chinese Characters

B1. 還 過 邊 遲 途

The above bottom radical is known as Boating Radical. It symbolizes on board a boat in water.

B2. 您 想 意 思

The above bottom radical is the character 心 XIN (heart) and is known as Heart Bottom Radical.

B3. 然 無

The above bottom radical is known as Four Dot Radical and is also used to represent the four legs of some animals.

More About Radicals:

More examples about radicals are explained below.
Some radicals are used on more than one side.
Example:

(L) 明 時 晚   (R) 旭   (T) 是 早   (B) 音 者

The character 日 RI$_4$ (*sun, day*) is a radical in the above characters. It is used as a radical on the left, right, top and bottom. The character 旭 XU$_4$ (bright) is not included in the 300 characters learned and is listed here to demonstrate the use of the radical only.

Examine this particular character as an example:

得 DE$_2$ obtain; get

The character 得 DE$_2$ has 2 radicals: a left radical (*double-standing-person radical*) and a top radical of the character 日 RI$_4$ (sun; day). Notice the left radical occupies the entire left side of the character while the character 日 is a top radical of the right hand side portion only. Thus the left radical is the major radical and is the radical used in finding the character in a dictionary.

Some radicals are characters by themselves. Above 日 is one example.

Examine the following characters:

學 XUE$_2$ 覺 JUE$_2$

Mastering Mandarin: Your Path to Proficiency

The top portion is the same in both characters but is not used as a radical for looking up the character. In looking up the dictionary, you can find the character easier by using the bottom portion as radical. There are 13 strokes in the top portion while there are only 3 strokes in 子 ZI3 (son) and 6 strokes in 見 JIAN4 (see) in the bottom portion of the characters.

The Use of Radicals:

Radicals are commonly used in Chinese dictionaries for sorting characters into different categories. Characters without radicals are categorized by type of the first stroke such as Dot, Horizontal, Vertical, Slanting (to the left or to the right) and Turn and Hook. Today's dictionaries usually provide different ways to find a character, predominantly 3 (1,2,3; 1,2,4) of the following:

1. By Radicals and Strokes. Radicals are arranged in a certain sequential order;
2. By the total number of strokes of the character in question.
3. By PINYIN (拼音). It is also known as Romanized Chinese (or Latinized Chinese) Phonetic Transcription;
4. By ZHUYIN (注音). It is a special set of symbols for phonetic notation. It is also known as the BO-PO-MO-FO System where O is pronounced like the o in 'or';

Radicals are very helpful in mastering Chinese characters as prefix and suffix are in learning English words. For instance:

明 --- 日 + 月
音 --- 立 + 日
意 --- 立 + 日 + 心 [曰 YUE1 say (classical)]
想 --- 相 + 心 [相 --- 木 MU4 wood + 目 MU4 eye]

Some radicals are characters themselves and are meaningful. There are special radicals for metals, chemicals, animals, plants and others.

4. TRADITIONAL CHARACTERS and SIMPLIFIED CHINESE CHARACTERS

"Keep it simple" has been practiced in language since ancient days. The word "sulphur" is written as "sulfer" is one example in English language used in America: and also "ad" for advertisement.

In an effort to expedite the process of eliminating illiteracy, two significant changes have been accomplished in China in the past decades (since 1950):

- *The use of Latin Alphabet for phonetic transcription based on Mandarin; and*
- *The simplification of some Chinese characters*

The accomplishment of the above is significant and the impact is long lasting. The process of learning how to read and write Chinese is expedited and, in addition, people get to learn to speak Mandarin.

Let us look at some examples:

(Left: traditional character; Right: simplified)

學　学

(16 strokes on the left and 8 strokes on the right)

(The top: 13 strokes simplified to 5.)

覺　觉

(19 strokes simplified to 9.)

(The simplified top is in existence: 当, 常..)

萬　万

(12 strokes reduced to 3. The simplified character is derived from an ancient writing style.)

辦　办

(16 strokes reduced to 4. Notice the left and right radicals are identical; 7 strokes each reduced to one each and the root word is enlarged to balance the look of the simplified character so that it looks nice.)

邊　边

(The character is simplified from 18 strokes to 4.)

Today, simplified characters and Latinized phonetic notation are adopted in China and South East Asia such as Malaysia and Singapore and are recognized by the United Nations.

Some individuals might have their own way of simplifying a character. In English some people tend to write 'doughnut' as 'donut', which is, however, not official. There is an official list of simplified characters in China based on official rules in simplifying characters set by a national commission in the central government.

5. NAMES IN CHINESE LANGUAGE:

(1) Chinese personal names when expressed in English can be pretty confusing: A Chinese name typically consists of three characters: the first one is the surname and the two characters that follow make up the given name. There is NO middle name in Chinese names.
- Some base on Mandarin and others base on their dialect;
- Even if it is based on Mandarin, some may use Latinized Chinese spelling while others use different phonetic systems;

Some stick with the Chinese tradition with the surname (family name) first followed by the given name. Others follow the American way with the surname last;
- Some spell the name of two characters in two words, some add a hyphen in between, and some spell it as one word with two syllables.
- In the U.S. a name of two characters is often incorrectly treated as the first character the name and the second as the middle name. This causes more confusion.
- There are a few surnames with two characters: and there are some people who choose one character for the name regardless of whether the surname is one character or two.

As an example, a very common Chinese surname 陳 can have different spellings such as:

Chen (Mandarin)   /   *Chan* (Cantonese)

Tan (Diejiu, Singapore)   /   *Chin* (Karkah)

Tran (Chinese from Vietnam)

(2) English personal names: In order to make it easy for the Chinese to address the name, it is not unusual to "simplify" the full name and make it easier to call and look more like a Chinese name even though it may exceed three characters. Each character is carefully chosen from the many characters of close sound so that it carries a good meaning and makes a good name whenever appropriate.

(3) Geographical names

    北京 BEI$_3$ JING$_1$ *Beijing* (Latinized Chinese)
                                    Peking (Based on a dialect)

    廣州 GUANG$_3$ ZHOU$_1$ *Guangzhou* (Latinized Chinese)
                                      Canton (Foreign name)

    廣東 GUANG$_3$ DONG$_1$ Guangdong (Latinized Chinese)
                                      Kwangtung (Other phonetics)

All geographical names in China are now expressed in Latinized Chinese: maps, street signs, etc. A name of two characters is often written as one word of two syllables, as in above examples. Sometimes it causes confusion. For instance:

西安 XI$_1$ AN$_1$ *Xian* (same as 先 XIAN$_1$, 現 XIAN$_4$)

To avoid confusion, Xi-an with a hyphen in between is more reasonable and is recommended here. Some Chinese dictionaries print it as Xi'an.

On the other hand, geographical names in English when translated into Chinese are simplified in some instances or based on historical translation:

U.S.A.   美利堅合眾國 MEI$_3$ LI$_4$ JIAN$_1$ HE$_2$ ZHONG$_4$ GUO$_2$
           一〉美國 MEI$_3$ GUO$_2$

Canada 加拿大 JIA$_1$ NA$_2$ DA$_4$ (加 is pronounced GA$_1$ based on Cantonese)

(4) Brand Names; Each Chinese character has a meaning or a variety of meanings depending on the matching with another character. Pretty often there are many characters with the same sound. Thus, this feature is particularly important in choosing the characters for names: make the name mean something good whenever possible.

A classic example is the brand name COCA COLA. Decades ago, the early translated name in Chinese was:

                可啃可蠟 KE$_3$ KEN$_3$ KE$_3$ LA$_4$

Literally it carries the meaning of 'chewing wax'. Obviously, this does not sound appealing for a soft drink. The Chinese brand name for COCA COLA was later changed to the following name and it has been used until now; and, presumably, will last forever:

可口可樂　KE³ KOU³ KE³ LE⁴

Literally it means Tasty and Happy. Isn't that significant to the brand name of a soft drink?

Notice that phonetically the new translated name is "KE LE" for the second word COLA, not so close but it carries a good meaning.

Therefore, name translation into Chinese, brand names in particular, really requires painstaking effort. A good translated brand name can help sales tremendously.

6. LANGUAGES OF CHINESE MINORITY

There are different nationalities in China, more than 50. The above explained written Chinese and speech Mandarin represent the official language of the entire China. In terms of nationality, this official language belongs to the language of the predominant nationality known as Han (漢 HAN$_4$). Han nationality (漢族 HAN$_4$ZU$_2$) is about 94% of the entire Chinese population. In domestic education in China, the language course CHINESE is called 漢語 HAN$_4$YU$_3$ instead of 中文 (ZHONG$_1$WEN$_2$) and thus the Latinized phonetic transcription is known as:

漢語拼音 HAN$_4$ YU$_3$ PIN$_1$ YIN$_1$. / 汉语拼音 (Simplified)

A Chinese-English Dictionary is often called:

漢英字典 HAN$_4$ YING$_1$ ZI$_4$ DIAN$_3$ / 汉英字典

An English-Chinese Dictionary is often known as:

英漢字典 YING$_1$ HAN$_4$ ZI$_4$ DIAN$_3$ / 英汉字典

The above mentioned dialects also belong to Han. Other than Han, some of the other nationalities have their own language(s) and culture. The major minority nationalities include:

滿族	MAN$_3$ ZU$_2$: Man nationality (Manchu);
蒙古族	MENG$_2$GU$_3$ZU$_2$: Meng Gu nationality (Mongolian);
回族	HUI$_2$ZU$_2$: Hui nationality;
藏族	ZANG$_4$ZU$_2$: Zang nationality (Tibetan);
苗族	MIAO$_2$ZU$_2$: Miao nationality;
瑤族	YAO$_2$ZU$_2$: Yao nationality;
壯族	ZHUANG$_4$ZU$_2$: Zhuang (Chuang) nationality; and
維吾爾族	WEI$_2$WU$_2$ER$_3$ZU$_2$: Uygur (Uigur) nationality.

7. PHONETICS:

A. LATIN ALPHABET IN PHONETIC TRANSCRIPTION OF CHINESE CHARACTERS

As mentioned in Section 4 of PART 1, this system, known as Romanized or Latinized Chinese, is based on Mandarin and was developed in the 1950s.

This section of phonetics is presented for readers' convenience. It is presented with one principle in mind: Keep it simple for all practical purposes. It provides basic guidelines. For detailed phonetics, please refer to other books and materials.

The ALPHABET:

The 26 letters from A to Z are used in Chinese with the exception of V which is only used for foreign words. The three letters of I, U and V are not applicable as the first letter of a word.

The VOWELS:

a:	as the *a* in 'father'	e.g.	他 TA	(he, him)
			八 BA	(eight)
			打 DA	(hit)
e:	as the *e* in 'her'	e.g.	二 ER	(two)
			和 HE	(and)
			客 KE	(guest)
	as the *e* in 'ten' (when following x)	e.g.	也 YE	(also)
			學 XUE	(learn)
			謝 XIE	(thank)
en:	as the *e* in 'often', 'siren', 'hidden'	e.g.	很 HEN	(very)
			甚 SHEN	(very)
			怎 ZEN	(why)
i:	as the *i* in 'tennis'.	e.g.	你 NI	(you)
			西 XI	(west)
			七 QI	(seven)
			必 BI	(must)

as the *y* in '*syringe*'	e.g.	資 ZI	(capital)
		次 CI	(time)
		思 SI	(think)
		日 RI	(day)
		知 ZHI	(know)
		遲 CHI	late)
		是 SHI	(is)
o: as the *o* in '*often*'	e.g.	握 WO	(grasp)
u: as the *u* in '*tuna*'	e.g.	途 TU	(trip)
as the *ü* in German with two dots on top	e.g.	女 NÜ	(female)
ai: as the *i* in '*tie*'	e.g.	太 TAI	(excessive)
ao: as the *o* in '*now*'	e.g.	到 DAO	(arrive)
an: as the *a* in '*Arnold*'	e.g.	安 AN	(peace)
ang: as the *a* in '*arng*' sound		當 DANG	(when)
ei: as the *a* in '*way*'	e.g.	為 WEI	(for)
iao: as combination: i + ao		了 LIAO	(end)
ian: as the *a* in '*Janet*'	e.g.	見 JIAN	(see)
iang: a combination: i + again which *a* is like the a in 'father'		講 JIANG	(say)
ie: as the e in 'network'		別 BIE	(other)
ou: as the o in 'motive'	e.g.	都 DOU	(all)
ong: as the o in 'only'.	e.g.	通 TONG	(through)
ua: as hw.	e.g.	話 HUA	(words)
uan: as in Spanish '*Juan*'	e.g.	歡 HUAN	(cheer)

uang: as in Spanish '*Juan*'+g.　　　　　光 GUANG (light)

ue:　as the e in 'er'.　　　e.g.　月 YUE　(moon, month)
　　　When *ue* follows x, as in　　　學 XUE　(learn),
　　　the e is like the e in '*ten*', like '*sweat*'.

uo:　as the *a* in '*war*'.　　e.g.　說 SHUO　(say)('sure')

The CONSONANTS:

b d g:　These three voiced or soft consonants
　　　　become non-voiced or hard.

g　　　is always a hard consonant as in '*gun*'.

c:　　　This letter is used as ts. e.g. 才 CAI (ability)
　　　　Refer to the word 'pizza' (peetsa) (not peesa).

q:　　　Similar to ts, lighter than c & ch when the tongue touches the upper jaw. 錢 QIAN (money)

ch:　　as ch in 'church'. e.g. 常 CHANG (often)

r:　　　Close to r in English but non-vibrating   e.g. 然 RAN (but)

x:　　　Similar to ks in which k is not pronounced   e.g. 心 XIN (heart)

y:　　　Always used as a consonant only. e.g. 英 YING (English)

z:　　　Hard z (non-voiced) close to English j, not z e.g. 在 ZAI (at, in)

zh:　　Similar to the s in 'pleasure' but hard,
　　　　not voiced or soft. e.g. 這 ZHE (this)

The rest of the consonants, *f h j k l m n p s t w,* are used pretty much like English. The letter v is only used for foreign words.

NOTE:

(1) The vowel i and e sometimes cause confusion to beginners. Let's examine these examples:

The vowel i is pronounced like y in the word 'syringe' only in syllables as follows:

zi　ci　si　ri　zhi　chi　shi
資　次　思　日　知　遲　師

When i follows other consonants, i is always pronounced like *i* in '*it*' (short) such as in 必 BI$_4$ or e in 'see' (long) as in 西 XI$_1$ (west). (XI$_1$ sounds like sea in 'sea gull.) So watch for the consonant before the *i*.

(2) The vowel *e* is pronounced like *e* in *er* except after consonant *y* as in *ye* or after vowel *i* or *u* as in ie, where the e is pronounced like the e in set. However, in *yue*, the e is like the *e* in '*her*'.

(3) The consonants q, c, ch: the tongue is behind the teeth touching the upper jaw. Just remember the two words: *pizza* and *church*, close enough to start. Every language has some special sounds. Just listen, compare and practice. As long as you treat ch as in church and pronounce *c* and *q* as the *z* in pizza ('peetsa'), it is close enough and is OK.

(4) The consonants s and x: Both can be followed by the vowel *i* but pronounced differently and so often cause confusion to beginners:

SI (思, 四) : The i is pronounced like the *y* in '*syringe*'.

XI (西, 習) : The i is pronounced like e in 'see'. Treat *x* like *s (ks)*, not *z*.

(5) Vowel u following *s (su)* and *x (xü)*:

SU as '*soo*' (souvenir); (蘇 SU$_1$, a surname)

XU (須, 需): *Like the German* u with 2 dots.

But in typing, type 'u' as usual except in 女 where the 'u' is 'nv' to represent the 'u' with 2 dots.

B. THE CONCEPT OF TONES OF CHINESE CHARACTERS:

There are many characters of the same spelling but in different tones. Basically there are four tones for most same-spelling characters. Some may have only 3, 2 tones or 1 tone. For simplicity, the four tones are named 1,2,3 and 4 as used in some computer programs for typing Chinese. Tone symbols in Chinese dictionaries are somewhat like these:

¯ ˊ ˇ ˋ (1 2 3 4)

There are no such tone notations in English. To understand the tones in Chinese language, consider the concept below:

1. A Chinese character is a single-syllable word
2. A Chinese character can lead or follow another character to form a two-syllable word
3. a two-syllable or multi-syllable word, there is an accent and the accent is always on ONE of the syllables. (Same as in English.)
4. Each character is independent and has its own sound or tone.

Before we get into examples of tones of Chinese characters, let us examine the accent of some words in English:

cargo ... Os_car_ :

Accent is on the first syllable in both words; The syllable car is in different sound in the two English words

The same spelling car demonstrates two tones.

This is the concept of tones in Chinese.

A further example:

target .. re**tar**da̠tion .. **mor**tar .. gui**tar**
 ¹   ²   ³   ⁴

The syllable _tar_ exists in each of the 4 words

The syllable _tar_ has a different sound (tone) in each of the above 4 words

Accent of each of the 4 words is in bold type

    read aloud the 4 words and compare the sound of the syllable _tar_ in each word

The 4 sounds of tar in sequential order is very, very close to the four tones in Chinese. The first and last reflect tone 1 and tone 4 like a perfect match while the second and third are close enough to tone 2 and tone 3 in Chinese.

So, there are tones in English words, too!

This is the concept of tones in Chinese characters.

    Now we can get into examples of Chinese characters to demonstrate the four tones. In the following examples, first demonstrate the single characters of a tone group and then each character matches with another character to form a two-syllable word. For all practical purposes, an example of a close sound in English is provided to help understand and compare, not perfect but better than none.

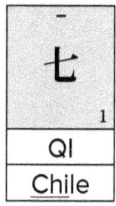 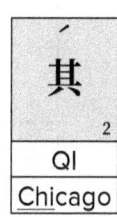  

QI	QI	QI	QI
Chile	Chicago	itchiness	cheese

The above 4 characters are all spelled QI, but the tones are different.

QI₁: High tone close to *chi* in Chile; (high pitch)

QI₂: Level tone somewhat like *chi* in Chicago

QI₃: Turning tone somewhat like *chi* in itchiness

QI₄: Ending tone somewhat like *chee* in cheese. (lower scale).

Remember that the *q* in Chinese is close to *ts* in English, not *ch*. {Cf. 'pizza' ('pi:tsa')} (pizza: not 'pi:cha' , nor 'pi:sa, but 'pi:tsa)

Focus on the vowel i and practice the four tones without the consonant *q*. Each of the vowels, including diphthongs, has four tones.

When each of the above characters matches with another character to form a word/term, such as in the following examples, it further demonstrates the significance of tones. (Key characters bold type.)

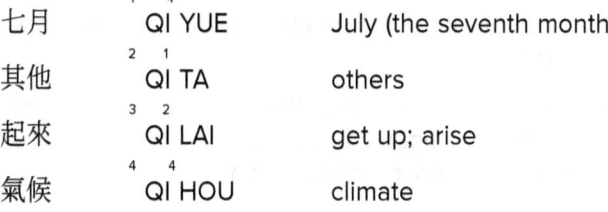

七月　　　QI YUE　　　July (the seventh month)

其他　　　QI TA　　　others

起來　　　QI LAI　　　get up; arise

氣候　　　QI HOU　　　climate

(In the above examples, each of the four characters *leads* another character to form a two-syllable word.)

A further example of TONES of Chinese characters:

 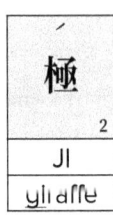 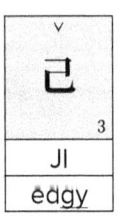 

1	2	3	4
JI	JI	JI	JI
Jesus	giraffe	edgy	gee,..

JI₁: High tone somewhat like *Je* in *Je*sus (high pitch)

JI₂: Level tone somewhat like gi in giraffe

JI₃: Turning tone somewhat like gy in edgy, and

JI₄: Ending tone somewhat like gee in "*Gee*, look at that." (short *gee*).

Let us match each of these four characters with another character to form a word/terra, such as in the following examples. It further demonstrates the significance of tones. (Key characters bold type)

成績	CHĒNG JÍ (2,1)	accomplishment; result
北極	BĚI JÍ (3,2)	North Pole
自己	ZÌ JǏ (4,3)	self
日記	RÌ JÌ (4,4)	diary

(In the above examples, each of the four characters follows another character to form a two-syllable word.)

In addition to the 4 tones described above, there is the light tone, the one without tone indicator. In some computer programs for typing Chinese, this tone is treated as tone 5. Only a few characters, mainly the auxiliary words, are in tone 5, such as:

嗎 MA: close to the *ma* in 'grand*ma*' , 'stig*ma*'

了 LE: as the ler in 'antler'

的 DE: as the der in 'gender'

麼 ME: as the mer in 'hammer', or the or in 'armo(u)r '.(Accent is on the first syllable.)

Now we understand: Tones of Chinese characters are not mysterious at all. It is an important feature of the language: Single-syllable characters are the basic units of the Chinese language.

To practice the tones of Chinese characters, it is highly recommended to follow these steps:

(1) Read aloud each and all of the above examples of tones in sequential order (tone 1, 2, 3, 4) repeatedly. Start with the 4 words in English and focus on the sound of the common syllable.

(2) Practice the four Chinese characters in each set of examples in the same way.

(3) Follow the same pattern, practice the four tones of each of the vowels and diphthongs.

(4) Further practice by adding a consonant to the front of the vowel or diphthong.

To practice tones, keep in mind: read aloud, by all means; the louder the better, please. The tone indicator and the spelling remind you the tone. Focus is always on the characters: recognize them.

8. CHINESE TYPING & WORD PROCESSING:

A. Input Method:

Chinese is based on characters. A character is a pictograph while the computer input is based on Latin alphabet. Thus it becomes necessary to use the computer keyboard to draw/call and display the character.

Different methods of input are available, such as the following: (This varies with programs.)

(1) PINYIN 拼音 also known as Romanized Chinese (or Latinized Chinese) as used in this book.
(2) Base on Radicals: The keys on the keyboard are assigned to represent specific radicals
(3) ZHUYIN (注音 or BO-PO-MO-FO System) Assign the keys to represent specific phonetic notation symbols
(4) Input by handwriting the character clearly.

For English speakers, the PINYIN (phonetic spelling) method is the most convenient way. This book is generated with PINYIN.

B. Input Based on Romanized Chinese or PINYIN:

Early computer programs required typing the letters as well as the tone to draw a character. Now you can input all the characters of a word of 2-syllables at one time like typing an English word and the display will show the word in Chinese. If the word displayed is not the word you want, then hit 'space bar' to display other same spelling words and choose the one you need.

All Chinese typing and word processing programs can accommodate the input of Chinese spelling to call the character or the input of English by switching the mode.

C. Chinese Character Codes:

Long before the computer era, Chinese characters were coded for sending telegram messages, known as telegram code which used 4-digit numerical combination. To make it accessible for computer programs to draw (call) the character, each of the Chinese characters is coded, known as Internal Code.

There is Big5 based on traditional characters and there is GB which is based on simplified characters only. Microsoft Windows uses Unicode. Chinese computer codes may not be compatible.

D. Computer Windows Environment:

(1) MS Windows versions: A Windows OS computer is equipped to read Chinese by default. To enable the writing Chinese feature, you need to select and add the Chinese language option under region settings in Control Panel.

(2) Mac OS versions: A Mac OS computer is equipped to read Chinese by default. To enable the writing Chinese feature, you need to select and add the Chinese language option under Language & Region in System Preferences.

PART 2
MODULES

- Learn 300 Chinese Characters and 500 bilingual sample sentences in 20 Modules
- Each Module of 15 Characters in 3 Sub-Modules
- Each Sub-Module of 5 Characters in 3 Sections:
    - A. Build Vocabulary and Expressions with the 5 new Characters
    - B. Expand Vocabulary and Expressions with all the Characters Learned in Previous Modules
    - C. Bilingual Sample Sentences; with Grammar and Analysis in Explanatory NOTES. Plus, Mandarin Romanized Phonetic Transcription.

MODULE 1

M1.1 FIRST GROUP OF 5 NEW CHARACTERS:

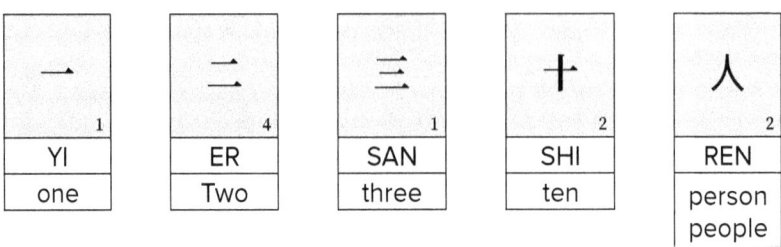

By learning these 5 characters, you can begin to build up your vocabulary with our block building technique as follows.

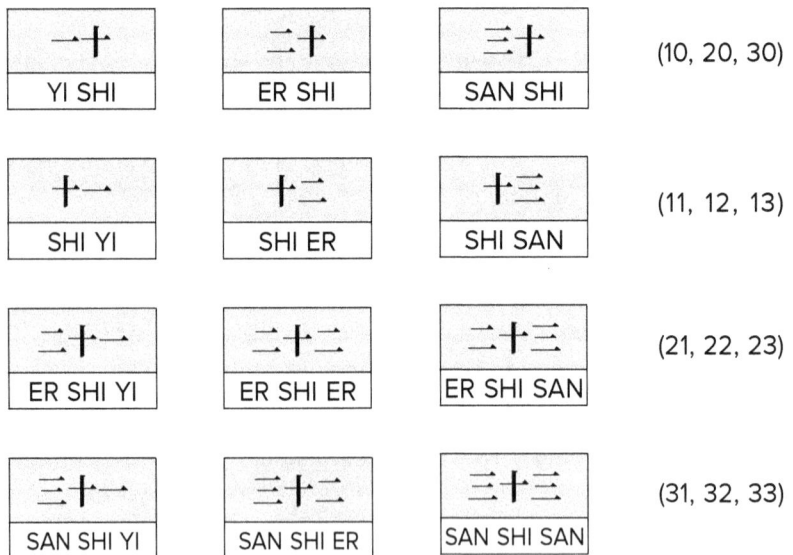

By adding one character, you can build phrases, such as:

ANNOTATIONS

(1) The Chinese character 人 is one word and has its own meaning. By adding a numerical number, it forms a phrase just like English.

(2) There is no plural form of nouns in Chinese language.

(3) WRITING Chinese characters: There are some basic ground rules in writing Chinese Characters:

- Each character occupies a rectangle or square regardless of the number of strokes a character has. For practice, 3/8" across and 1/2" high is a good size (approximately 10 X 13 mm).
- A character is composed of strokes:

    一 YI (one) has one stroke

    二 ER (two), 十 SHI (ten) and 人 REN (person) each has two strokes

    三 SAN (three) has three strokes.

- There is a sequential order in writing the strokes of a character:
    - *Horizontal strokes first, then vertical*: such as 十
    - *Top stroke first, bottom one last*: such as 二 and 三
    - *Strokes on left first, then right*: such as 人
        - *Horizontal strokes are written from left to right* and *vertical* strokes (including slanting strokes) are written *from top down*. (There is one exception to this rule: the Hand Tick Radical is from southwest moving upward to the northeast direction. (cf: Radical in PART 3)
- There is a starting point and an ending point for each stroke. Notice that even the simplest character 一 YI (one) is not a random line.
- The following three lines of printing of the same characters demonstrate the different styles or fonts:

    † Line 1 is regular print

    † Line 2 is hand written form

    † Line 3 is hand written with a traditional brush pen.

一	二	三	十	人
一	二	三	十	人
一	二	三	十	人

(4) PHONETICS: In Latinized (Romanized) Chinese, (cf. PART 1 Section 7 for further information)

- 一 YI (one): i is like the e in 'yeast'.
- 二 ER (two): like the er in 'her'.
- a or 'a + consonant': a is always pronounced as a in 'father'. 三 SAN (three): like 'sarn'.
  - 人 REN (person): the e is like the e in 'siren', 'listen', 'often'; r: non-vibrating.
  - 十 SHI (ten): the i has no equivalent in English, but very close to the y in 'syringe'.
- There are four tones in each vowel (including diphthongs) in Chinese. For simplicity, they are labeled as 1 2 3 4. (cf. PART 1 Section 7: **The Concept of Tones of Chinese Characters**.)

  一 YI$_1$ (one) and 三 SAN$_1$ (three) belong to tone 1;

  人 REN$_2$ (person) and 十 SHI$_2$ (ten) are in tone 2;

  二 ER$_4$ (two) is tone 4.

MODULE 1

M1.2 SECOND GROUP OF 5 NEW CHARACTERS

		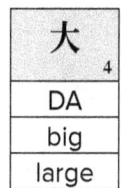		
RI	YUE	DA	XIAO	TIAN
day	month / moon	big / large	small / little	sky / day

M1.2A Apply our block building technique to these five characters:

日日	RI^4 RI^4	daily (Tends to be Southern usage as in Cantonese.)
天天	TIAN^1 TIAN^1	daily (Tends to be Northern usage as in Mandarin.)
大小	DA^4 XIAO^3	size
大大	DA^4 DA^4	huge
小小	XIAO^3 XIAO^3	very small; a little bit
大大小小	DA^4 DA^4 XIAO^3 XIAO^3	all sizes; people of all ages

M1.2B You can expand your vocabulary by using all the ten characters learned so far; you can even develop expressions:

大人	DA^4 REN^2	adult (casual)
小人	XIAO^3 REN^2	villain; vile person
一月	YI^1 YUE^4	January
二月	ER^4 YUE^4	February
三月	SAN^1 YUE^4	March
十月	SHI^2 YUE^4	October
十一月	SHI^2 YI^1 YUE^4	November

MODULE 1

十二月	SHÍ ÈR YUÈ	December
一月大	YĪ YUÈ DÀ	January is a long month. (31 days in January)
十一月小	SHÍ YĪ YUÈ XIĂO	November is a short month. (30 days)
三月二十一日	SĀN YUÈ ÈR SHÍ YĪ RÌ	March 21
一人一天	YĪ RÉN YĪ TIĀN	one day per person
一天三人	YĪ TIĀN SĀN RÉN	three persons per day

一	二	三	十	人
一	二	三	十	人
一	二	三	十	人

日	月	大	小	天
日	月	大	小	天
日	月	大	小	天

ANNOTATIONS ───

(1) More about Chinese character writing:

日: Four strokes in sequential order:
   1. Left vertical stroke from top down
   2. Right turning stroke from top left to right and then turns downward
   3. Horizontal stroke in the middle
   4. Horizontal stroke at the bottom.

月: Four strokes in sequential order:
   1. Left bending stroke from top down bending outward to the left
   2. Right turning stroke from top left to right, turns downward and ends with a tick upward
   3. Upper horizontal stroke in the middle
   4. Lower horizontal stroke in the middle.

大: Three strokes in sequential order:
   1. Horizontal stroke from left to right
   2. Left bending stroke from top downward bending outward to the left
   3. Right bending stroke from below the horizontal stroke bending outward to the right, southeast direction.

小: Three strokes in sequential order:
   1. Vertical stroke from top down and turns upward like a tick
   2. Left dot from top downward, from north-east to southwest direction
   3. Right dot from top downward, from northwest to southeast direction.

天: Four strokes in sequential order:
   1. Top horizontal stroke
   2. Second horizontal stroke
   3. Left bending stroke
   4. Right bending stroke.

(2) Pictographic Expression:

Look at these Chinese characters:

人 REN$_2$ person : It looks like the symbol of a person standing with two legs wide apart

大 DA$_4$ big : It looks like a person standing with two hands stretching out

小 XIAO$_3$ small : It looks like a person standing with two legs close together and two hands hanging downward

日 RI$_4$ sun : Symbol of the sun; (round to rectangle)

月 YUE$_4$ moon : Symbol of the moon when it is not a full moon.

Characters such as above examples are pictographic characters. They reflect the initial development of Chinese written language.

Characters are basic units of the Chinese language. A Chinese character can be viewed as an atom which can form molecules with other atoms of the same or different element. A character alone is a single syllable word. A character can also lead or follow another character to form a two-syllable word. The spelling can help you pronounce the character, look up in a dictionary and draw the character from the computer. Always focus on practicing the Chinese characters: read, write and recognize them.

MODULE 1

M1.3 THIRD GROUP OF 5 NEW CHARACTERS:

不 (4)	是 (4)	很 (3)	好 (3)	嗎 (1)
BU	SHI	HEN	HAO	MA
no; not	yes; is	very	good	(question)

M1.3A Apply our block building technique to these five characters, you can now have thirteen expressions as follows:

是	SHI⁴	yes
不是	BU⁴ SHI⁴	no; not
不好	BU⁴ HAO³	no good; not good
很好	HEN³ HAO³	very good
是嗎?	SHI MA³?	Is that right?
是不是?	SHI⁴ BU⁴ SHI⁴?	Is that right?
不是嗎?	BU⁴ SHI⁴ MA?	Isn't it true?
好不好?	HAO³ BU⁴ HAO³?	Is that good? Is that OK?
不好嗎?	BU⁴ HAO³ MA?	Isn't that nice?
很好嗎?	HEN³ HAO³ MA?	Is it very good?
是不是很好?	SHI⁴ BU⁴ SHI⁴ HEN³ HAO³	Is it very good?
不是很好嗎?	BU⁴ SHI⁴ HEN³ HAO³ MA	Isn't it very good?
很好,不是嗎?	HEN³ HAO³, BU⁴ SHI⁴ MA?	Very good, isn't it?

ANNOTATIONS ———

(1) 嗎 MA is a character that has no equivalent in English. It is used to express a question. A statement followed by this character at the end becomes a question and a question mark is used.

(2) Each of the above 9 expressions ending with "嗎"?" is a sentence in Chinese language. Notice that there is no subject word such as "it" or "that" in the Chinese expressions.

(3) 嗎 MA without tone indicator: light tone. Some computer programs treat it as tone 5.

M1.3B Expand vocabulary and expressions by using all the 15 characters learned:

好人	HAO³ REN²	nice person
很大	HEN³ DA⁴	very big
很小	HEN³ XIAO³	very small
好大	HAO³ DA⁴	very big (casual, oral)
好小	HAO³ XIAO³	very small (casual, oral)
好天	HAO³ TIAN¹	fine day

M1.3C Sample sentences:

一人三天, 不是很好嗎?

YI REN SAN TIAN, BU SHI HEN HAO MA?

Each person for three days, isn't that very nice?

十二月是月大, 是不是?

SHI ER YUE SHI YUE DA, SHI BU SHI?

December is a long month. Isn't it?

ANNOTATIONS ———

The above last sample sentence demonstrates a difference in sentence structure between English and Chinese. In Chinese, a sentence expresses an idea and there is a comma between the two segments; while in English, it is in two sentences.

一	二	三	十	人
日	月	大	小	天
不	是	很	好	嗎
一	二	三	十	人
日	月	大	小	天
不	是	很	好	嗎

MODULE 2

M2.1 FIRST GROUP OF 5 NEW CHARACTERS:

上⁴	下⁴	午³	工¹	作⁴
SHANG	XIA	WU	GONG	ZUO
up	down	noon	work	do

M2.1A Build vocabulary and expressions with these 5 characters:

上午	SHÀNG WǓ	morning; a.m.
下午	XIÀ WǓ	afternoon; p.m.
工作	GŌNG ZUÒ	work
上工	SHÀNG GŌNG	go to work
上下	SHÀNG XIÀ	up and down; leaders and subordinates
上上下下	SHÀNG SHÀNG XIÀ XIÀ	from top to bottom; people at all levels

M2.1B Expand vocabulary and expressions by using all the 20 characters learned:

工人	GŌNG RÉN	worker
人工	RÉN GŌNG	manual; labor; wage (casual)
天上	TIĀN SHÀNG	in the sky
天下	TIĀN XIÀ	on earth; the world
工作日	GŌNG ZUÒ RÌ	workday
不上不下	BÙ SHÀNG BÙ XIÀ	hung up halfway; hanging in the air

ANNOTATIONS ———

工 GONG and 人 REN are two characters. 工人 GONG REN means 'worker' while 人工 REN GONG means 'manual', 'labor' or 'wage'. This is not unusual. It demonstrates the use of characters.

M2.1C Sample sentences:

上午工作, 下午不工作。
SHANG WU GONG ZUO, XIA WU BU GONG ZUO.
Work in the morning, no work in the afternoon.

天下人人工作, 不是很好嗎?
TIAN XIA REN REN GONG ZUO, BU SHI HEN HAO MA?
Everybody in the world works. Isn't that very nice?

天天工作, 好不好?
TIAN TIAN GONG ZUO, HAO BU HAO?
Work every day. Is it good?

MODULE 2

M2.2 SECOND GROUP OF 5 NEW CHARACTERS:

左 ³	右 ⁴	手 ³	用 ⁴	力 ⁴
ZUO	YOU	SHOU	YONG	LI
left	right	hand	use	force

M2.2A Build vocabulary and expressions with these 5 characters:

左手	ZUǑ SHǑU	left hand
右手	YÒU SHǑU	right hand
手力	SHǑU LÌ	hand force
用力	YÒNG LǏ	use force (physically)
用手力	YÒNG SHǑU LÌ	use hand force
用左手	YÒNG ZUǑ SHǑU	use left hand
用右手	YÒNG YÒU SHǑU	use right hand
左右手	ZUǑ YÒU SHǑU	left and right hands; key assistants

2.2B Expand vocabulary and expressions by using all the 25 characters learned:

人力	RÉN LÌ	manual; manpower
大力	DÀ LÌ	strongly; vigorously
人手	RÉN SHǑU	helper
手工	SHǑU GŌNG	handmade; hand craft
手上	SHǑU SHÀNG	in hand
手下	SHǑU XIÀ	subordinate (casual) (Literally: under one's hand.)

42 Mastering Mandarin: Your Path to Proficiency

M2.2C Sample sentences:

用右手出力,不是左手出力。
YONG YOU SHOU CHU LI, BU SHI ZUO SHOU CHU LI.
Use right hand to apply force, not the left hand.

出大力。CHU DA LI
Apply strong force. / Devote major efforts.

手下十人。　　SHOU XIA SHI REN.
Ten subordinates.

十天左右。　　SHI TIAN ZUO YOU.
About ten days. (Approximately ten days.)

左手力小,右手力大。
ZUO SHOU LI XIAO, YOU SHOU LI DA.
Left hand is not as strong; right hand is strong.

上下午工作,左右手用力。
SHANG XIA WU GONG ZUO. ZUO YOU SHOU YONG LI.
Work in the morning and afternoon. Use left hand and right hand to apply force.

MODULE 2

M2.3 THIRD GROUP OF 5 NEW CHARACTERS:

肯 ³	自 ⁴	己 ³	出 ⁴	入 ⁴
KEN	ZI	JI	CHU	RU
willing to	from	self	out	in

M2.3A Build vocabulary and expressions with these 5 characters:

自己	ZI JI (⁴ ³)	oneself
出入	CHU RU (¹ ⁴)	in and out; discrepancy
肯自己出入	KEN ZI JI CHU RU (³ ⁴ ³ ¹ ⁴)	willing to be in and out by oneself

2.3B Expand vocabulary and expressions by using all the 30 characters learned:

出力	CHU LI (¹ ⁴)	use force; put in effort
肯出力	KEN CHU LI (³ ¹ ⁴)	willing to force; willing to in effort
肯不肯	KEN BU KEN (³ ⁴ ³)	willing or not
肯	KEN (³)	willing to
不肯	BU KEN (⁴ ³)	not willing to

M2.3C Sample sentences:

工作不肯出力。

GONG ZUO BU KEN CHU LI.

Not willing to put in effort at work.

上上下下, 人人肯出力。

SHANG SHANG XIA XIA, REN REN KEN CHU LI.

From leaders to subordinates, everybody is willing to put in effort.

很多好工人, 很肯自己出力。

HEN DUO HAO GONG REN, HEN KEN ZI JI CHU LI.

Many good workers are very willing to put in effort on their own.

一二三十人	日月大小天	不是很好嗎
上下午工作	左右手用力	肯自己出入
一二三十人	日月大小天	不是很好嗎
上下午工作	左右手用力	肯自己出入
一二三十人	**日月大小天**	**不是很好嗎**
上下午工作	**左右手用力**	**肯自己出入**

MODULE 3

M3.1 FIRST GROUP OF 5 NEW CHARACTERS:

我 ₃	請 ₃	你 ₃	來 ₂	看 ₄
WO	QING	NI	LAI	KAN
I	please	you	come	see
me	invite	you		look

M3.1A Build vocabulary and expressions with these 5 characters:

請看	QING KAN (3 4)	Please see (this). /Please look at it.
你看	NI KAN (3 4)	Look. / Look at it.
看看	KAN KAN (4 4)	Let's see.
看來	KAN LAI (4 2)	It looks./ it appears.
我看	WO KAN (3 4)	I think.
我來	WO LAI (3 2)	I come. /Let me do it
我請	WO QING (3 3)	Be my guest. (I pay)
我請你來看。	WO QING NI LAI KAN. (3 3 3 2 4)	I invite (request) you to come over and have a look.

M3.1B Expand vocabulary and expressions by using all the 35 characters learned:

請人	QING REN (3 2)	hire people
請人工作	QING REN GONG ZUO (3 2 1 4)	hire people to
我自己	WO ZI JI (3 4 3)	myself
你自己	NI ZI JI (3 4 3)	yourself

46 Mastering Mandarin: Your Path to Proficiency

M3.1C Sample sentences:

上午自己工作,下午請人。〔自己:我自己〕
SHANG WU ZI JI GONG ZUO, XIA WU QING REN.
I myself work in the morning and hire people for the afternoon. (It could also be "He himself... ")

你我是自己人。
NI WO SHI ZI JI REN.
You and I are on the same side.

你請十三人來工作。〔cf. M10.1: 個 GE₄〕
NI QING SHI SAN REN LAI GONG ZUO.
Go and hire thirteen people to come to work.

看來你不肯用力。
KAN LAI NI BU KEN YONG LI.
It looks like you are not willing to apply force.

我看出來,你是好人。
WO KAN CHU LAI, NI SHI HAO REN.
I can tell; you are a nice person.

你看,我請你來,你不肯來,很不好,是不是?
NI KAN, WO QING NI LAI, NI BU KEN LAI, HEN BU HAO, SHI BU SHI?
Look, I requested you to come and you were not willing to come. That's not good at all. Is it?

ANNOTATIONS ───────

The Chinese sentence is not double negative. The last phrase "是不是?" is asking the entire statement before it: "Is it true?"

請。
QING.
Please. / After you.

請出力。
QING CHU LI.
Please apply force. / Please put in effort.

請出來工作。
QING CHU LAI GONG ZUO.
Please come out and work.

一二三十人　　　日月大小天　　　不是很好嗎
上下午工作　　　左右手用力　　　肯自己出入
我請你來看

一二三十人　　　日月大小天　　　不是很好嗎
上下午工作　　　左右手用力　　　肯自己出入
我請你來看

───────

MODULE 3

M3.2 SECOND GROUP OF 5 NEW CHARACTERS:

她₁	和₂	他₁	們₂	問₄
TA	HE	TA	MEN	WEN
she, her	and	he, him	(plural)	ask

M3.2A Build vocabulary and expressions with these 5 characters:

他們	TA MEN (1 2)	they, them
她們	TA MEN (1 2)	they, them (feminine)
她和他們問。	TA HE TA MEN WEN. (1 2 1 2 4)	She and they ask.

M3.2B Expand vocabulary and expressions by using all the 40 characters learned:

我們	WO MEN (3 2)	we, us
你們	NI MEN (3 2)	you (plural)
人們	REN MEN (2 2)	people (general sense, written form)
他們自己	TA MEN ZI JI (1 2 4 3)	themselves
他自己	TA ZI JI (1 4 3)	himself
她自己	TA ZI JI (1 4 3)	herself

M3.2C Sample sentences:

她問他們。

TA WEN TA MEN.   She asks them. / She asked them.

他們問她。

TA MEN WEN TA.   They ask her. / They asked her.

她請你和我,看看請不請他。

TA QING NI HE WO, KAN KAN QING BU QING TA.

She invited you and me. See if she invites him.

他們請她來,我看她不肯來。

TA MEN QING TA LAI, WO KAN TA BU KEN LAI.

They invited her. I don't think she would come.

ANNOTATIONS

(1) There is no subjective case or objective case of Pronouns in Chinese: 她 is used for *she* or *her*

(2) 們 is a character to be added to a pronoun to make it plural: 我 is *I* or *me* while 我們 is *we* or *us*.

(3) In the above last two sample sentences, there is a comma between the two segments of each Chinese sentence while in English each of the two segments is a separate sentence. This demonstrates an important feature of sentence structure between Chinese and English. In Chinese language, the two segments convey the context of the sentence and thus are treated as parts of the sentence. Based on English grammar, the two segments have to be separate simple sentences or form a complex sentence.

MODULE 3

M3.3 THIRD GROUP OF 5 NEW CHARACTERS:

說¹	您²	還²	在⁴	家¹
SHUO	NIN	HAI	ZAI	JIA
say	you	still	at	home

M3.3A Build vocabulary and expressions with these 5 characters:

在家	ZAI⁴ JIA¹	at home
還在家	HA1² ZAI⁴ JIA¹	still at home
說您還在家。	SHUO¹ NIN² HAI² ZAI⁴ JIA¹.	(Somebody) says you are still at home. (Somebody) said you were still at home.

NOTE:

您 NIN₂ is a courteous and respectful expression of 你 NI₃ (you) in Mandarin, typical in Northern China, Beijing in particular. It is used in the singular form to show special respect to a senior, higher ranking official, a guest or visitor.

M3.3B Expand vocabulary and expressions by using all the 45 characters learned:

大家	DA⁴ JIA¹	all; everybody
人家	REN² JIA¹	people (general sense, oral form)
自己家	ZI⁴ JI³ JIA¹	home of oneself
您好!	NIN² HAO³	How are you? / Hi!/ How do you do?

M3.3C Sample sentences:

人家說您是好人。

REN JIA SHUO NIN SHI HAO REN.

People say (that) you are a nice person.

請您來我家一下, 好嗎?

QING NIN LAI WO JIA YI XIA, HAO MA?

Would you mind come over to my home, please?

我們請她來, 您看好不好?

WO MEN QING TA LAI, NIN KAN HAO BU HAO?

Let's invite her to come. How would you think?

她說你還在家, 不肯來。

TA SHUO NI HAI ZAI JIA, BU KEN LAI.

She said you were still at home and didn't want to come.

ANNOTATIONS ⎯⎯⎯⎯

The last sample sentence above is in past tense while the other three are in present tense in English. There is no verb conjugation in Chinese; tense of a verb (time of action) is based on context. This will be explained further.

MODULE 4

M4.1 FIRST GROUP OF 5 NEW CHARACTERS:

學²	習²	中¹	英¹	文²
XUE	XI	ZHONG	YING	WEN
learn	practice	Chinese	English	language

M4.1A Build vocabulary and expressions with these 5 characters:

學習	XUE² XI²	learn; study
英文	YING WEN²	English language
中文	ZHONG¹ WEN²	Chinese language
中英	ZHONG¹ YING¹	Chinese & English; Sino-Britain
英中	YING¹ ZHONG¹	Britain-China
中學	ZHONG¹ XUE²	middle/high school
文學	WEN² XUE²	literature
學英文	XUE² YING¹ WEN²	learn English
學習中文	XUE² XI² ZHONG WEN²	middle/high school
學習中英文	XUE² XI² ZHONG¹ YING¹ WEN²	Learn Chinese and English.

ANNOTATIONS

學英文 = 學習英文; 學 = 學習 learn; study

學習 is the complete word, it can be used as a verb or as a noun.

學 is the short form as a verb for 學習.

學 when used with other characters, will form other words, such as: 中學, 文學.

This is an example of one important feature of Chinese characters: A character can be a word by itself or can form a word with another one or two characters like a word with 2 or 3 syllables.

M4.1B Expand vocabulary and expressions by using all the 50 characters learned:

大學	DÀ XUÉ	university/college
小學	XIǍO XUÉ	elementary/primary school
日學	RÌ XUÉ	day school
上學	SHÀNG XUÉ	go to school (attend class)
入學	RÙ XUÉ	register for school/class
自學	ZÌ XUÉ	self study
力學	LÌ XUÉ	Mechanics (science)
好學	HÀO XUÉ	love learning (HAO4)
學好	XUÉ HǍO	learn the good; do well in studies
學說	XUÉ SHUŌ	theory, doctrine
學問	XUÉ WÈN	knowledge (gained through education)

M4.1C Sample sentences

她天天在家自學中文。

TA TIAN TIAN ZAI JIA ZI XUE ZHONG WEN.

She self-studies Chinese at home everyday.

他很好學，在大學學英文，在家學中文。

TA HEN HAO XUE, ZAI DA XUE XUE YING WEN, ZAI JIA XUE ZHONG WEN.

He loves learning. He studies English in college and learns Chinese at home.

ANNOTATIONS

好 HAO$_3$ when used to mean good as an adjective or adverb is at tone 3.

In the above sentence, 好學 HAO$_4$ XUE$_2$ means love learning; the character 好 is used as a verb and is pronounced at tone 4.

一二三十人	日月大小天	不是很好嗎
上下午工作	左右手用力	肯自己出入
我請你來看	她和他們問	說您還在家
學習中英文		

MODULE 4

M4.2 SECOND GROUP OF 5 NEW CHARACTERS:

美³	國²	都¹	去⁴	了³
MEI	GUO	DUO; DU	QU	LE; LIAO
pretty	country	all; also	go	(already)

M4.2A Build vocabulary and expressions with these 5 characters:

美國	MEI GUO (3 2)	U.S.A.
國都	GUO DU (2 2)	capitol (of a nation)
都去了	DUO QU LE (1 4)	all gone; all left
美國都去了。	MEI GUO DOU QU LE. (3 2 1 4)	(了: light tone.) Had even been to the U.S.

M4.2B Expand vocabulary and expressions by using all the 55 characters learned:

美人	MEI REN (3 2)	beauty
很美	HEN MEI (3 3)	very pretty; beautiful
中國	ZHONG GUO (1 2)	China
英國	YING GUO (1 2)	U.K.
國家	GUO JIA (2 1)	nation, country

M4.2C Sample sentences:

他們學習英文, 美國、英國都去了。

TA MEN XUE XI YING WEN, MEI GUO, YING GUO DOU QU LE.

They studied English and had been to the U.S. as well as to the U.K.

"你和我去中國學中文, 他們去不去?"
"NI HE WO QU ZHONG GUO XUE ZHONG WEN, TA MEN QU BU QU?"
"You and I are going to China to study Chinese. Are they going? "

"大家都去。"
"DA JIA DOU QU. "
"Everybody is going. "

你們都來了, 很好。
NI MEN DOU LAI LE, HEN HAO.
All of you are here (have come). Very good.

"他們都去了嗎?"
"TA MEN DOU QU LE MA? "
"Did they all go?"

"都去了。"
"DOU QU LE. "
"All of them." (Literally: "All gone.")

都是他自己不好。
DOU SHI TA ZI JI BU HAO.
It's all his own fault.

MODULE 4

M4.3 THIRD GROUP OF 5 NEW CHARACTERS:

叫	謝	又	再	見
4	4	4	4	4
JIAO	XIE	YOU	ZAI	JIAN
call	thank	also	again	see

M4.3A Build vocabulary and expressions with these 5 characters:

謝謝	XIE XIE (4 4)	thank you
再見	ZAI JIAN (4 4)	good-bye; (Literally: see again)
叫謝又再見。	JIAO XIE YOU ZAI JIAN.	Say thank you and good-bye.

M4.3B Expand vocabulary and expressions by using all the 60 characters learned:

叫作	JIAO ZUO (4 4)	known as; called
叫人	JIAO REN (4 2)	call, greet people
叫好	JIAO HAO (4 3)	applaud
看見	KAN JIAN (4 4)	see
一再	YI ZAI (1 4)	time and again
再三	ZAI SAN (4 1)	repeatedly

M4.3C Sample sentences:

她學中文, 又學英文文學。
TA XUE ZHONG IEN, YOU XUE YING WEN WEN XUE.
She studies Chinese; and she also studies English Literature.

他去了英國, 又去美國。
TA QU LE YING GUO, YOU QU MEI GUO.
He went to the U.K., and then to the U.S.

我一再叫他來, 他不肯來。我看見他還在家。
WO YI ZAI JIAO TA LAI. TA BU KEN LAI. WO KAN JIAN TA HAI ZAI JIA.
I told him again and again. He didn't want to come. I saw him still at home.

他又來了?
TA YOU LAI LE?
He has come again? (He is here again?)

謝謝您來, 請您再來。再見。
XIE XIE NIN LAI, QING NIN ZAI LAI. ZAI JIAN.
Thank you for coming. Please come again. Goodbye.

Q: "你叫了他來嗎?"
"NI JIAO LE TA LAI MA?"
"Did you tell him to come?"

A: "叫了。我看他是不肯來。"
"JIAO LE. WO KAN TA SHI BU KEN LAI."
"Yes, I did. I think he doesn't want to come."

"你看,他又叫你去了。再不去不好。"

"NI KAN, TA YOU JIAO NI QU LE. ZAI BU QU BU HAO."

"Look. He is asking you to go again. It's not fine if you miss again."

ANNOTATIONS ———

(1) There is no Conjugation of Verbs in Chinese language; no such things as *do, did, done, doing* or *go, went gone, going*.

(2) "是" is the only form of Verb 'to be'; there is no such things as *am, is, are, was, were, be, been, or being*.

(3) Tense of a verb or time of action is expressed in the context. There are some characters such as 了 (LE) that can be used to specify the completion of an action. Other characters for that purpose will be learned in later Modules.

(4) Compare the above sample sentences, some are in present tense and others are in past tense by context or by past-tense indicator such as the character 了.

(5) The character 了 LE/LIAO$_3$ when used as a past tense or perfect tense indicator, such as in the format "*verb* + 了"(e.g. 叫了、去了), the character 了 is pronounced LE without tone indicator, i.e. tone 5.

MODULE 5

M5.1 FIRST GROUP OF 5 NEW CHARACTERS:

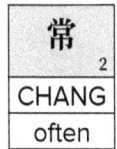				
2	4	4	4	2
CHANG	ZUO	GUAN	JIU	XING
often	do	get used to	exactly	fine

M5.1A Build vocabulary and expressions with these five characters:

常常	CHÁNG CHÁNG	often
做慣	ZUÒ GUÀN	get used to doing something
常做慣就行。	CHÁNG ZUÒ GUÀN JIÙ XÍNG.	Do it often and get used to it; that would be fine.

ANNOTATIONS ———

"常做慣就行。"is a sentence in Chinese language. It is not unusual to have a sentence without a subject word in Chinese.

M5.1B Expand vocabulary and expressions by using all the 65 characters learned:

習慣	XÍ GUÀN	habit, get used to
行人	XÍNG RÉN	pedestrian
就來了	JIÙ LÁI LE	coming soon; on the way
就是	JIÙ SHÌ	is; exactly; even if
就是說	JIÙ SHÌ SHUŌ	that is to say; in other words

M5.1C Sample sentences:

"你學中文, 習慣嗎?"   (written)

NI XUE ZHONG WEN, XI GUAN MA?

"你學中文, 慣不慣?"   (oral, casual)

NI XUE ZHONG WEN, GUAN BU GUAN?

"You study Chinese. Get used to it?"

學中文, 常常學, 天天學, 習慣了就行。

XUE ZHONG WEN, CHANG CHANG XUE, TIAN TIAN XUE, XI GUAN LE JIU XING.

To study Chinese, (one needs to) study often, study everyday, and get used to it. Then it will be fine.

學中文, 學英文, 不常常學就是不行。   (就是: just)

XUE ZHONG WEN, XUE YING WEN, BU CHANG CHANG XUE JIU SHI BU XING.

In studying Chinese or English, (if you) don't study frequently, it just wouldn't work.

我學中文, 學不好, 就是不行。   (就是: just)

WO XUE ZHONG WEN, XUE BU HAO, JIU SHI BU XING.

I studied Chinese and didn't do well. (No matter what I did,) It just didn't work.

我們工作上用中文, 我不學中文就是不行。   (就是: no matter what)

WO MEN GONG ZUO SHANG YONG ZHONG WEN, WO BU XUE ZHONG WEN JIU SHI BU XING.

We use Chinese at work. I have to learn Chinese no matter what.

就是不叫我學中文，我還是學。(就是：even if)
JIU SHI BU JIAO WO XUE ZHONG WEN, WO HAI SHI XUE.
Even if I am not asked to, I still learn Chinese.

叫他來我家，行不行？
JIAO TA LAI WO JIA, XING BU XING?
Tell him to come to my home. Would that be OK (all right)?

行。那就好了。
XING. NA JIU HAO LE.
Fine. That would be nice.

Q: "你做，行嗎？"
"NI ZUO, XING MA?"
"You do it. Would that be fine with you?"

A: "行。我來。"
"XING, WO LAI."
"Sure. Let me do it."

A: "就來了。"
"JIU LAI LE."
"I'm on my way." (Literally: coming soon.)

Q: "叫了他來，他就不來，很不好。" (就=就是)
"JIAO LE TA LAI, TA JIU BU LAI. HEN BU HAO."
"He was told to come and he knowingly didn't come. That's too bad."

A: "就是。"

"JIU SHI."

"Exactly."

就是他。

JIU SHI TA.

It's he. (That's the guy.)

ANNOTATIONS

(1) "就" is a Chinese character which has a variety of meanings depending on the context and application. Examples shown above are only a small portion of it. Basically, it is used as an Adverb to add emphasis. This character is used pretty often.

(2) 習慣 is a word made up of two characters. One character 慣 can be used to mean the same in simplified usage. This is a feature of common occurrence in Chinese. (cf. M4.1: 學 = 學習)

3) 行不行？= 行嗎？

慣不慣？= 習慣嗎？

來不來？= 來嗎？

These are examples of different ways of expressing the same meaning.

MODULE 5

M5.2 SECOND GROUP OF 5 NEW CHARACTERS:

今₁	年₂	並₄	沒₂	有₃
JIN	NIAN	BING	MEI	YOU
present	year	at all	no, not	have

M5.2A Build vocabulary and expressions with these five characters

今年	JĪN NIÁN	this year
年年	NIÁN NIÁN	year after year
沒有	MÉI YǑU	not available, there is nothing
今年並沒有。	JĪN NIÁN BÌNG MÉI YǑU.	This year there is nothing at all.

M5.2B Expand vocabulary and expressions by using all the 70 characters learned

今天	JĪN TIĀN	today
今日	JĪN RÌ	today
去年	QÙ NIÁN	last year
有人	YǑU RÉN	occupied; somebody
年月日	NIÁN YUÈ RÌ	year/month/day
上一年	SHÀNG YĪ NIÁN	the previous year
下一年	XIÀ YĪ NIÁN	the following year
有出入	YǑU CHŪ RÙ	there is inconsistency/discrepancy
有出有入	YǑU CHŪ YǑU RÙ	gain some and lose some
有好有不好	YǑU HǍO YǑU BÙ HǍO	pros and cons

M5.2C Sample sentences:

Q: "有人嗎?" "YOU REN MA?" "Anybody in?"
A: "有。" "YOU." "Yes."

你有沒有? NI YOU MEI YOU? Do you have it?

"你有沒有看見她,有沒有?" --- "有。"
"NI YOU MEI YOU KAN JIAN TA, YOU MEI YOU?" --- "YOU."
"Did you see her, yes or no?" --- "Yes."

    ("有,我有看見她。") ("YOU, WO YOU KAN JIAN TA.")

    ("Yes, I did see her.")

"你並沒有看見他,是不是?" --- "是。"
"NI BING MEI YOU KAN JIAN TA, SHI BU SHI?" --- "SHI."
"You did not see him, did you?" --- "No."

    ("是,我並沒有看見他。") (是 here means true.)

    ("That's true: I did not see him.")

ANNOTATIONS ———

Analyse the above last 2 sample groups:

1. Sometimes a YES in Chinese is equivalent to a NO in English in a response to a question;

2. "有沒有 + verb" -- "Do (you/they/we...) verb"

3. 他 he/him 她 she/her -- same sound when orally spoken. Without knowing the gender, he or she (or him or her) is used in interpreting.

Q: "你們在大學有沒有學中文?"

"NI MEN ZAI DA XUE YOU MEI YOU XUE ZHONG WEN?"

"Do you people study Chinese in College? " (University)

A: "沒有。""MEI YOU.""No." (有沒有學? -- 沒有。)

Q: "你們在大學學不學中文?"

"NI MEN ZAI DA XUE XUE BU XUE ZHONG WEN?"

"Do you people study Chinese in College?

A: "不學。"   "BU XUE." "No."   (學不學? -- 不學。)

ANNOTATIONS

(1) A brief response such as "No" in English could be in many different forms in Chinese because the verb is used in response. e.g.:

是不是你?	SHI BU SHI NI?	Is that you?
--- 不是。	BU SHI.	No.
你有嗎?	NI YOU MA?	Do you have it?
--- 沒有。	MEI YOU.	No. (Don't have it.)
你來不來?	NI LAI BU LAI?	Are you coming over?
--- 不來。	BU LAI.	No. (Not coming.)
你學嗎?	NI XUE MA?	Do you learn?
--- 不學。	BU XUE.	No. (Not learning it.)
行不行?	XING BU XING?	Is that OK?
--- 不行。	BU XING.	No. (Not OK.)

(2). The same holds true for a brief response of Yes. In the above examples, the responses to The questions are:

是不是? --- 是。	SHI.	Yes. (Yes.)
有沒有? --- 有。	YOU.	Yes. (Have.)
來不來? --- 來。	LAI.	Yes. (Come.)
學不學? --- 學。	XUE.	Yes. (Learn.)
行不行? --- 行。	XING.	Yes. (OK.)

他並不是不肯來, 他是來不了。

TA BING BU SHI BU KEN LAI, TA SHI LAI BU LIAO.

Not that he didn't want to come. He couldn't make it.

並不是我。 BING BU SHI WO. Not me at all.

今年並不行; 去年就很好。(就 is used, not 就是)

JIN NIAN BING BU XING, QU NIAN JIU HEN HAO.

This year no good at all, Last year it was very nice.

叫我學中文, 我學來學去, 就是不習慣, 沒學好。

JIAO WO XUE ZHONG WEN, WO XUE LAI XUE QU, JIU SHI BU XI GUAN, MEI XUE HAO.

I was asked to learn Chinese. I learned and learned, but still didn't get used to it and couldn't make it.

他學中文, 並沒有去中國學, 就在美國學, 很好。

TA XUE ZHONG WEN, BING MEI YOU QU ZHONG GUO XUE, JIU ZAI MEI GUO XUE, HEN HAO.

He studies Chinese. He didn't go to China for his studies. He studies in the U.S. Pretty good (result).

MODULE 5

M5.3 THIRD GROUP OF 5 NEW CHARACTERS:

要₄	多₁	少₃	才₂	夠₄
YAO	DUO	SHAO	CAI	GOU
need, want	much, many	little	ability	enough

M5.3A Build vocabulary and expressions with these five characters:

多少?	DUO¹ SHAO³	how many? how much?
多少	DUO¹ SHAO³	somewhat
多多	DUO¹ DUO¹	a lot
多多少少	DUO¹ DUO¹ SHAO³ SHAO³	more or less, somewhat
要多少才夠?	YAO⁴ DUO¹ SHAO³ CAI² GOU⁴?	How much (many) would be enough?

M5.3B Expand vocabulary and expressions by using all the 75 characters learned:

要是	YAO⁴ SHI⁴	If; in case
要人	YAO⁴ REN²	VIP (very important person)
要好	YAO⁴ HAO³	be good friends
好多	HAO³ DUO¹	a lot
多好	DUO¹ HAO³	how nice
多出	DUO¹ CHU¹	extra
多謝	DUO¹ XIE⁴	thank you

(Tends to be Southern usage as in Cantonese; in Mandarin: 謝謝 XIE₄ XIE₄ is used more often.)

人才	RÉN CÁI	talent
天才	TIĀN CÁI	genius
夠了	GÒU LE	enough; that's enough

M5.3C Sample sentences:

我學英文學了三年, 美國都去了, 還是不夠用, 還要學 多少年才夠?

WO XUE YING WEN XUE LE SAN NIAN, MEI GUO DOU QU LE, HAI SHI BU GOU YONG, HAI YAO XUE DUO SHO NIAN CAI GOU?

I have been studying English for three years. I have even been to the United States. Still not enough. How many more years do I have to study to be enough?

ANNOTATIONS ———

In the above sentence, notice the use of punctuation is very different between Chinese and English. A sentence in Chinese conveys a complete idea with a comma used several times.

我多多少少學了中文。

WO DUO DUO SHAO SHAO XUE LE ZHONG WEN.

I have learned some Chinese.

她是人才。　　(人才: talent)

TA SHI REN CAI.

She is a talent.

———

ANNOTATIONS ───────

The Chinese character 才 CAI$_2$ carries different meanings in different applications, as in the case of the character 就 JIU$_4$ (cf. M5.1). Compare the following examples, notice the same character 才 CAI$_2$ is used like an adverb:

你才來? (才: so)

NI CAI LAI?

You are so late? (Literally, "You just got here?")

我才看見她。 (才: just)

WO CAI KAN JIAN TA.

I just saw her.

來才好。 (才: better do)

LAI CAI HAO.

Better come. (It's better for you to come.)

我才不去。 (才: certainly)

WO CAI BU QU.

I certainly wouldn't go.

MODULE 6

M6.1 FIRST GROUP OF 5 NEW CHARACTERS

這 ⁴	裡 ³	非 ¹	那 ⁴	邊 ¹
ZHE	LI	FEI	NA	BIAN
this	place	not	that; then	side; edge

M6.1A Build vocabulary and expressions with these five characters:

這裡	ZHE LI ⁴ ³	here
這邊	ZHE BIAN ⁴ ¹	here; this side
那邊	NA BIAN ⁴ ¹	there; that side
那裡	NA LI ⁴ ³	there
裡邊	LI BIAN ⁴ ¹	inside
這裡非那邊。	ZHE LI FEI NA BIAN. ⁴ ³ ¹ ⁴ ¹	Here is different from there.

ANNOTATIONS ———

非 used alone means 不是 (not, is not).

M6.1B Expand vocabulary and expressions by using all the 80 characters learned:

這天	ZHE TIAN ⁴ ¹	this day
那天	NA TIAN ⁴ ¹	that day
這年	ZHE NIAN ⁴ ²	this year
那年	NA NIAN ⁴ ²	that year
非常	FEI CHANG ¹ ²	unusually, very

Mastering Mandarin: Your Path to Proficiency

並非	BÌNG FĒI	not at all
(並非 = 並不是)		
是非	SHÌ FĒI	right and wrongs; gossip
是是非非	SHÌ SHÌ FĒI FĒI	the rights and wrongs; gossip

ANNOTATIONS ———

Beijing Mandarin is considered to be the perfect and standard Mandarin, similar to English in London which represents the King's English.

The character 那 such as in 那天、那邊、那裡 is pronounced as NEI4 instead of NA4 in Beijing local dialect; but NA4 is perfectly fine in general.

———

M6.1C Sample sentences:

他沒有請我, 那我就不去了。　　(那…: then …)
TA MEI YOU QING WO, NA WO JIU BU QU LE.
He didn't invite me, then I'm not going.

她一邊學英文, 還一邊學中文。　(一邊…, 一邊…)
TA YI BIAN XUE YING WEN, HAI YI BIAN XUE ZHONG WEN.
She studies Chinese while she's studying English.

今天很多人沒有來, 那裡夠人?　(那裡…: how …)
JIN TIAN HEN DUO REN MEI YOU LAI, NA LI GOU REN?
Today many people didn't show up. How can we have enough people?

今天人手不夠, 那就請大家多出力。　(那就…: so…)
JIN TIAN REN SHOU BU GOU, NA JIU QING DA JIA DUO CHU LI.
Today we don't have enough helping hands. So please, everybody, work harder.

是她自己要去那裡的，並非我叫她去的。
SHI TA ZI JI YAO QU NEI LI DE, BING FEI WO JIAO TA QU DE.
She wanted to go there herself. I didn't ask her to go.

這邊工作多，今天你就不要去那邊了。
ZHE BIAN GONG ZUO DUO, JIN TIAN NI JIU BU YAO QU NEI BIAN LE.
It is busy here, so today you don't go there.

ANNOTATIONS

去那邊 = 到那邊去 (Cf. **M9.3**)

不要說是非了，是是非非多了不好。
BU YAO SHUO SHI FEI LE. SHI SHI FEI FEI DUO LE BU HAO.
Don't gossip. It doesn't do any good to have too much gossip.

那年非常不好，是非多。
NEI NIAN FEI CHANG BU HAO, SHI FEI DUO.
It was very bad that year, a lot of gossip.

MODULE 6

M6.2 SECOND GROUP OF 5 NEW CHARACTERS:

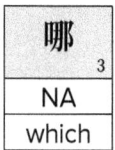				
NA	XIE	XIANG	TONG	DE / DI
which	some	each other	same	of

ANNOTATIONS ———

Above character 的 DE without tone sign indicates a half sound, pronounced light.

M6.2A Build vocabulary and expressions with these five characters:

哪些?	NĂ XIE?	which (plural)
相同	XIĀNG TÓNG	the same
哪些(是)相同的?	NĂ XIE XIĀNG TÓNG DE?	Which are the same?

ANNOTATIONS ———

(1) A Chinese sentence can be complete without a verb. In the above example, the verb 是 (is, are) can be omitted.

(2) 哪 is a character only used in a question to Ask "which?", "where" or "who" in singular or plural leaning.

M6.2B Expand vocabulary and expressions by using all the 85 characters learned:

哪裡?	NĂ LĬ	where
哪天?	NĂ TIĀN	which day? (NEI₃ TIAN₁?)
or:哪一天?	NĂ YĪ TIĀN?	(cf. **M6.1B** Note)
一些	YĪ XIĒ	some
一同	YĪ TÓNG	together
不同	BÙ TÓNG	different
同年	TÓNG NIÁN	the same year
相好	XIĀNG HÁO	getting intimate, going steady
這些	ZHÈ XIĒ	these
那些	NÀ XIĒ	those
多一些	DUŌ YĪ XIĒ	some more; a little more
少一些	SHĂO YĪ XIĒ	a little less; not quite enough

M6.2C Sample sentences:

"謝謝您!"
XIE XIE NIN.
"Thank you!"

"哪裡, 哪裡, 不謝。"   (哪裡: Oh, no)
NA LI, NA LI, BU XIE.   (Notice 哪裡 is repeated.)

ANNOTATIONS ────

In the above colloquial expression, the Response 哪裡 NA₃ LI₃ which usually means "where", does not mean "where" at all. Notice that there is no question mark used in the above sentence. Compare the above sentence with the colloquial expression below.

(哪裡？：where?)

"我看見了！"/ "哪裡？" ("在哪裡？")

WO KAN JIAN LE! / NA₃LI₃? (ZAI₄NA₃LI₃?)

"I can see it! "/ "Where? " ("Where is it?)

我的中文不好。　　　　　(我的：my ...)

WO DE ZHONG WEN BU HAO.

My Chinese (language) is not good.

都是我的。　　　　　　　(我的：...mine)

DOU SHI WO DE.

All belong to me. ("These are all mine. ")

Q: "你在學中文嗎?" (在學 = 在學習)

　　NI ZAI XUE ZHONG WEN MA?

　　"Are you studying Chinese? "

A: "是。"　　　　SHI　　　　　　"Yes."
　　"是的。"　　　SHI DE　　　　"Yes, I am."

────

"在 + verb" such as above "在學習" indicates that the verb is in Continuous Tense.

Q: "還有人要來嗎?"

    HAI YOU REN YAO LAI MA?

    "Are there any other people coming?"

A: "有。"   YOU.   "Yes."

   "有的。"   YOU DE.   "Yes, there are."

這些人和那些人是不同的。(同 $TONG_2$ = 相同 $XIANG_1\ TONG_2$)
ZHE XIE REN HE NEI XIE REN SHI BU TONG DE.
These people are different from those people.

去年很少的, 今年就多了, 大不相同。
QU NIAN HEN SHAO DI, JIN NIAN JIU DUO LE, DA BU XIANG TONG.
Last year there was very little. This year there is plenty. Big difference."

這些都是相同的, 看不出有哪些不同。
ZHE XIE DOU SHI XIANG TONG DE, KAN BU CHU YOU NA XIE BU TONG.
These are all the same. (I) don't see which are different.

───────

1. 的 is a very common character which has two major uses:
   (1) 我的手 WO DE/DI SHOU my hand: 的 carries possessive meaning;
   (2) 是的 SHI DE yes: 的 used at the end of an expression to affirm the answer.
2. The character 的 has two sounds: DI and DE, when used at the end of an expression, it is often pronounced as DE.

你說的那些是哪些?
NI SHI DE NA$_4$ XIE$_1$ SHI NA$_3$ XIE$_1$? (cf. **M6.1C** NOTE)
NI SHUO DE NEI$_4$ XIE$_1$ SHI NEI$_3$ XIE$_1$? (Beijing dialect)
Which ones do you mean when you said those?

MODULE 6

M6.3 THIRD GROUP OF 5 NEW CHARACTERS

爲 4/2	甚 4	麼 1	難 2	懂 3
WEI	SHEN	ME / MO	NAN	DONG
for; do	very	what	difficult	understand

M6.3A Build vocabulary and expressions with these five characters:

甚麼?	SHÉN ME?	what?
甚麼	SHÉN ME	what, whatever, everything, nothing
爲甚麼?	WÈI SHÉN ME?	why?
甚難	SHÉN NÁN	very difficult (written style)
(很難	HĚN NÁN	very difficult)

ANNOTATIONS ———

(1) 甚難 is used in written form of classical style Chinese.
(2) 很難 is used in written and spoken form of today's Chinese (vernacular style).

爲難	WÉI NÁN	cause a hard time; a tough decision
難爲	NÁN WÉI	hard, tough; cause a hard time
難懂	NÁN DǑNG	hard to understand
爲甚麼難懂?	WÈI SHÉN ME NÁN DǑNG?	Why (is it) hard to understand?

M6.3B Expand vocabulary and expressions by using all the 90 characters learned:

爲了	WEI⁴ LE	for; for the sake of; in order to
爲人	WEI² REN²	conduct oneself
人爲	REN² WEI²	caused by human
難看	NAN² KAN	ugly
難得	NAN² DE²	hard to come by
難道	NAN² DAO	(isn't it; can't it)
那麼	NA⁴ ME	like that; such; then
這麼	ZHE⁴ ME	like this; so ...

M6.3C Sample sentences:

他不肯學中文,要他學,他學來學去學不好,難爲了他。　　(難爲: tough)

TA BU KEN XUE ZHONG WEN, YAO TA XUE, TA XUE LAI XUE QU XUE BU HUI. NAN WEI LE TA.

He didn't want to study Chinese, but was required to. He studied and studied and still didn't do well. It's tough for him.

你爲甚麼要爲難我?　　(爲難: hard time)

NI WEI SHEN ME YAO WEI NAN WO?

Why are you giving me a hard time?

叫你學英文,是爲了你自己好。　　(爲了: for)

JIAO NI XUE YING IEN, SHI WEI LE NI ZI JI HAO.

Ask you to learn English. It's for your own good.

爲了要去中國工作,他天天學中文。　　(爲了: in order to)

WEI LE YAO QU ZHONG GUO GONG ZUO, TA TIAN TIAN XUE ZHONG WEN.

In order to work in China, he is studying Chinese every day. (cf. PART 1 Section 1 and M9.3: 到 DAO4)

做甚麼都好, 習慣了就不難。　　(甚麼: whatever)
ZUO SHEN ME DOU HAO, XI GUAN LE JIU BU NAN.
Whatever (you) do, it isn't hard at all once (you) get used to it.

ANNOTATIONS ───────

甚麼 in the above example means "whatever".
There is a verb in front of it. Here 做 ZUO (do) is the verb.

他甚麼都學, 甚麼都沒有學好。(甚麼: everything)
TA SHEN ME DOU XUE, SHEN ME DOU MEI YOU XUE HAO.
He studied everything and nothing was done well.

───────

甚麼 here means everything and then nothing.

"他有甚麼? 他甚麼都沒有。" (甚麼: nothing)
TA YOU SHEN ME? TA SHEN ME DOU MEI YOU.
"What does he have? He has nothing at all."

───────

甚麼 in this example means "what" and then "nothing".

"甚麼? 你說甚麼?　　(甚麼: what)
SHEN ME? NI SHUO SHEN ME?
"What? What did you say?"

───────

The exact meaning is based largely on the tone and voice at the time of speaking, English and Chinese alike. Use it with caution.

這麼說,你就要去中國了? 多好!(多好 = 多麼好)
ZHE ME SHUO, NI JIU YAO QU ZHONG GUO LE? DUO HAO!
So, pretty soon you are leaving for China? How nice!

這麼難,叫我學? 我就學不了。
ZHE ME NAN, JIAO WO XUE? WO JIU XUE BU LIAO.
It's so hard. Ask me to learn this? I just can't do it.

那麼你要學甚麼?
NA ME NI YAO XUE SHEN ME?
Then what do you want to study?

你甚麼都不肯學,那還行嗎?
NI SHEN ME DOU BU KEN XUE, NA HAI XING MA?
You are not willing to learn anything. How come?

難道 is an adverb used to emphasize a rhetorical question. Compare the following sample sentences:

(1) 你知道嗎?   NI ZHI DAO MA?
你知道不知道?   NI ZHI DAO BU ZHI DAO?
Do you know?   (Question)

(2) 你不知道嗎?   NI BU ZHI DAO MA?
Don't you know? (Rhetorical question)

(3) 難道你不知道嗎?   NAN DAO NI BU ZHI DAO MA?
Aren't you aware of it? / Didn't you know about it?

(4) 你是知道的, 難道不是嗎?

   Isn't it true that you knew about it?

Different responses reflect the extent or degree of emphasis as shown in the following examples:

(1)　我不知道。　　　　　　　　WO BU ZHI DAO.
　　 I don't know.

(2)　我不知道的。　　　　　　　WO BU ZHI DAO DI.
　　 I'm not aware of it.

(3)　我就不知道了。　　　　　　WO JIU BU ZHI DAO LE.
　　 Not to my knowledge.

(4)　那我就不知道了。　　　　　NA WO JIU BU ZHI DAO LE.
　　 Not that I know of.

(5)　我怎麼知道?　　　　　　　WO ZEN ME ZHI DAO?
　　 How do I know?

MODULE 7

M7.1 FIRST GROUP OF 5 NEW CHARACTERS:

已 ³	經 ¹	過 ⁴	各 ⁴	地 ⁴
YI	JING	GUO	GE	DI
already	through	pass	different	place

M7.1A Build vocabulary and expressions with these five characters:

已經	YĪ JĪNG (3 1)	already (已 is the short form of 已經)(cf. **M2.3** 己 JĪ self)
經過	JĪNG GUÒ (1 4)	via; after
各地	GÈ DÌ (4 4)	different places, everywhere
已經過各地。	YĪ JĪNG GUÒ GÈ DÌ. (3 1 4 4 4)	Had already passed through different places. / (We/They) had already been to different places.

M7.1B Expand vocabulary and expressions by using all the 95 characters learned:

經手	JĪNG SHǑU (1 3)	handle(verb); deal with
經常	JĪNG CHÁNG (1 2)	often (經常 = 常常)
月經	YUÈ JĪNG (4 1)	menstruation; monthly Period
過年	GUÒ NIÁN (4 2)	New Year, New Year celebration
過問	GUÒ WÈN (4 4)	inquire with concern
過手	GUÒ SHǑU (4 3)	change hands
過去	GUÒ QÙ (4 4)	in the past
過來人	GUÒ LÁI RÉN (4 2 2)	a person who has had same experience

過不去	GUO⁴ BU⁴ QU⁴	cannot get through; not getting along
難過	NAN² GUO⁴	having a hard time; feel sorry
說不過去	SHUO¹ BU⁴ GUO⁴ QU⁴	not convincing

ANNOTATIONS ─────

'Verb + 過' indicates the definite past tense or perfect tense of the verb. e.g. 去過 QU GUO: went; had been there.

各人	GE⁴ REN²	everybody
天地	TIAN¹ DI⁴	Heaven and Earth; world

─────

M7.1C Sample sentences:

去年我們一行十人,經過英國去中國的,各人都看了不同的天地。

QU NIAN WO MEN YI XING SHI REN, JING GUO YING GUO QU ZHONG GUO, GE REN DOU KAN LE BU TONG DI TIAN DI.

Last year our group of ten went to China via the U.K. Everybody saw a different world.

ANNOTATIONS ─────

一行 YI₁ XING₂ (group, a group in a trip) is an expression used in written language of classical style Chinese writing, still in common use today.

你不是說過要去中國嗎?已經是十月了,還沒有去?

NI BU SHI SHUO GUO YAO QU ZHONG GUO MA? YI JING SHI SHI YUE LE, HAI MEI YOU QU?

Didn't you say you were going to China? It's October already and you are still not going?

你要去美國?問她好了,她去年去過。

NI YAO QU MEI GUO? WEN TA HAO LE, TA QU NIAN QU GUO.

You are going to America? Just ask her. She went there last year.

你不是說過她要來嗎?

NI BU SHI SHUO GUO TA YAO LAI MA?

Didn't you say that she was coming here?

我見過她。

WO JIAN GUO TA.

I met her before.

經過一年學習,她的中文很好。

JING GUO YI NIAN XUE XI, TA DE ZHONG WEN HEN HAO.

After one year study, her Chinese is pretty good.

他們已經有三年沒有相見了。

TA MEN YI JING YOU SAN NIAN MEI YOU XIANG JIAN LE.

They have not seen each other for three years already.

各地都有好有不好。

GE DI DOU YOU HAO YOU BU HAO.

Each place has its pros and cons.

他們說的都不相同,各人說各人的。
TA MEN SHUO DE DOU BU XIANG TONG, GE REN SHUO GE REN DE.
What they said was all different. Everybody had a different story.

你爲甚麼要和我過不去? 　　　(過不去)
NI WEI SHEN ME YAO HE WO GUO BU QU?
Why are you giving le a hard time? Literally: Why are you not getting along with me?

這裡過那邊?過不去的。 　　　(過不去)
ZHE LI GUO NEI BIAN? GUO BU QU DI.
From here to that side? Can't get through.

你這麼說, 說不過去的。 　　　(說不過去)
NI ZHE ME SHUO, SHUO BU GUO QU DE.
What you say is not convincing.

"你去過中國嗎?" 　　　　　　"去過了。"
"NI QU GUO ZHONG GUO MA?" 　　"QU GUO LE."
"Have you been to China?" 　　"Oh, yes."

過去, 學中文的美國人不多的。(過去)
GUO QU, XUE ZHONG WEN DI MEI GUO REN BU DUO DI.
In the past, not many Americans studied Chinese.

不要難過, 他明天就會來的。 　(難過)
BU YAO NAN GUO, TA MING TIAN JIU HI LAI DI.
Don't feel bad; he is coming tomorrow.

MODULE 7

M7.2 SECOND GROUP OF 5 NEW CHARACTERS:

心₁	完₂	全₂	明₂	白₂
XIN	WAN	QUAN	MING	BAI
heart/mind	finish	complete	bright	white

M7.2A Build vocabulary and expressions with these five characters:

完全	WÁN QUÁN (2 2)	fully, completely
全心	QUÁN XIN (2 1)	whole-hearted
明白	MÍNG BÁI (2 2)	understand

(明白 = 懂 DONG₃ (M6.3))

明明	MÍNG MÍNG (2 2)	obviously, clearly
白白	BÁI BÁI (2 2)	in vain
明明白白	MÍNG MÍNG BÁI BÁI (2 2 2 2)	clearly; undoubtedly
心完全明白 =	XIN WÁN QUÁN MÍNG BÁI. (1 2 2 2 2)	Fully understand in (my, his,...) mind.
心裡完全明白	XIN LI WÁN QUÁN MÍNG BÁI. (1 3 2 2 2 2)	

M7.2B Expand vocabulary and expressions by using all the 100 characters learned:

人心	REN XIN (2 1)	human heart, human mind
好心	HAO XIN (3 1)	good heart; good intention
有心	YOU XIN (3 1)	caring; intentional
多心	DUO XIN (1 1)	not sticking to; oversensitive
完好	WAN HAO (2 3)	in good condition
完人	WAN REN (2 2)	perfect person

完了	WAN² LE	finished; it's over
全文	QUAN² WEN²	full text; entire copy
全力	QUAN² LI⁴	full effort; all-out
全國	QUAN² GUO²	entire nation; national; nation-wide
全年	QUAN² NAN²	whole year: year round
明年	MING² NIAN²	next year
明天	MING² TIAN¹	tomorrow
天明	TIAN¹ MING²	daybreak
英明	YING¹ MING²	brilliant, wise
白人	BAI² REN²	white person; Caucasian
白天	BAI² TIAN¹	day time

M7.2C Sample sentences:

我懂多少中文的,人家說中文,我的心完全明白說的是甚麼,我自己說不出來就是了。(我的心=我心裡)

WO DONG DUO SHAO ZHONG WEN DE, REN JIA SHUO ZHONG WEN, WO DE XIN WAN QUAN MING BAI SHUO DE SHI SHEN ME, WO ZI JI SHUO BU CHU LAI JIU SHI LE.(WO DE XIN = WO XIN LI)

I understand some Chinese. When people speak in Chinese, I know in my mind what it is about; but I just can't speak.

他來美國學英文,英文並沒有學好,白白地過了三年。

TA LAI MEI GUO XUE YING WEN, YING WEN BING MEI YOU XUE HAO, BAI BAI DI GUO LE SAN NIAN.

He came to America to study English. He didn't do well in English. Three years were spent in vain.

明明叫他不要說,他還是說了,這不就完了?

MING MING JIAO TA BU YAO SHUO, TA HAI SHI SHUO LE, ZHE BU JIU WAN LE?

He was clearly told not to talk about it, and yet he still said it. Isn't that over?

不要說了,沒有用的,白說。

BU YAO SHUO LE, MEI YOU YONG DI, BAI SHUO.

Stop talking. It wouldn't help, talking in vain.

MODULE 7

M7.3 THIRD GROUP OF 5 NEW CHARACTERS:

知	道	或	者	對
1	4	4	3	4
ZIN	DAO	HUO	ZHE	DUI
know	way	or	(which)	correct; to

M7.3A Build vocabulary and expressions with these five characters:

知道	ZHI¹ DAO⁴	know (知 is the short form)
或者	HUO⁴ ZHE³	or (或 is the short form)
或者....或者....	either....or....	
知道或者對。	ZHI¹ DAO⁴ HUO⁴ ZHE³ DUI⁴.	(I, we, ..) know that maybe it's correct.

M7.3B Expand vocabulary and expressions by using all the 105 characters learned:

知心	ZHI¹ XIN¹	intimate
知己	ZHI¹ JI³	intimate (friend)
自知	ZI⁴ ZHI¹	self knowing
明知	MING² ZHI¹	being aware of; knowingly
大道	DA⁴ DAO⁴	road; avenue
小道	XIAO³ DAO⁴	sideway, path
地道	DI⁴ DAO⁴	tunnel; genuine, pure (casual)
人道	REN² DAO⁴	humanity
人行道	REN² XING² DAO⁴	pavement, side-walk, pedestrian crossing
說道	SHUO¹ DAO⁴	say(s): "..."
(...說: = ...道:)		

ANNOTATIONS ────────

("道:..." is more often used in novels.)

學者	XUÉ ZHĚ	scholar
對手	DUÌ SHǑU	rival; opponent
作對	ZUÒ DUÌ	oppose
相對	XIĀNG DUÌ	relatively; facing one another
不對	BÙ DUÌ	not correct; wrong
一對	YĪ DUÌ	pair, couple
一對對	YĪ DUÌ DUÌ	pairs, couples
完全對	WÁN QUÁN DUÌ	exactly right

───────

M7.3C Sample sentences:

他對我說過要來我家的, 還沒有來, 或者來不了。

TA DUI WO SHUO GUO YAO LAI WO JIA DE, HAI MEI YOU LAI, HUO ZHE LAI BU LIAO.

He told me that he was coming to my home. He is not showing up yet. Maybe he can't make it.

要學英文, 或者去英國, 或者去美國, 都非常好。

YAO XUE YING WEN, HUO ZHE QU YING GUO, HUO ZHE QU MEI GUO, DOU FEI CHANG HAO.

To study English, either go to the U.K., or go to the U.S. Both are very good.

他是對的, 我知道他是懂的。　　(對: correct)

TA SHI DUI DE, WO ZHI DAO TA SHI DONG DE.

He is right. I know he is knowledgeable.

(對: to)

對她來說, 學中文並不難, 她已經在中學學過中文的。

DUI TA LAI SHUO, XUE ZHONG WEN BING BU NAN, TA YI JING ZAI ZHONG XUE XUE GUO ZHONG WEN DE.

For her, it isn't difficult to study Chinese at all. She already had Chinese in high school.

M1	一二三十人	日月大小天	不是很好嗎
M2	上下午工作	左右手用力	肯自己出入
M3	我請你來看	她和他們問	說您還在家
M4	學習中英文	美國都去了	叫謝又再見
M5	常做慣就行	今年並沒有	要多少才夠
M6	這裡非那邊	哪些相同的	爲甚麼難懂
M7	已經過各地	心完全明白	知道或者對

Encouraging Review

From Modules 1 to 7, we have learned 105 Chinese characters so far. Let's see what we can do with the limited knowledge of just the first one hundred characters (**M1.1** to **M7.3**). Below is an example of composition:

我們工作上經常要用中文。自今年三月,我就在學中文,爲的是做好工作。爲了學好中文,我哪裡都不去了,上午工作,下午在家自學。中文和英文,完全不同。不過,不是很難懂,並不是非要去中國學不行。我在美國學中文就很好。有些人去過英國的,看過他們那邊學甚麼,都說美國還好一些。

有一同學非常用心學,才不過十來天,她已經習慣了看中文,還說好些,一看見我就和我說中文,不明白就問人家。這同學和我很要好,我們要一同去中國工作。中國地大人多,不要說是人家請我們去,就是自己去我都肯。

謝天謝地,這一天就要來了,我們要去中國了,多好!

(cf. PART 1 Section 1 and M9.3: 去中國 = 到中國去)

(Latinized Chinese) (*Fill in Tone Indicators as a practice.*)

    WO MEN GONG ZUO SHANG JING CHANG YAO YONG ZHONG WEN. ZI JIN NIAN SAN YUE, WO JIU ZAI XUE ZHONG WEN, WEI DE SHI ZUO HAO GONG ZUO. WEI LE XUE HAO ZHONG WEN, WO NA LI DOU BU QU LE, SHANG WU GONG ZUO, XIA WU ZAI JIA ZI XUE. ZHONG WEN HE YING WEN WAN QUAN BU TONG. BU GUO, BU SHI HEN NAN DONG, BING BU SHI FEI

YAO QU ZHONG GUO XUE BU XING. WO ZAI MEI GUO XUE ZHONG WEN JIU HEN HAO. YOU XIE REN QU GUO YING GUO DE, KAN GUO TA MEN NA BIAN XUE SHEN ME, DOU SHUO MEI GUO HAI HAO YI XIE.

    YOU YI TONG XUE FEI CHANG YONG XIN XUE, CAI BU GUO SHI LAI TIAN, TA YI JING XI GUAN LE KAN ZHONG WEN, HAI SHUO HAO XIE, YI KAN JIAN WO JIU HE WO SHUO ZHONG WEN, BU MING BAI JIU WEN REN JIA. ZHE TONG XUE HE WO HEN YAO HAO, WO MEN YAO YI TONG QU ZHONG GUO GONG ZUO. ZHONG GUO DI DA REN DUO, BU YAO SHUO REN JIA QING WO MEN QU, JIU SHI ZI JI QU WO DOU KEN XIE TIAN XIE DI, ZHE YI TIAN JIU YAO LAI LE, WO MEN YAO QU ZHONG GUO LE, DUO HAO!

(English)

    We often have to use Chinese at work. Since March of this year, I have been studying Chinese so that I can do a better job. In order to do well in studying Chinese, I give up going anywhere, go to work in the morning and stay home self-study in the afternoon. Chinese is totally different from English. However, it is not too hard to understand, nor is it a must to learn Chinese in China. I learn Chinese in America and it is pretty good. Some people who have been to the U.K. and have seen what they learned there, all say that it is even better in the U.S.

    One classmate studies very attentively. Only ten days or more she can get used to reading Chinese already and can even speak quite a bit. Whenever she sees me, she speaks Chinese to me. Whatever she doesn't understand, she asks people. This classmate and I are good friends and we are going together to work in China. China is big and has many people. Even if I go on my own I would go, not to mention that people invite us to go there. Thank God, the day is coming that we are going to China. How nice!

AMAZING

Invest ten to fourteen hours to learn 100 Chinese characters in seven Modules, and one can write a decent essay of 200-character length (actual number 221 characters) in Chinese. Isn't that amazing? Very efficient.

CHALLENGE

Now, activate your creativity brain cells and write your own essay based on the 105 characters (M1.1 to M7.3) learned. You will surprise yourself.

Good Luck!

MODULE 8

M8.1 FIRST GROUP OF 5 NEW CHARACTERS:

每	次	前	面	快
3	4	2	4	4
MEI	CI	QIAN	MIAN	KUAI
every/each	time	front, before	face	fast

M8.1A Build vocabulary and expressions with these five characters:

每次	MEI³ CI⁴	every time
次次	CI⁴ CI⁴	every time
每每	MEI³ MEI³	often times
前面	QIAN² MIAN⁴	in front; front part
面前	MIAN⁴ QIAN²	in front of
快快	KUAI⁴ KUAI⁴	hurry up
每次前面快。	MEI³ CI⁴ QIAN² MIAN⁴ KUAI⁴.	Every time the front part is fast.

M8.1B Expand vocabulary and expressions by using all the 110 characters learned:

每人	MEI³ REN²	each person; everyone
每年	MEI³ NIAN²	each year
每月	MEI³ YUE⁴	each month
每天	MEI³ TIAN¹	everyday; daily
每對	MEI³ DUI⁴	each pair; every couple
次要	CI⁴ YAO⁴	secondary
次年	CI⁴ NIAN²	the following year

人次	RÉN CÌ (2 4)	person-time
前天	QIÁN TIĀN (2 1)	day before yesterday
前年	QIÁN NIÁN (2 2)	year before last
前者	QIÁN ZHĚ (2 3)	the former
見面	JIÀN MIÀN (4 4)	meet with
出面	CHŪ MIÀN (1 4)	appear in person; exercise one's capacity
面對	MIÀN DUÌ (4 4)	facing
對面	DUÌ MIÀN (4 4)	opposite side
面對面	MIÀN DUÌ MIÀN (4 4 4)	face to face
多面手	DUŌ MIÀN SHŎU (1 4 3)	versatile; handyman

M8.1C Sample sentences:

他看見他前面有一些人，很快就不見了。

TA KAN JIAN TA QIAN MIAN YOU YI XIE REN, HEN KUAI JIU BU JIAN LE.

He saw some people in front of him; very soon they disappeared.

三年來，他一面上大學，一面工作，看來他還好。

SAN NIAN LAI, TA YI MIAN SHANG DA XUE, YI MIAN GONG ZUO, KAN LAI TA HAI HAO.

For three years, he has been attending college while working. It appears that he is doing fine.

ANNOTATIONS ────

一面…一面… == 一邊…一邊… (MODULE 6.1)

他經常說要來,每每就是來不了。

TA JING CHANG SHUO YAO LAI, MEI MEI JIU SHI LAI BU LIAO.

He often said that he would come over; often times he just couldn't make it.

他自己來,面對面對我說才行。

TA ZI JI LAI, MIAN DUI MIAN DUI WO SHUO CAI XING.

The only way is to have him come over and talk to me face to face.

他經常說要做快一點,每次都快不了。

TA JING CHANG SHUO YAO ZUO KUAI YI DIAN, MEI CI DOU KOAI BU LIAO.

He often said that he would speed it up and every time he missed.

────

ANNOTATIONS ────

Compare the Tense of Verbs (time of action) in the above sample sentences.

────

MODULE 8

M8.2 SECOND GROUP OF 5 NEW CHARACTERS:

M8.2A Build vocabulary and expressions with these five characters:

後半	HOU BAN	latter half
放慢	FANG MAN	slow down
慢點	MAN DIAN	slow down; late
放後	FANG HOU	set aside; push behind
慢慢	MAN MAN	slowly
後半放慢點。	HOU BAN FANG MAN DIAN.	The rear half slows down a little bit.

M8.2B Expand vocabulary and expressions by using all the 115 characters learned:

後來	HOU LAI	later on
後年	HOU NIAN	year after next
後天	HOU TIAN	day after tomorrow
後面	HOU MIAN	behind; rear
後邊	HOU BIAN	behind; rear
後者	HOU ZHE	the latter
今後	JIN HOU	from now on

ANNOTATIONS ———

"Verb + 後" indicates "after (the action)": e.g. 來後 LAI₂ HOU₄ after (somebody) came.

前後	QIAN₂ HOU₄	front and rear; beginning to end (altogether)
前前後後	QIAN₂ QIAN₂ HOU₄ HOU₄	(same as 前後)
半年	BAN₄ NIAN₂	half year
半天	BAN₄ TIAN₁	half day
一半	YI₁ BAN₄	one half
對半	DUI₄ BAN₄	fifty fifty split
過半	GUO₄ BAN₄	more than half
大半	DA₄ BAN₄	more than half
放下	FANG₄ XIA₄	put down
放行	FANG₄ XING₂	release
放心	FANG₄ XIN₁	relieved; don't worry
放手	FANG₄ SHOU₃	let go; a free hand
放過	FANG₄ GUO₄	let off; miss
一點點	YI₁ DIAN₃ DIAN₃	a little bit
一點	YI₁ DIAN₃	some (一點 = 一些)

———

M8.2C Sample sentences:

我們一行十二人,大半沒有去過中國的,甚麼都不放過,都要看一看。

WO MEN YI XING SHI ER REN, DA BAN MEI YOU QU GUO ZHONG GUO DE, SHEN ME DOU BU FANG GUO, DOU YAO KAN YI KAN.

In our team of twelve, more than half had never been to China. We didn't want to miss anything; we wanted to see everything.

學中文，我是慢慢來的，一天學一點，前後學了一年，很好。

XUE ZHONG WEN, WO SHI MAN MAN LAI DE, YI TIAN XUE YI DIAN, QIAN HOU XUE LE YI NIAN, HEN HAO.

In studying Chinese, I work on it slowly, a little bit every day. So far it has been one year and it's pretty good.

我很好，請放心。

WO HEN HAO, QING FANG XIN.

I am fine. Please don't worry about me.

MODULE 8

M8.3 THIRD GROUP OF 5 NEW CHARACTERS:

原²	因¹	太⁴	方¹	便⁴
YUAN	YIN	TAI	FANG	BIAN
source	cause	too	side	convenient

M8.3A Build vocabulary and expressions with these five characters:

原因	YUÁN YIN (2 1)	reason
方便	FĀNG BIÀN (1 4)	convenient; convenience
太	TÀI (4)	too; excessive (太 = 太過 TAI₄ GUO₄)

ANNOTATIONS ─────

太 or 太過 is used as an adverb to modify verbs, adjectives or other adverbs.

原因太方便。 YUÁN YIN TÀI FĀNG BIÀN (2 1 4 1 4). The reason is too convenient.

─────

M8.3B Expand vocabulary and expressions by using all the 120 characters learned:

原來	YUÁN LÁI (2 2)	original; previous; turn out to be
原文	YUÁN WÉN (2 2)	original text
原地	YUÁN DÌ (2 1)	original place
原作	YUÁN ZUÒ (2 4)	original piece of work
還原	HUÁN YUÁN (2 2)	restore to original; (chemical) reduction
因爲	YIN WÈI (1 4)	because

方面	FĀNG MIÀN	aspect; regard
方才	FĀNG CÁI	just a while ago
地方	DÌ FĀNG	place
前方	QIÁN FĀNG	ahead
後方	HÒU FĀNG	rear; rear area
自便	ZÌ BIÀN	help yourself; up to you
大便	DÀ BIÀN	stool, shit
小便	XIǍO BIÀN	urine; pass water

M8.3C Sample sentences:

外面看不見甚麼人，原來都在這裡。　　　(原來)

WAI MIAN KAN BU JIAN SHEN ME REN, YUAN LAI DOU ZAI ZHE LI.

There isn't anybody outside. It turns out that everybody is here.

去中國很方便，原來沒有去過的都說要去。　　　(原來)

QU ZHONG GUO HEN FANG BIAN, YUAN LAI MEI YOU QU GUO DE DOU SHUO YAO QU. (cf. PART 1 Section 1 and M9.3) It's very convenient to go to China. All those who have not been there say that they want to go.

原來是你！YUAN LAI SHI NI! Oh, it's you! (原來)

他學中文是有原因的：他明年要去中國工作。

TA XUE ZHONG WEN SHI YOU YUAN YIN DE: TA MING NIAN YAO QU ZHONG GUO GONG ZUO.

There is a reason why he is studying Chinese. He is going to work in China next year.

做快一點才行, 太慢了。這些太少, 不夠。

ZUO KUAI YI DIAN CAI XING, TAI MAN LE. ZHE XIE TAI SHAO, BU GOU.

Too slow, (you've) got to speed up. These are not enough, too little.

這裡不方便, 過那邊才說。

ZHE LI BU FANG BIAN, GUO NEI BIAN CAI SHUO.

Here is not the right place to talk. Get over there and talk.

這裡是中心, 去哪裡都很方便。

ZHE LI SHI ZHONG XIN, QU NA LI DOU HEN FANG BIAN.

Here is the center. It's very convenient to go anywhere.

你方便就來我家。

NI FANG BIAN JIU LAI WO JIA.

Come to my home at your convenience.

MODULE 9

M9.1 FIRST GROUP OF 5 NEW CHARACTERS:

想₃	起₃	幾₃	件₄	事₄
XIANG	QI	JI	JIAN	SHI
think	up	several	piece	matter

M9.1A Build vocabulary and expressions with these five characters:

想起	XIĂNG QĬ (3 3)	think of; recall
幾件	JĬ JIÀN (3 4)	several pieces
事件	SHÌ JIÀN (4 4)	incident

想起幾件事。 XIĂNG QĬ JĬ JIÀN SHÌ. (3 3 3 4 4)

A few things come into mind.
(Literally: Think of a few things.)

M9.1B Expand vocabulary and expressions by using all the 125 characters learned:

想家	XIĂNG JIĀ (3 1)	home sick
起家	QĬ JIĀ (3 1)	build up (wealth); make one's fortune
起行	QĬ XÍNG (3 2)	start on a journey
起見	QĬ JIÀN (3 4)	爲....起見: for the sake of; in order to
起來	QĬ LÁI (3 2)	get up; arise
家事	JIĀ SHÌ (1 4)	family matter
要事	YÀO SHÌ (4 4)	important matter (cf. **M5.3B**: 要是 YAO₄ SHI₄)

人事	RÉN SHÌ	personnel
出事	CHŪ SHÌ	accident; something happened
了事	LIǍO SHÌ	get something over
有事	YǑU SHÌ	something to be taken care of
懂事	DǑNG SHÌ	sensible (child)
這件事	ZHÈ JIÀN SHÌ	this matter / affair
一件件事	YÍ JIÀN JIÀN SHÌ	each of the matters
對事不對人	DUÌ SHÌ BÚ DUÌ RÉN	against the subject matter, not against the person

M9.1C Sample sentences:

這件事是他不對;不過,爲了大家和好地一同工作起見,我們對事不對人。

ZHE JIAN SHI SHI TA BU DUI; BU GUO, WEI LE DA JIA HE HAO

DI YI TONG GONG ZUO QI JIAN, WO MEN DUI SHI BU DUI REN.

He is wrong in this matter. However, for the sake of working together in a friendly way, we are against the subject matter and not against the person.

好幾年前的事了,完全沒有人想起這件事。

HAO JI NIAN QIAN DE SHI LE, WAN QUAN MEI YOU REN XIANG QI ZHE JIAN SHI.

It has been quite a few years. Nobody recalls this matter at all.

想來想去,就是想不起來。

XIANG LAI XIANG QU, JIU SHI XIANG BU QI LAI.

Keep thinking it over and over again; (I) just don't recall.

ANNOTATIONS ———

There is no subject in the above last sentence. It implies the pronoun "I". This kind of sentence structure is not unusual in Chinese language. In English a subject is required to satisfy the grammatical rules of sentence structure.

出事了。

CHU SHI LE.

Some kind of accident happened.
Something went wrong.

出了甚麼事?

CHU LE SHEN ME SHI?

What happened?

沒有出甚麼事。

MEI YOU CHU SHEN MO SHI.

Nothing happened.

沒事了。

MEI SHI LE.

The problem is over.

Q: "在想甚麼?"　　　ZAI XIANG SHEN MO?

　"What are you thinking about?"

A: "沒甚麼。有點想家。"　　MEI SHEN MO. YOU DIAN XIANG JIA.

　"Nothing. A little home-sick."

他是非常小心的人,事事都自己做,不懂就問,一學就明。

TA SHI FEI CHANG XIAO XIN DE REN, SHI SHI DOU ZI JI ZUO, BU DONG JIU WEN, YI XUE JIU MING.

He is a very careful person. He handles everything by himself. Anything he doesn't understand, he asks and he learns fast.

這件事,他說的和你說的有出入。

ZHE JIAN SHI, TA SHUO DE HE NI SHUO DE YOU CHU RU.

There is inconsistency in what he said and what you said about this matter.

In the last sentence above, notice the two clauses:

他說的 'what he said' and 你說的 'what you said'. There is no relative pronoun 'what' in the Chinese sentence. 有出入 = 是有出入的.

MODULE 9

M9.2 SECOND GROUP OF 5 NEW CHARACTERS:

	得	可	以	搞
JUE²	DE²	KE³	YI³	GAO³
feel	obtain	may	use	do

M9.2A Build vocabulary and expressions with these five characters:

覺得	JUE² DE²	feel; think
可以	KE³ YI³	may, can (可 = 可以)
覺得可以搞。	JUE² DE² KE³ YI³ GAO³.	(I) think it can be done.

M9.2B Expand vocabulary and expressions by using all the 130 characters learned:

得力	DE² LI⁴	helpful
得人心	DE² REN² XIN¹	gain people's support
不得人心	BU⁴ DE² REN² XIN¹	being unpopular
可行	KE³ XING²	feasible
可是	KE³ SHI⁴	however
可見	KE³ JIAN⁴	it is thus clear that
以前	YI³ QIAN²	before; in the past
以後	YI³ HOU⁴	after; thereafter
以來	YI³ LAI²	since then
以上	YI³ SHANG⁴	more than; above
以下	YI³ XIA⁴	less than; below

以便	YI³ BIAN⁴	in order to; so that
以爲	YI³ WEI²	think; assume
以...爲	YI³...WEI²	use...as...

ANNOTATIONS ———

搞 is a character used widely. Basically it is a word of action 'do' for casual use. It could substitute just about any verb of action; however, avoid overusing it by choosing the appropriate verb.

搞工作	GAO³ GONG¹ ZUO⁴	do the work (做工作)
搞好(做好)	GAO³ HAO³	get it done nicely
難搞	NAN² GAO³	hard to do; tough
難得	NAN² DE²	hard to come by
不好搞	BU⁴ HAO³ GAO³	it's tough

———

M9.2C Sample sentences:

以美國爲中心。〔以...爲...:use ... as ... 〕

YI MEI GUO WEI ZHONG XIN.

Take America as the center. / America is the center.
(可以: can, may)

他原來覺得可以做的, 後來做來做去搞不出來, 這就難

搞了。(覺得 JUE² DE⁴ = 以爲 YI³ WEI²)

TA YUAN LAI JUE DE KE YI ZUO DE, HOU LAI ZUO LAI ZUO QU GAO BU CHU LAI, ZHE JIU NAN GAO LE.

Originally he thought it could be done. Later he did it this way and that way and still nothing done. This makes it tough.

做得好。 ZUO DE HAO. Well done.
看得見嗎? KAN DE JIAN MA? Can (you) see it?
看得見了。 KAN DE JIAN LE. (Now I) can see it.

看得見了 = 看見了 --- 得 is used to add emphasis.

難得很 NAN₂ DE₂ HEN₃ very tough; very difficult.
(難得很=很難:難得很 is typical Mandarin orally.)
(cf. M6.3)

我看得出來, 你是好人。(cf. M3.1C 4th sample.)
WO KAN DE CHU LAI, NI SHI HAO REN.
I can tell; you are a nice person.

(以… : per…)
以我看, 他並不懂。 YI WO KAN, TA BING BU DONG.
I think he doesn't understand.

你來我家, 以便一起去。 (以便… : so that…)
NI LAI WO JIA, YI BIAN YI QI QU. (一起 = 一道)
You come to my home so that we can go together.

ANNOTATIONS

The above last sentence in Chinese is typical. In daily use, more often than not, the word "we" is omitted in the Chinese sentence.

(你來我家, 以便我們一起去。 Same meaning.)

得了, 我做就是了。
DE LE, WO ZUO JIU SHI LE. (Notice 了 is LE, not LIAO.)
OK. I'll do it.

他並不懂, 可是他又不肯學。

TA BING BU DONG, KE SHI TA YOU BU KEN XUE.

他並不懂, 可又不肯學。

TA BING BU DONG, KE YOU BU KEN XUE.

He doesn't understand and yet he is not willing to learn.

Both Chinese expressions are fine. The second one is typical Mandarin in speaking.

我可以看一看嗎?   /   "可以看一下嗎?"

WO KE YI KAN YI KAN MA? / "KE YI KAN YI XIA MA? "

May I see it? / Can I have a look?

Q "你覺得好不好?"   /   "你覺得好嗎?"

"NI JUE DE HAO BU HAO? " / "NI JUE DE HAO MA? "

"Do you think it's good? "

A "我看是好的。"   /   "我想是好的。"

"WO KAN SHI HAO DE." / "WO XIANG SHI HAO DE."

"I think it's good. "

"很好。" "HEN HAO. " / "好得很" "HAO DE HEN. "

"Very good."

MODULE 9

M9.3 THIRD GROUP OF 5 NEW CHARACTERS:

討₃	論₄	給₃	提₂	到₄
TAO	LUN	GEI	TI	DAO
ask for	discuss	give; being	lift; mention	arrive

M9.3A Build vocabulary and expressions with these five characters:

討論	TAO³ LUN⁴	discuss, discussion
提到	TI² DAO⁴	mention
給	GEI³	give
給提到	GEI³ TI² DAO⁴	being mentioned

ANNOTATIONS ———

"給 + verb" makes the verb become passive voice.

討論給提到。TAO³ LUN⁴ GEI³ TI² DAO⁴.

Being mentioned at the discussion.

M9.3B Expand vocabulary and expressions by using all the 135 characters learned:

討好	TAO³ HAO³	ingratiate oneself with
討還	TAO³ HUAN²	ask for return or payment
提出	TI² CHU¹	put forward, raise (request, propose)
提起	TI² QI³	lift (something); raise (a subject)

Mastering Mandarin: Your Path to Proficiency

提前	TI² QIAN²	ahead of time/schedule
到家	DAO⁴ JIA¹	highly skillful; arrive home
到手	DAO⁴ SHOU³	in hand; in possession
來到	LAI² DAO⁴	come; arrive
到來	DAO⁴ LAI²	arrival
看到	KAN⁴ DAO⁴	see (看到 = 看見)

M9.3C Sample sentences:

給我。　　　　　GEI WO.　　　　　Give it to me.

我給了他,你看見的。　　WO GEI LE TA, NI KAN JIAN DE.
I gave it to him. You saw that.

ANNOTATIONS ———

The character 了 here gives the definite past tense of the action 給. The second portion is in past tense based on the context.

我看見他出去的。
WO KAN JIAN TA CHU QU DE. I saw him leaving.

我不想給他知道我常來你家,可我每次來都給他看到。
WO BU XIANG GEI TA ZHI DAO WO CHANG LAI NI JIA, KE WO MEI CI LAI DOU GEI TA KAN DAO.
I don't want him to know that I often come to your home; but every time I came, he saw me.

———

The above example demonstrates 3 features of the difference between Chinese and English:

(1) While passive voice is used in a Chinese sentence, active voice is preferred in English. The character 給 GEI₃ makes the verb that follows the passive expression (給他看到: was seen by him);

(2) Tense of a verb in Chinese is mainly based on context; notice the tense in Chinese sentence;

(3) There are no relative pronouns such as 'that' or 'which' in Chinese language for a complex sentence. A subordinate clause follows the verb directly. (知道我常來你家).

我提出這件事來，請大家討論討論，看看好不好給他做。

WO TI CHU ZHE JIAN SHI LAI, QING DA JIA TAO LUN TAO LUN, KAN KAN HAO BU HAO GEI TA ZUO.

I bring up this matter to let all of you discuss it over and see if it would be fine to let him do it.

---

(1) 請大家 here means 請你們 in a courteous my. This kind of indirect expression is common in Chinese.

(2) 討論討論 means 討論; 看看 means 看. Repeating the verb is often used in oral usage to put some emphasis.

論學問, 他好得多。　　　　　　(論...: speaking about...)

LUN XUE WEN, TA HAO DE DUO.

As far as knowledge is concerned, he is much better. (..., he is more knowledgeable.)

這件事, 非給他做不可。

ZHE JIAN SHI, FEI GEI TA ZUO BU KE.

This matter must be handled by him and nobody else.

提起他, 人人都說是好人。

TI QI TA, REN REN DOU SHUO SHI HAO REN.

Whenever he is mentioned, everybody says that he is a nice person.

他還在家。	(還 HAI: still)
TA HAI ZAI JIA.	He is still at home. (cf. M3.3)
他還沒有做完。	(還 HAI: yet)
TA HAI MEI YOU ZUO WAN.	He has not completed yet.
還好, 他不知道。	(還 HAI: fortunately)
HAI HAO, TA BU ZHI DAO.	Not bad, he doesn't know. (Fortunately, he doesn't know)
明天是你來還是他來?	(還 是 HAI SHI: or)
MING TIAN SHI NI LAI HAI SHI TA LAI?	Tomorrow you come or he comes? (Who is going to come tomorrow: you or he?)
你來過了, 今天還是你來?	(還是 HAI SHI: still)
NI LAI GUO LE, JIN TIAN HAI SHI NI LAI?	You had been here before. And today it is you again?
還是我來好。	(還是 HAI SHI: better)
HAI SHI WO LAI HAO.	It is better for me to come. / (... to do it.)
叫他還。	(還 HUAN: return (something))
JIAO TA HUAN.	Ask him to return it.

還給他。　　　　　　　　　　(還 HUAN: return (something))
HUAN GEI TA.　　　　　　　　Return to him.

我給了他好多天了,還沒有還,要討還。　(還 HAI₂: still; 還 HUAN₂: return)
WO GEI LE TA HAO DUO TIAN LE,　I gave it to him many days ago and he
HAI MEI YOU HUAN, YAO TAO HUAN.　didn't return it. Ask him to return it.

他會說中文,常到中國去。
TA HUI SHUO ZHONG WEN,　　　He can speak Chinese.
CHANG DAO ZHONG GUO QU.　　He goes to China often.

到中國去=去中國;去美國=到美國去。

到中國去 is a typical expression in Mandarim;

去中國 is a general expression, often used in the south such as Cantonese.

(Try to locate all the 去中國、去美國、去英國 in sample sentences of previous Modules and change them to 到中國去、到美國去、到英國去 respectively as a practice.)

MODULE 10

M10.1 FIRST GROUP OF 5 NEW CHARACTERS:

五³	六⁴	個⁴	項⁴	目⁴
WU	LIU	GE	XIANG	MU
five	six	piece	item	list; eye

M10.1A Build vocabulary and expressions with these five characters:

項目	XIĀNG MÙ	project
個	GE⁴	(indicate the number of persons, objects, ...)
五六個項目。	WŪ LIÙ GÈ XIĀNG MÙ	Five or six projects.

M10.1B Expand vocabulary and expressions by using all the 140 characters learned:

五月	WŪ YUÈ	May (the month of May)
六月	LIÙ YUÈ	June
事項	SHÌ XIÀNG	matter; item; point
目的	MÙ DÌ	purpose
目前	MÙ QIÁN	at present; currently
個個	GÈ GÈ	each and every one
每個	MĚI GÈ	each; every
個人	GÈ RÉN	individual; personal

120 Mastering Mandarin: Your Path to Proficiency

M10.1C Sample sentences:

我們這裡工作的六個人，個個都懂多少中文。

WO MEN ZHE LI GONG ZUO DE LIU GE REN, GE GE DOU DONG DUO SHAO ZHONG WEN.

Of the six people who work here, everybody more or less understands some Chinese.

我個人覺得可以做到。

WO GE REN JUE DE KE YI ZUO DAO.

Personally I think it can be done.

工作就工作，不要做個人的事。

GONG ZUO JIU GONG ZUO, BU YAO ZUO GE REN DE SHI.

work is work; don't do personal things.

學中文學得快還是慢，這要看個人了。

XUE ZHONG WEN XUE DE KUAI HAI SHI MAN, ZHE YAO KAN GE REN LE.

In learning Chinese, whether fast or slow, it all depends on the individual.

ANNOTATIONS

個 GE is used to express unit similar to 'piece', 'sheet', 'drop' and the like. There are specific characters for different uses, very specific.

六個人	six persons	(六人 means the same.)
六個月	six months	(六月: June; 個 must be used to mean number of months)
五天	five days	(個 is not used at all.)

五項	five items	(項 is used)
五件事	five things	(matters) (件 is used instead of 個)
五個項目	five projects	(個 is used; not 五項目)

目前我們有五個項目在做，明年又要多一個了。

MU QIAN WO MEN YOU WU GE XIANG MU ZAI ZUO, MING NIAN YOU YAO DUO YI GE LE.

Currently we have five projects ongoing. Next year we will have one more.

這個項目難搞得很。

ZHE GE XIANG MU NAN GAO DE HEN.

This project is tough enough.

三年前中國來的那個項目，提前了一年做完。

SAN NIAN QIAN ZHONG GUO LAI DE NEI GE XIANG MU, TI QIAN LE YI NIAN ZUO WAN.

The project from China three years ago was completed one year ahead of schedule.

The above last sentence provides an example to show the feature of sentence structure between Chinese and English.

(1) Descriptive phrases are in front of the subject "項目" in Chinese while inEnglish the subject word "project" stands out first followed by descriptive phrase(s).

(2) Active voice is used in this Chinese sentence without a subject; passive voice is used in the English sentence.

MODULE 10

這個, 我就不要了。

ZHE GE, WO JIU BU YAO LE.

This one, I don't want it.

工作不少, 我們有五個人, 一個人做一項, 還行。

GONG ZUO BU SHAO, WO MEN YOU WU GE REN, YI GE REN ZUO YI XIANG, HAI XING.

Quite a bit of work. We have five people. Each of us works on one item. We're still OK.

目前我們的工作有的是。 (有的是: plenty)

MU QIAN WO MEN DE GONG ZUO YOU DE SHI.

At present we have plenty of work to do.

這些人, 有的是懂中文的。 (有的是…: some)

ZHE XIE REN, YOU DE SHI DONG ZHONG WEN DE.

Some of these people understand Chinese.

他學中文的目的就是要到中國去工作。

TA XUE ZHONG WEN DE MU DI JIU SHI YAO DAO ZHONG GUO QU GONG ZUO.

他學中文, 目的就是要到中國去工作。

TA XUE ZHONG WEN, MU DI JIU SHI YAO DAO ZHONG GUO QU GONG ZUO.

He studies Chinese with the purpose of going to work in China.

The 2 Chinese sentences mean the same.

The second one is more typical.

MODULE 10

M10.2 SECOND GROUP OF 5 NEW CHARACTERS:

共	七	百	萬	元
4	1	3	4	2
GONG	QI	BAI	WAN	YUAN
total	seven	hundred	ten thousand	dollar

M10.2A Build vocabulary and expressions with these five characters:

七百	QI BAI (1 4)	seven hundred
萬萬	WAN WAN (4 4)	absolutely; hundred million
百萬	BAI WAN (3 4)	million

ANNOTATIONS ———

萬 which means ten thousand is a basic unit in Chinese to express large numbers as thousand is used in English.

共七百萬元。 GONG QI BAI WAN YUAN (4 1 3 4 2). Total of seven million dollars.

———

M10.2B Expand vocabulary and expressions by using all the 145 characters learned:

一共	YI GONG (1 4)	total (共 is the short form)
中共	ZHONG GONG (1 4)	The Chinese Communist Party
	(abbreviated form in Chinese for: 中國共產黨)	
共同	GONG TONG (4 2)	common; together
共有	GONG YOU (4 3)	total of; commonly owned
共和	GONG HE (4 2)	republic

共和國	GÒNG HÉ GUÓ	republic (nation)
元月	YUÁN YUÈ	January (Same as 一月)
美元	MĚI YUÁN	U.S. Dollar
日元	RÌ YUÁN	Japanese YEN
七月	QĪ YUÈ	July

M10.2C Sample sentences:

七個項目,每個一百萬,一共七百萬元。〔一共;共有〕

QI GE XIANG MU, MEI GE YI BAI WAN, GONG QI BAI WAN YUAN.

Seven projects at one million each; the total is seven million dollars.

ANNOTATIONS ———

一共 in the above sentence can be replaced by 共有 or 一共有.

———

他們到中國去,一共用了七百萬美元,搞幾個項目。

TA MEN DAO ZHONG GUO QU, YI GONG YONG LE QI BAI WAN MEI YUAN, GAO JI GE XIANG MU.

They went to China and spent a total of seven million U.S. Dollars for several projects.

ANNOTATIONS ———

Sentence structure: Comma, the punctuation mark, is used quite differently in Chinese. It is often used where a conjunction (such as 'and' in a clause) or a preposition (such as 'for' in a phrase) is used in English.

這一百萬元是五個人共有的。　　　　　(共有)

ZHE YI BAI WAN YUAN SH WU GE REN GONG YOU DE.

These one million dollars are owned by five people.

那個項目是他們和我們共同做的。　　　(共同)

NEI GE XIANG MU SHI TA MEN HE WO MEN GONG TONG ZUO DE.

That project was handled by them along with us.

五、六、七三個月,每個月要一萬元。

WU, LIU, QI SAN GE YUE, MEI GE YUE YAO YI WAN YUAN.

Need ten thousand dollars for each of the three months of May, June and July.

The pause mark (、) is a punctuation mark used in Chinese language where a comma is used in English. It is used to separate each item in a series. Notice 五、六、七: no "and" before 七.

他年過半百,是個非常好的人。

TA NIAN GUO BAN BAI, SHI GE FEI CHANG HAO DI REN.

He is over fifty years old, a very nice person.

做事做到一半就不做,萬萬不可。

ZUO SHI ZUO DAO YI BAN JIU BU ZUO, WAN WAN BU KE.

Never ever quit halfway in doing something.

MODULE 10

M10.3 THIRD GROUP OF 5 NEW CHARACTERS:

投²	資¹	八¹	九³	千¹
TOU	ZI	BA	JIU	QIAN
put in	capital	eight	nine	thousand

M10.3A Build vocabulary and expressions with these five characters:

投資	TOU² ZI¹	invest; investment
八千	BA¹ QIAN¹	eight thousand
投資八九千。	TOU² ZI¹ BA¹ JIU³ QIAN¹.	Invest eight to nine thousand (dollars).

M10.3B Expand vocabulary and expressions by using all the 150 characters learned:

投入	TOU² RU⁴	put in
資方	ZI¹ FANG¹	investor party; capital
工資	GONG¹ ZI¹	wage; salary
八月	BA¹ YUE⁴	August
九月	JIU³ YUE⁴	September
千萬	QIAN¹ WAN⁴	be sure; ten million
千千萬萬	QIAN¹ QIAN¹ WAN⁴ WAN⁴	thousands and thousands

M10.3C Sample sentences:

去年他們到中國去, 投入不少人力, 投資過千萬。

QU NIAN TA MEN DAO ZHONG GUO QU, TOU RU BU SHAO REN LI, TOU ZI GUO QIAN WAN.

Last year they went to China, put in quite some manpower and investment was over ten million.

這個項目投資一百萬還不夠的, 目前搞不了。

ZHE GE XIANG MU TOU ZI YI BAI WAN HAI BU GOU DE, MU QIAN GAO BU LIAO. (搞不了=做不來 ZUO$_4$ BU$_4$ LAI$_2$.)

An investment of one million is still not enough for this project. Can't do it at this time.

美方是資方, 出資, 中方出人出地, 一共有八百萬美元。

MEI FANG SHI ZI FANG, CHU ZI, ZHONG FANG CHU REN CHU DI, YI GONG YOU BA BAI WAN MEI YUAN.

The American party is investor providing capital, the Chinese party provides man power and land, and the total is eight million U.S. Dollars.

M1	一二三十人	日月大小天	不是很好嗎
M2	上下午工作	左右手用力	肯自己出入
M3	我請你來看	她和他們問	說您還在家
M4	學習中英文	美國都去了	叫謝又再見
M5	常做慣就行	今年並沒有	要多少才夠
M6	這裡非那邊	哪些相同的	爲甚麼難懂
M7	已經過各地	心完全明白	知道或者對
M8	每次前面快	後半放慢點	原因太方便
M9	想起幾件事	覺得可以搞	討論給提到
M10	五六個項目	共七百萬元	投資八九千

ANNOTATIONS ⎯⎯⎯⎯

Armed with the 150 characters learned so far, you can write a short paragraph of a certain topic. The following is just an example.

提出來的投資項目很多，我們不懂的就不過問了。知道好的，目前我們做得來的，就非搞不可。今天請大家來，爲的是要大家一起來討論討論。爲方便起見，每個項目的中文、英文都有，英文在前，中文在後。

TI CHU LAI DE TOU ZI XIANG MU HEN DUO, WO MEN BU DONG DE JIU BU GUO WEN LE. ZHI DAO HAO DE, MU QIAN WO MEN ZUO DE LAI DE, JIU FEI GAO BU KE. JIN TIAN QING DA JIA LAI, WEI DE SHI YAO DA JIA YI QI LAI TAO LUN TAO LUN. WEI FANG BIAN QI JIAN, MEI GE XIANG MU DE ZHONG WEN, YING WEN DOU YOU, YING WEN ZAI QIAN, ZHONG WEN ZAI HOU.

There are many investment projects proposed. Those we don't understand, we are not concerned about. Those we do know that they are good and that we can handle at this time, we must take them. Today you are invited to come and discuss these things together. For convenience's sake, each project is listed in both Chinese and English; English in front followed by Chinese.

*   *   *

Review each of the characters, words, expressions and sentences. Focus on "That's HOW it works!" Get familiar with the nature of Chinese language.

⎯⎯⎯⎯

MODULE 11

M11.1 FIRST GROUP OF 5 NEW CHARACTERS:

只₃	四₄	成₂	把₃	握₄
ZHI	SI	CHENG	BA	WO
only	four	become fraction	handle	grip

M11.1A Build vocabulary and expressions with these five characters:

四成	SI⁴ CHENG²	forty percent
把握	BA³ WO⁴	certainty; sure; grip
只四成把握。	ZHI³ SI⁴ CHENG² BA³ WO⁴.	(只=只有) Only forty percent certain.

M11.1B Expand vocabulary and expressions by using all the 155 characters learned:

只有	ZHI³ YOU³	only (只 is the short form)
只得	ZHI³ DE²	only (只得 = 只有 = 只)
只是	ZHI³ SHI¹	only, just
只不過	ZHI³ BU⁴ GUO⁴	only, not over; nothing but
只好	ZHI³ HAO³	obliged to; no choice but
只要	ZHI³ YAO⁴	as long as; only if
四月	SI⁴ YUE⁴	April
四方	SI⁴ FANG¹	square; four sides
四面八方	SI⁴ MIAN⁴ BA¹ FANG¹	everywhere; all directions
成爲	CHENG² WEI²	become
成天	CHENG² TIAN²	all day long

成年	CHÉNG NIÁN	all year round; adulthood
成年人	CHÉNG NIÁN RÉN	adult person (Cf. M1.2B: 大人)
成事	CHÉNG SHÌ	completed; completion
成家	CHÉNG JIĀ	get married (form a family)
成對	CHÉNG DUÌ	in pairs, couple
把手	BǍ SHǑU	handle; grip; knob
握手	WÒ SHǑU	shake hands; handshake

M11.1C Sample Sentences:

我對這方面完全不懂，沒有把握做好。

WO DUI ZHE FANG MIAN WAN QUAN BU DONG, MEI YOU BA WO ZUO HAO.

I totally don't understand this field; I'm not sure if I can do well.

他做過相同的項目的，我想他這一次完全有把握做好。

TA ZUO GUO XIANG TONG DE XIANG MU DE, WO XIANG TA ZHE YI CI WAN QUAN YOU BA WO ZUO HAO.

He handled a similar project before. I think it is pretty sure that he will do well this time.

ANNOTATIONS ———

The word 'before' does not occur in the Chinese sentence. It can be added on and it becomes：他以前做過…。No difference in meaning. In Chinese, 做過 already specifies that it is past tense whether the word 以前 is added or not.

他把這件事給了我做。(把....(給)...)

TA BA ZHE JIAN SHI GEI LE WO ZUO.

He let me handle this latter. (Literally: He gave this matter to me and let me do it.)

他以前把這些給我看過。

TA YI QIAN BA ZHE XIE GEI WO KAN GUO.

He showed these to me before. (Literally: He gave these to me before and let me have a look at them.)

這個項目把我給爲難了。

ZHE GE XIANG MU BA WO GEI WEI NAN LE.

This project puts me in a tough situation.

這個項目爲難了我。

ZHE GE XIANG MU WEI NAN LE WO.

This project puts me in a tough situation.

ANNOTATIONS

The above last two sentences in Chinese give the same meaning; the first one more like passive voice while the second active voice. The first one tends to be northern China oral usage. The second one is a direct expression. Both are perfect Chinese expressions. This is an example of expression variations in Chinese language.

我只見過他一面。　　(只: only)

WO ZHI JIAN GUO TA YI MIAN.

I only met him once.

不是很多人知道的,只有他一個人知道,他經手做過。　　(只有: only)

BU SHI HEN DUO REN ZHI DAO DE, ZHI YOU TA YI GE REN ZHI DAO, TA JING SHOU ZUO GUO.

Not many people know. He is the only one who knows. He handled that before.

只有他和你一起來,我才說。　　(只有...才...: only If)

ZHI YOU TA HE NI YI QI LAI, WO CAI SHUO.

I will talk about it only if he and you come together.

只要他和你一起來,我就說。　　(只要...就...: as long as)

ZHI YAO TA HE NI YI QI LAI, WO JIU SHUO.

As long as he and you come together, I will talk about it.

他不肯去,那只好你去了。　　(只好: no choice)

TA BU KEN QU, NA ZHI HAO NI QU LE.

He doesn't want to go. Then no choice, you go.

這個項目,我們投資過百萬,只好做下去。(只好: obligated)

ZHE GE XIANG MU, WO MEN TOU ZI GUO BAI WAN, ZHI HAO ZUO XIA QU.

We have invested more than one million in this project. We are obligated to continue.

他來看我,只不過是想要我投資。(只不過: nothing but)

TA LAI KAN WO, ZHI BU GUO SHI XIANG YAO WO TOU ZI.

He came to see me. It was nothing but to ask me to invest.

那次到中國去不只五個人。　　（不只: more than）

NA CI (NEI CI) DAO ZHONG GUO QU BU ZHI WU GE REN.

There were more than five people in that trip to China.

他們每次見面都大力握手。

TA MEN MEI CI JIAN MIAN DOU DA LI WO SHOU.

They shake hands firmly every time they meet together.

美國有很多外地來的人，來自四面八方。

MEI GUO YOU HEN DUO WAI DI LAI DE REN, LAI ZI SI MIAN BA FANG.

In America, many people come from foreign places from all directions.

ANNOTATIONS ———

四面八方: Literally means four sides and eight directions.

MODULE 11

M11.2 SECOND GROUP OF 5 NEW CHARACTERS:

分¹	别²	记⁴	办⁴	法³
FEN	BIE	JI	BAN	FA
separate divide	part other	remember record	do process	way method

M11.2A Build vocabulary and expressions with these five characters:

分别	FEN¹ BIE²	separate; difference; respectively
分法	FEN¹ FA³	way of distributing or separating
记法	JI⁴ FA³	method of remembering or recording
记分	JI⁴ FEN¹	keep the score (record)
办法	BAN⁴ FA³	ways, means; method
法办	FA³ BAN⁴	bring to justice; punish by law
分别记办法。	FEN¹ BIE² JI⁴ BAN⁴ FA³.	Remember the methods separately.

M11.2B Expand vocabulary and expressions by using all the 160 characters learned:

分工	FEN¹ GONG¹	divide the work; division of labor
分手	FEN¹ SHOU³	part company; say goodbye
分家	FEN¹ JIA³	divide the family
分得	FEN¹ DE²	receive the share

分行	FEN¹ HANG²	branch office (NOTE: 行 pronounced XING₂ in Module 5)
分明	FEN¹ MING²	clearly demarcated distinctly
分心	FEN¹ XIN¹	divert (distract) attention
學分	XUE² FEN¹	credit (of a course)
對分	DUI⁴ FEN¹	split into halves; 50/50
得分	DE² FEN²	score; earn a point
別人	BIE² REN²	other people

ANNOTATIONS

The character 別 BIE₂ needs special attention:

(1) When used in "別 + noun" format : 別 means "other ... " :such as: 別人、別家、別地

(2) When used in "別 + verb" format: 別=不要 meaning "don't", "not to", such as:別說、別提、別看、別學、別做

(3) In strictly Beijing local dialect oral usage, 別 in above (2) (but not in (1)) is replaced by 甭 BENG₂ and so it becomes:
別說—> 甭說 BENG₂ SHUO₁ (don't say; not to mention)
別提—> 甭提 BENG₂ TI₂ (don't mention).
(Notice the character 甭 is made up of 不用.)
(甭 is an example of dialect character.)

記得	JI⁴ DE²	remember; keep in mind
記事	JI⁴ SHI⁴	record events
記過	JI⁴ GUO⁴	record a demerit
日記	RI⁴ JI⁴	diary
辦事	BAN⁴ SHI⁴	handle things; work
難辦	NAN² BAN⁴	tough (situation); hard to handle

好辦	HǍO BÀN	easy to handle; ("a piece of cake")
方法	FĀNG FǍ	method, way
法人	FǍ RÉN	legal person
法國	FǍ GUÓ	France
法國人	FǍ GUÓ RÉN	French (person, people)
國法	GUÓ FǍ	national laws and regulations
法文	FǍ WÉN	French (language)
文法	WÉN FǍ	grammar (language rules)

M11.2C Sample Sentences:

學英文和學中文都要經常學才行, 在這方面沒有甚麼分別。

XUE YING WEN HE XUE ZHONG WEN DOU YAO JING CHANG XUE CAI XING, ZAI ZHE FANG MIAN MEI YOU SHEN ME FEN BIE.

No matter learning English or Chinese, one must study frequently. There is no difference in this regard.

他們分別有三年了, 沒有見過面。

TA MEN FEN BIE YOU SAN NIAN LE, MEI YOU JIAN GUO MIAN.

They have not seen each other for three years since they parted.

這件事給你辦, 看看有甚麼辦法。

ZHE JIAN SHI GEI NI BAN, KAN KAN YOU SHEN ME BAN FA.

I let you handle this matter. See if there is any way.

他有工作日記, 辦了甚麼事都記下來。

TA YOU GONG ZUO RI JI, BAN LE SHEN ME SHI DOU JI XIA LAI.

He keeps a work diary, recording whatever is done.

記得明天到我家來。

JI DE MING TIAN DAO WO JIA LAI.

Remember (or: Be sure) to come to my home tomorrow.

這是十幾年前的事了，我甚麼都記不得了。

ZHE SHI SHI JI NIAN QIAN DE SHI LE, WO SHEN ME DOU JI BU DE LE.

This is something that happened more than ten years ago. I don't remember anything at all.

投資好是好，可我懂的不多，沒有把握。

TOU ZI HAO SHI HAO, KE WO DONG DE BU DUO, MEI YOU BA WO.

In a way it is good to invest. But I don't know much about it. I'm not sure.

一共有五個項目，分別給五個人辦。

YI GONG YOU WU GE XIANG MU, FEN BIE GEI WU GE REN BAN.

There are five projects altogether, to be handled by five people respectively.

只要你肯學，別說中文，甚麼文都可以學好。

ZHI YAO NI KEN XUE, BIE SHUO ZHONG WEN, SHEN ME WEN DOU KE YI XUE HAO.

As long as you are willing to learn, you can learn any language, not to mention Chinese.

ANNOTATIONS ————

別說=不要說= not to mention; let alone. 別提=不要提= don't mention (提：提出, 提到)

"別 + verb" -- tends to be northern China usage.

"不要 + verb" -- tends to be southern China usage.

Both in written form acceptable, people understand.

MODULE 11

M11.3 THIRD GROUP OF 5 NEW CHARACTERS:

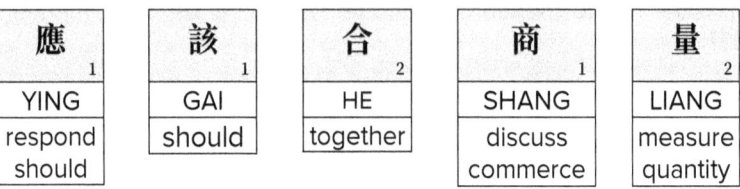

M11.3A Build vocabulary and expressions with these five characters:

應該	YĪNG GĀI	ought to
商量	SHĀNG LIANG	discuss, negotiate
應該合商量。	YĪNG GĀI HÉ SHĀNG LIANG.	Ought to discuss it together.

(合=合起來 HÉ QǏ LÁI together) (LIÀNG)

M11.3B Expand vocabulary and expressions by using all the 165 characters learned:

合力	HÉ LÌ	work together
合作	HÉ ZUÒ	cooperate, cooperation
合同	HÉ TÓNG	contract
合法	HÉ FǍ	legal; lawful
合成	HÉ CHÉNG	synthesize, synthesis
合資	HÉ ZĪ	joint venture (capital)
合辦	HÉ BÀN	joint venture
應用	YÌNG YÒNG	apply; use in (YÌNG)
應有	YĪNG YǑU	proper; deserve (YĪNG)
商人	SHĀNG RÉN	business people; merchant
力量	LÌ LIÀNG	strength; force (LIÀNG)

大量	DÀ LIÀNG	large quantity
少量	SHǍO LIÀNG	small quantity

M11.3C Sample Sentences:

他要你和他一起去,你應該去。
TA YAO NI HE TA YI QI QU, NI YING GAI QU.
He wants you to go with him. You should go.

工作是工作,應該好好做。
GONG ZUO SHI GONG ZUO, YING GAI HAO HAO ZUO.
Work is work; ought to do well.

我們大家在一起工作,應該好好合作。
WO MEN DA JIA ZAI YI QI GONG ZUO, YING GAI HAO HAO HE ZUO.
All of us work together and we should cooperate smoothly.

你沒有把握就不應該投資。
NI MEI YOU BA WO JIU BU YING GAI TOU ZI.
You should not invest if you are not sure.

1. 應該做的事就要做。
   YING GAI ZUO DI SHI JIU YAO ZUO.
2. 應該辦的事就要辦。
   YING GAI BAN DI SHI JIU YAO BAN.

3. 該做就做。

   GAI ZUO JIU ZUO.

4. 該辦就辦。

   GAI BAN JIU BAN.

   Whatever should be done, just do it.

ANNOTATIONS

(1) All of the 4 sample sentences in Chinese carry the same meaning.
(2) 做 = 辦：辦 tends to be Northern usage.
(3) 該 = 應該 = 應. the short form 應 or 該, either one is fine. 該 is used more often.
(4) The first 2 sentences are longer and the last 2 are shorter, close to classical style. In Chinese writing, conciseness is always valued.

各人有各人的想法，這沒甚麼不好。不過，有事大家要 好好商量。

GE REN YOU GE REN DE XIANG FA, ZHE MEI SHEN ME BU HAO. BU GUO, YOU SHI DA JIA YAO HAO HAO SHANG LIANG.

Everybody has a different thought. There is nothing wrong with that. However, all of us should discuss together if there is a problem.

這個項目太大，我們力量不夠，要請人合作，搞合資。

ZHE GE XIANG MU TAI DA, WO MEN LI LIANG BU GOU, YAO QING REN HE ZUO, GAO HE ZI.

This project is too big. We don't have enough resources. We need partners; go for joint venture.

他們三個人合起來,可以搞到一百萬美元。
TA MEN SAN GE REN HE QI LAI, KE YI GAO DAO YI BAI WAN MEI YUAN.
The three of them together can come up with one million U.S. Dollars.

這項目是和中國合資,是合法的。
ZHE XIANG MU SHI HE ZHONG GUO HE ZI, SHI HE FA DE.
This project is a joint venture with China. It is legal.

我們的中美合資項目,都有合同的。
WO MEN DE ZHONG MEI HE ZI XIANG MU, DOU YOU HE TONG DE.
We have contracts for all our Sino-American joint venture projects.

那個項目要很大工作量才完得成。
NEI GE XIANG MU YAO HEN DA GONG ZUO LIANG CAI WAN DE CHENG.
That project requires a lot of work to get it completed.

這兩個項目是不同的,不應該合在一起。
ZHE LIANG GE XIANG MU SHI BU TONG DE, BU YING GAI HE ZAI YI QI.
These two projects are different and should not be combined together.

MODULE 12

M12.1 FIRST GROUP OF 5 NEW CHARACTERS:

兩	朋	友	之	間
3	2	3	1	1
LIANG	PENG	YOU	ZHI	JIAN
two	friend	friend	of	between among

M12.1A Build vocabulary and expressions with these five characters:

朋友	PÉNG YǑU	friend
之間	ZHĪ JIĀN	between; among
兩朋友之間	LIǍNG PÉNG YǑU ZHĪ JIĀN	between two friends

M12.1B Expand vocabulary and expressions by using all the 170 characters learned:

好友	HǍO YǑU	good friend
友好	YǑU HǍO	friendly
友人	YǑU RÉN	friend (友人 = 朋友)
知心朋友	ZHĪ XĪN PÉNG YǑU	intimate friend; close friend
小朋友	XIǍO PÉNG YǑU	'little friend' -- an endearment expression by adults in addressing a child or children (equivalent to saying "honey")

M12.1C Sample sentences:

他們兩個是同事，又是知心朋友。

TA MEN LIANG GE SHI TONG SHI, YOU SHI ZHI XIN PENG YOU.

The two of them are colleagues and are intimate friends as well.

學中文和學英文,兩者之間,很大不同。　　　(之間: between)

XUE ZHONG WEN HE XUE YING WEN, LIANG ZHE ZHI JIAN, HEN DA BU TONG.

In learning Chinese and English, there is big difference between the two.

他們三個人之間是好朋友,甚麼都可以說。　　(之間: among)

TA MEN SAN GE REN ZHI JIAN SHI HAO PENG YOU, SHEN ME DOU KE YI SHUO.

The three of them are good friends. They can talk about anything among themselves.

我們要在三月到五月之間到中國去。

WO MEN YAO ZAI SAN YUE DAO WU YUE ZHI JIAN DAO ZHONG GUO QU.

We are going to China some time between March and May.

ANNOTATIONS ———

中國之友 = 中國的朋友: Friends of China.

(1) 中國之友 is a typical expression of classical style Chinese: concise. 友 is the short form of 朋友; more often used in writing.

(But not 中國之朋).

(2) 中國的朋友 is a typical expression of vernacular Chinese. 的 is used instead of 之, like 'of' in English; lore often used in speaking.

他學了中文之後,就要到中國去工作了。

TA XUE LE ZHONG WEN ZHI HOU, JIU YAO DAO ZHONG GUO QU GONG ZUO LE.

After he has learned some Chinese, he is going to work in China.

他到英國來之前,學過一些英文的。

TA DAO YING GUO LAI ZHI QIAN, XUE GUO YI XIE YING WEN DE.

He learned some English before he came to the U.K.

---

(1) Above 2 sentences demonstrate the expression of TENSE of verbs (time of action). In Chinese it is often based on context. The second sentence is in past tense in English.

(2) Also notice the different uses of the character 之 ZHI₁: 之前、之後 means before and after an incident or action respectively.

(3) 他來了之後 = 他來了以後 (After he came) or (After he comes).

.... 之後, 他就到中國去了。

.... ZHI BOU, TA JIU DAO ZHONG GUO QU LE.

.... After that, he went to China.

以後, 不要再去了。　　　　　　(以後 = 今後)

YI HOU, BU YAO ZAI QU LE.

今後, 不要再去了。　　　　　　(=今後, 別再去了。) (Cf. M11.2B)

JIN HOU, BU YAO ZAI QU LE.　　(...BIE ZAI QU LE.)

From now on, don't go there anymore.

Notice the different use of '...之後' and '以後'

in the above sample sentences.

才兩三個人, 有甚麼事都好說。　　(好說: easy)

CAI LIANG SAN GE REN, YOU SHEN ME SHI DOU HAO SHUO.

There are only two or three people involved. Whatever happens, it is easy to handle.

Notice the brief expression in Chinese in the above sample sentence. To make the sentences complete in English, some words have to be filled in.

Q: "這件事給你做, 好嗎?"

"ZHE JIAN SHI GEI NI ZUO, HAO HA? "

"Let you handle this matter. Is that OK? "

A: "你我之間, 好說。我來。"　　　　　　(好說: fine)

"NI WO ZHI JIAN, HAO SHUO. WO LAI."

"Between you and me, that's fine. I'll do it."

Q: "太謝謝你了。"

"TAI XIE XIE NI LE. "

"Thank you so much. "

A: "好說, 好說。不謝。"　　　　　　(好說: so nice)

"HAO SHUO, HAO SHUO. BU XIE."

"Oh, it's so kind of you. Don't mention."

MODULE 12

M12.2 SECOND GROUP OF 5 NEW CHARACTERS:

談	話	題	也	廣
²	⁴	²	³	³
TAN	HUA	TI	YE	GUANG
talk	conversation	topic	also	broad

M12.2A Build vocabulary and expressions with these five characters:

談話	TAN² HUA⁴	conversation
話題	HUA⁴ TI²	conversation topics
談話題也廣。	TAN² HUA⁴ TI² YE³ GUANG³.	Topics of conversation (are) also broad.

M12.2B Expand vocabulary and expressions by using all the 175 characters learned:

說話	SHUO¹ HUA⁴	speak, talk, say
問話	WEN⁴ HUA⁴	question; interrogation
對話	DUI⁴ HUA⁴	dialogue
大話	DA⁴ HUA⁴	lie; boast (casual)
好話	HAO³ HUA⁴	good words (comment)
問題	WEN⁴ TI²	problem; question; issue
題目	TI² MU⁴	title; topic; subject
題外話	TI² WAI⁴ HUA⁴	words away from the topic or theme
廣大	GUANG³ DA⁴	broad
談天	TAN² TIAN¹	chat
談心	TAN² XIN¹	heart-to-heart talk

也好   YE³ HAO³   might as well

M12.2C Sample sentences:

我去，你也去。   (也: also, too)
WO QU, NI YE QU.
I am going there, and you too.

他不去，我也就不去了。   (也就: then. ...too)
TA BU QU, WO YE JIU BU QU LE.
He is not going. Then I wouldn't go either.

他去，你一起去也好。   (也好: might as well)
TA QU, NI YI QI QU YE HAO.
He is going and you might as well go together.

他去，你一起去，也好。   (也好: That's fine.)
TA QU, NI YI QI QU, YE HAO.
He is going, and you go together. That's fine.

他去也好，不去也好，都可以。   (也好, ...也好。whether ... or ...)
TA QU YE HAO, BU QU YE HAO, DOU KE YI.
It will be fine whether he is going or not. ((If) he goes, fine. (If) he doesn't go, fine, too, either way.)

ANNOTATIONS ———

(1) The above 5 examples provide an idea how a simple character 也 YE is used in different applications based on the context.

(2) In the above sentence #4, 也好 = 也是好的: That's fine.

(3) 非也。FEI₁ YE₃ = 不是的。BU₄ SHI₄ DI.: No, it isn't. -- The former is a classical style Chinese expression which is always very brief. The latter is a vernacular Chinese expression. Even in modern Chinese writing or speaking, people sometimes still use 非也 to put emphasis and add fun into their expression. In English, one can write "Know Thyself." instead of "Know yourself."

他說他要去。　　　　　　　　　　(說: say, said)

TA SHUO TA YAO QU.

He says he is going. (He said he would go.)

他說話很快。　　　　　　　　　　(說話: speak, talk)

TA SHUO HUA HEN KUAI.

He speaks (talks) very fast.

他說話一就一、二就二。　　　　　(說話: words)

TA SHUO HUA YI JIU YI, ER JIU ER.

He talks briefly and precisely. (He speaks no nonsense.)

———

一就一、二就二 = 一就是一、二就是二；

就 = 就是. In Chinese, concise expressions are always preferred: the shorter the better, in writing especially.

他的談話是友好的。

TA DE TAN HUA SHI YOU HAO DE.

His conversation is friendly.

朋友見面,話就多了,談天說地,沒完沒了。

PENG YOU JIAN MIAN, HUA JIU DUO LE, TAN TIAN SHUO DI, MEI WAN MEI LIAO.

When friends get together, they have a lot to talk about. They keep chatting and never ends.

---

(1) In the above last Chinese sentence, the word 'when' does not occur; but by context, it is used. This is another example of concise expression in Chinese language.

(2) 談天說地 : chatting; literally it says "talk about the sky and the earth." Note that 談 and 說 mean the same thing: talk, speak. In Chinese it is preferable to use different characters (word) to mean the same thing in one expression to make it more lively. 談天說地 is preferred to 談天談地 or 說天說地.

(3) 沒完沒了: no ending; never ends. 完 and 了 mean the same: end. By using both 沒完 and 沒了 together, the phrase becomes more lively, descriptive and emphasized,

(4) Notice that in this particular sentence, there are 4 segments with 4 characters each; a total of 16 characters. This is another feature of typical writing style in Chinese: concise and symmetrical if possible and appropriate.

這個項目,問題很多,還是不搞好些。　　(問題: problem)

ZHE GE XIANG MU, WEN TI HEN DUO, HAI SHI BU GAO HAO XIE.

這個項目,問題很多,還是不搞爲好。

ZHE GE XIANG MU, WEN TI HEN DUO, HAI SHI BU GAO WEI HAO.

There are many problems in this project. It's better not to do it.

爲好 = 好些

他學了中文的, 到中國去工作沒問題。　　(問題: problem)

TA XUE LE ZHONG WEN DE, DAO ZHONG GUO QU GONG ZUO MEI YOU WEN TI.

He has studied Chinese. He has no problem to work in China.

我想提個問題。　　(問題: question)

WO XIANG TI GE WEN TI.

I'd like to ask a question.

今天作文的題目是:學中文。　　(題目: topic)

JIN TIAN ZUO WEN DE TI MU SHI: XUE ZHONG WEN.

Today the topic of composition is: Learning Chinese.

Articles such as "a" and "the" are not used in Chinese language. The above last two sentences clearly indicate 'a question' and 'the topic' by context.

這是小事, 不要小題大作。　　(小題大作: Make a fuss over a trifle.)

ZHE SHI XIAO SHI, BU YAO XIAO TI DA ZUO.

This is a trifle. Don't make a fuss over it.

MODULE 12

M12.3 THIRD GROUP OF 5 NEW CHARACTERS:

當¹	然²	高¹	興⁴	講³
DĀNG	RÁN	GĀO	XÌNG	JIĂNG
when	yet	high	excitement	talk

M12.3A Build vocabulary and expressions with these five characters:

當	DĀNG¹	when
當然	DĀNG¹ RÁN²	certainly; of course
高興	GĀO¹ XÌNG⁴	happy, glad
講	JIĂNG³	talk
當然高興講。	DĀNG¹ RÁN² GĀO¹ XÌNG⁴ JIĂNG³.	Certainly (they, we, ..) talk happily.

M12.3B Expand vocabulary and expressions by using all the 180 characters learned:

當年	DĀNG¹ NIÁN²	the very same year; in those days
當天	DĀNG¹ TIĀN¹	the very same day
當心	DĀNG¹ XĪN¹	caution; beware of
當中	DĀNG¹ ZHŌNG¹	among; in which
當地	DĀNG¹ DÌ⁴	local
當面	DĀNG¹ MIÀN⁴	in the presence of; face to face
應當 (應當 = 應該)	YĪNG¹ DĀNG¹	should, ought to

相當	XIĀNG DĀNG	quite; equivalent
上當	SHÀNG DÀNG	being duped (當 MNG4)
家當	JIĀ DÀNG	belongings (casual)
便當 (便當 = 方便)	BIÀN DÀNG (便當 Take-out lunch -- Taiwan)	handy, convenient
自然	ZÌ RÁN	natural; eventual
大自然	DÀ ZÌ RÁN	Nature; Mother Nature
天然	TIĀN RÁN	natural
不然 (不然 = 要不然 YÀO4 BU RAN = 再不然 ZÀI4 BU RAN)	BÙ RÁN	if not; otherwise
然後	RÁN HÒU	and then
高大	GĀO DÀ	tall and big
高中	GĀO ZHŌNG	senior high school
高明	GĀO MÍNG	clever, brilliant
高見	GĀO JIÀN	brilliant idea
高地	GĀO DÌ	highland
高原	GĀO YUÁN	plateau
高手	GĀO SHǑU	master-hand
提高	TÍ GĀO	raise; bring... to a higher level
興起	XĪNG QǏ	rise; spring up; something in fashion
興辦	XĪNG BÀN	set up; establish (a business, school,...)
講學	JIǍNG XUÉ	give lectures
講話	JIǍNG HUÀ	speak, talk (= 說話); presentation

講習	JIĂNG XÍ	lecture and study (workshop)
講和	JIĂNG HÉ	settle a dispute; make peace; reconcile
講明	JIĂNG MÍNG	state explicitly; make Clear
講好	JIĂNG HĂO	agree upon; make arrangement
講過	JIĂNG GUÒ	said; mentioned before

M12.3C Sample sentences:

兩朋友之間，談話題也廣，當然高興講。

LIANG PENG YOU ZHI JIAN, TAN HUA TI YE GUANG, DANG RAN GAO XING JIANG.

Between two friends, conversation topics are broad and of course they chat happily.

他那天來見我，我當天就對他當面講明了的。

TA NEI TIAN LAI JIAN WO, WO DANG TIAN JIU DUI TA DANG MIAN JIANG MING LE DI.

The other day he came to see me, and I made clear to him face to face the very same day.

朋友相見，一起談心，可高興了。

PENG YOU XIANG JIAN, YI QI TAN XIN, KE GAO XING LE.

When friends get together and have a heart-to-heart talk, they are so happy.

ANNOTATIONS ———

In the last sentence above:

(1) 當 can be added to the sentence in Chinese as the first character to mean "when" explicitly; but it can also be omitted without compromise in meaning. The nature of this complex sentence in Chinese is based on the context.

(2) cf. NOTE for a sample sentence in M12.2C.

想當年, 學中文哪有今天這麼方便?

XIANG DANG NIAN, XUE ZHONG WEN NA YOU JIN TIAN ZHE ME FANG BIAN?

Recalling in those days, how could we learn Chinese in such a convenient way as today?

這方法來學中文, 相當好, 當然學得快些。

ZHE FANG FA LAI XUE ZHONG WEN, XIANG DANG HAO, DANG RAN XUE DE KUAI XIE.

This method to learn Chinese is pretty good.

For sure, one learns faster.

你又不要這個, 不然就給你那個, 好嗎?

NI YOU BU YAO ZHE GE, BU RAN JIU GEI NI NEI GE, HAO MA?

You don't like this one. If not, how about (I, we) give you that one?

當年他到英國去, 然後又到美國去了。

DANG NIAN TA DAO YING GUO, RAN HOU YOU DAO MEI GUO QU LE.

In those days, he went to the United Kingdom and then to the United States.

他爲甚麼不高興, 你知道嗎?

TA WEI SHEN ME BU GAO XING, NI ZHI DAO MA?

你知道他爲甚麼不高興嗎?

NI ZHI DAO TA WEI SHEN ME BU GAO XING MA?

Do you know why he is unhappy?

In the last example above, the two sentences in Chinese mean the same. In practice, the first one, in shorter segments, is used more often. (cf. M10.1C: last sample sentence.)

MODULE 13

M13.1 FIRST GROUP OF 5 NEW CHARACTERS:

由 [2]	於 [2]	決 [2]	定 [4]	遲 [2]
YOU	YU	JUE	DING	CHI
cause	at	decide	calm	late
reason		determined	decided	

M13.1A Build vocabulary and expressions with these five characters:

由於	YOU YU [2,2]	due to; since
決定	JUE DING [2,4]	decide; decision
定於	DING YU [4,2]	decided to be (set on a (定於=決定於) certain date or at a certain place)
由於決定遲, ...	YOU YU JUE DING CHI, ... [2,2,2,4,2]	Since the decision was made late, ...

M13.1B Expand vocabulary and expressions by using all the 185 characters learned:

事由	SHI YOU [4,2]	subject matter; in reference to (such as "Re: ... " in a business letter topic)
於是	YU SHI [2,4]	hence; as a result
決心	JUE XIN [2,1]	determination
定做	DING ZUO [4,4]	made to order; custom-made
定了	DING LE [4]	determined; decision made
一定	YI DING [1,4]	specified; definitely
不定	BU DING [4,4]	irregular; undetermined

遲到	CHI² DAO⁴	being late (at arrival)
遲遲	CHI² CHI²	slow, tardy
太遲	TAI⁴ CHI²	too late

M13.1C Sample sentences:

由於他要到中國去工作三年,他就下定決心學中文。

YOU YU TA YAO DAO ZHONG GUO QU GONG ZUO SAN NIAN, TA JIU XIA DING JUE XIN XUE ZHONG WEN.

Since he is going to work in China for three years, he has made up his mind to learn Chinese.

他天天都和中國人一起工作,好些年了,於是不知不覺地學會了講好些中文。

TA TIAN TIAN DOU HE ZHONG GUO REN YI QI GONG ZUO, HAO XIE NIAN LE, YU SHI BU ZHI BU JUE DI XUE HUI LE JIANG HAO XIE ZHONG WEN.

He has been working together with Chinese people for a number of years. As a result he has learned to speak quite some Chinese without even realizing it.

這件事,決定了沒有?

ZHE JIAN SHI, JUE DING LE MEI YOU?

這件事,定了沒有?

ZHE JIAN SHI, DING LE MEI YOU?

這件事,定下來沒有?

ZHE JIAN SHI, DING XIA LAI MEI YOU?

Any decision made on this matter?

ANNOTATIONS ─────

The above last example shows that the three expressions in Chinese have the same meaning. The first expression is complete and formal; the other two are more casual.

對不起, 太遲了, 沒辦法。

DUI BU QI, TAI CHI LE, MEI BAN FA.

Sorry, it's too late. Can't help.

他們決心很大, 決定了的事, 一定全力完成。

TA MEN JUE XIN HEN DA, JUE DING LE DI SHI, YI DING QUAN LI WAN CHENG.

They are well determined. Once a decision is made, they will definitely complete it with full effort.

─────

The last sample sentence above demonstrates the difference in the use of comma and period in an expression. In Chinese, it is treated as one sentence in which the last two segments carry extended content of the first segment.

他有個不好習慣, 非要遲到不可。

TA YOU GE BU HAO XI GUAN, FEI YAO CHI DAO BU KE.

He has an undesirable habit: bound to be late.

還是由他們來做好。

HAI SHI YOU TA MEN LAI ZUO HAO.

It's better to let them do it.

不一定由你自己來做, 給其他人做也可以的。

BU YI DING YOU NI ZI JI LAI ZUO, GEI QI TA REN ZUO YE KE YI DE.

It is not necessary that you do it yourself. It is fine to let other people do it.

Q: "一定是他搞的。"
"YI DING SHI TA GAO DE.'
"It must be he who did it."

A: "不一定,還不能肯定的。"
"BU YI DING, HAI BU NENG KEN DING DI."
"Not really. Can't be certain yet."

他的決心很大,要一邊工作一邊學中文。
TA DE JUE XIN HEN DA, YAO YI BIAN GONG ZUO YI BIAN XUE ZHONG WEN.
He is well determined to study Chinese while he is working.

我們定於下個月到中國去。(cf. M9.3)
WO MEN DING YU XIA GE YUE DAO ZHONG GUO QU.
We have decided to go to China next month.

MODULE 13

M13.2 SECOND GROUP OF 5 NEW CHARACTERS:

需¹	立⁴	即²	幫¹	助⁴
XU	LI	JI	BANG	ZHU
need	stand / set	reach	help	assist

M13.2A Build vocabulary and expressions with these five characters:

立即	LI⁴ JI²	immediate; immediately
幫助	BANG¹ ZHU⁴	help; assist
需立即幫助。	XU¹ LI⁴ JI² BANG¹ ZHU⁴.	Need immediate assistance.

M13.2B Expand vocabulary and expressions by using all the 190 characters learned:

需要	XU¹ YAO⁴	need (需 = 需要, short form)
立法	LI⁴ FA³	legislation (Literally: 'establish laws'.)
立定	LI⁴ DING⁴	Halt! (command)
立面	LI⁴ MIAN⁴	elevated view (construction drawing)
即是	JI² SHI⁴	that is (i.e.)
即便	JI² BIAN⁴	even if; even though
幫工	BANG¹ GONG¹	casual worker
幫手	BANG¹ SHOU³	helping hand; helper
助手	ZHU⁴ SHOU³	assistant

M13.2C Sample sentences:

由於決定遲, 需立即幫助。

YOU YU JUE DING CHI, XU LI JI BANG ZHU.

Since the decision came late, immediate assistance is needed.

這件事我不懂, 很難辦, 請你多多幫助。

ZHE JIAN SHI WO BU DONG, HEN NAN BAN, QING NI DUO DUO BANG ZHU.

I don't know about this. It's tough. Please give me all the help you can.

我一有甚麼需要, 他都立即來幫手。

WO YI YOU SHEN ME XU YAO, TA DOU LI JI LAI BANG SHOU.

Whenever I am in need, he always gives me a hand immediately.

你需要甚麼, 請提出來, 我一定想辦法幫助。

NI XU YAO SHEN ME, QING TI CHU LAI, WO YI DING XIANG BAN FA BANG ZHU.

If you need any help, please let me know. I'll definitely do my best to help.

(Literally: If you need anything, please put forward and I'll definitely try to figure out a way to help.)

ANNOTATIONS ———

(1) In the last sample sentence above, 需要 is used as a verb while it is a noun in the sentence before it.

(2) "If" is not used in the Chinese sentence but it exists by context. It could be added to the sentence, too; however it's more commonly used without it.

這個項目,需要立即投資一千萬美元。以我們目前的力量,做不來。

ZHE GE XIANG MU, XU YAO LI JI TOU ZI YI QIAN WAN MEI YUAN. YI WO MEN MU QIAN DE LI LIANG, ZUO BU LAI.

This project requires immediate investment of ten million U.S. Dollars. With our current resources, it is beyond our reach.

力量 literally means strength. (MODULE 11.3).

便當即是方便。　　　　　　　　(便當= 方便)

BIAN DANG JI SHI FANG BIAN.

Handy means the same as convenient.

我當即就給了他的。　　　　　　(當即= 立即= 當時立即)

WO DANG JI JIU GEI LE TA DI.

I gave it to him right away.

即便沒有你來,我也完成得了。

JI BIAN MEI YOU NI LAI, WO YE WAN CHENG DE LIAO.

Even if you didn't come, I could have completed it.

不是不想幫,已經太遲了,即便再幫也幫不了。

BU SHI BU XIANG BANG, YI JING TAI CHI LE, JI BIAN ZAI BANG YE BANG BU LIAO.

Not that (I/we) don't want to help. It's all too late. It wouldn't help even if there is further assistance.

由於那個項目是不合法的,我不想幫助甚麼。

YOU YU NEI GE XIANG MU SHI BU HE FA DE, WO BU XIANG BANG ZHU SHEN ME.

Since that project is unlawful, I don't want to give any help.

去請十個得力的幫工來。

QU QING SHEN GE DE LI DI BANG GONG LAI.

Go and hire ten capable casual workers.

幫不幫, 看需要。

BANG BU BANG, KAN XU YAO.

要幫助還是不幫助, 這就要看需要了。

YAO BANG ZHU HAI SHI BU BANG ZHU, ZHE JIU YAO KAN XU YAO LE.

Whether to help or not, it depends on the need.

In the last example above, notice the first of the 2 Chinese sentences is very concise. The first segment of each sentence is obviously not complete and is completed by the second segment.

你要幫就幫, 這是你的事。

NI YAO BANG JIU BANG, ZHE SHI NI DI SHI.

If you want to help, go ahead. It's your business.

MODULE 13

M13.3 THIRD GROUP OF 5 NEW CHARACTERS:

靠 ⁴	及 ²	時 ²	管 ³	理 ³
KAO	JI	SHI	GUAN	LI
rely on	and	time	control	manage

M13.3A Build vocabulary and expressions with these five characters:

及時	JI² SHI²	timely; on time
管理	GUAN³ LI³	manage
靠及時管理。	KAO⁴ JI² SHI² GUAN³ LI³	Count on timely management.

M13.3B Expand vocabulary and expressions by using all the 195 characters learned:

以及	YI³ JI²	and (及 = 以及, short form)
又及	YOU⁴ JI²	postscript; (PS)
不及	BU⁴ JI²	not as good as
來不及	LAI² BU⁴ JI²	can't make it on time; miss schedule
時間	SHI² JIAN¹	time
時事	SHI² SHI⁴	news
當時	DANG¹ SHI²	at that time
同時	TONG² SHI²	at the same time; simultaneous
過時	GUO⁴ SHI²	obsolete; out of date
有時	YOU³ SHI²	sometimes

即時	JI² SHI²	immediately; instantly (cf.及時 JI₂ SHI₂)
小時	XIAO³ SHI²	hour
工時	GONG¹ SHI²	work hour (工作小時)
管工	GUAN³ GONG¹	foreman
管人	GUAN³ REN²	managing people
管事	GUAN³ SHI⁴	be in charge; managing
管道	GUAN³ DAO⁴	pipeline; piping
管家	GUAN³ JIA¹	steward
經理	JING¹ LI³	manager; manage
道理	DAO⁴ LI³	principle
道家	DAO⁴ JIA¹	Daoist (a school of thought in philosophy prevailing in China 770-220 BC.)
定理	DING⁴ LI³	theorem
原理	YUAN² LI³	principle; fundamentals
助理	ZHU⁴ LI³	assistant
講理	JIANG³ LI³	straighten up something with somebody; reasoning (講理 = 講道理)

M13.3C Sample sentences:

管理要及時，不然就太遲了。

GUAN LI YAO JI SHI, BU RAN JIU TAI CHI LE.

Management should be timely provided, otherwise it's too late.

管理不好, 就難辦了。

GUAN LI BU HAO, JIU NAN BAN LE.

If not managed properly, it would be rough.

我完全不知道, 就靠你了。

WO WAN QUAN BU ZHI DAO, JIU KAO NI LE.

I know nothing about it. I count on you.

要幫助他們就要及時, 太遲了就沒有用。

YAO BANG ZHU TA MEN JIU YAO JI SHI, TAI CHI LE JIU MEI YOU YONG.

If (you/we/...) want to help them, do it timely. Otherwise, it wouldn't help if it is too late. (Note: Subject is omitted in the Chinese sentence. The real subject depends on the context.)

他不講理, 我不管了。　　　　(講理 = 講道理)

TA BU JIANG LI, WO BU GUAN LE.

他不講理, 我不理了。

TA BU JIANG LI, WO BU LI LIAO.

He is not reasonable. I don't care.

ANNOTATIONS

The last two sample sentences above express the same idea. Notice that 管=管理=理. Both expressions are Chinese expressions. However, 不理 is more often used in southern China such as in Cantonese.

管他三七二十一, 我才不理。

GUAN TA SAN QI ER SHI YI, WO CAI BU LI.

Whatever happens, I just don't care.

三七二十一 is a slang, literally meaning 3 times 7 equals to 21.

我要出去, 就靠你來管這些幫工了。
WO YAO CHU QU, JIU KAO NI LAI GUAN ZHE XIE BANG GONG LE.
I'm taking off. I count on you to manage these casual workers.

他學的是心理學。
TA XUE DI SHI XIN LI XUE.
What he is studying is Psychology.

他心理不高興, (他) 不說就是了。
TA XIN LI BU GAO XING, (TA) BU SHUO JIU SHI LE.
He is unhappy in his mind, but he doesn't say.

MODULE 14

M14.1 FIRST GROUP OF 5 NEW CHARACTERS:

意₄	思₁	等₃	候₄	信₄
YI	SI	DENG	HOU	XIN
idea	think	wait	wait	letter

M14.1A Build vocabulary and expressions with these five characters:

意思	YI⁴ SI	idea; meaning
等候	DENG³ HOU⁴	wait; wait for
等等	DENG³ DENG³	etc.; and so forth
意思等候信	YI⁴ SI DENG⁴ HOU⁴ XIN⁴.	The idea is to wait for the letter.

M14.1B Expand vocabulary and expressions by using all the 200 characters learned:

意见	YI⁴ JIAN⁴	opinion
天意	TIAN¹ YI⁴	God's will; act of Nature
用意	YONG⁴ YI⁴	intention
心意	XIN¹ YI⁴	regards; heartily
有意	YOU³ YI⁴	intentional
好意	HAO³ YI⁴	good faith; good intention
大意	DA⁴ YI⁴	careless; idea in brief
思想	SI¹ XIANG³	thought; thinking
思家	SI¹ JIA¹	home sick (思家 = 想家 XIANG₃ JIA₁ (M9.1))

170 Mastering Mandarin: Your Path to Proficiency

思想家	SI¹ XIANG³ JIA¹	thinker
相等	XIANG¹ DENG³	equal
等量	DENG³ LIANG⁴	equal quantity
時候	SHI² HOU	moment; a point in time
信件	XIN⁴ JIAN⁴	letter （信=信件）
家信	JIA¹ XIN⁴	family letter
相信	XIANG¹ XIN⁴	believe; trust
有意思	YOU³ YI⁴ SI	interesting
有意見	YOU³ YI⁴ JIAN⁴	having a complaint
沒意思	MEI² YI⁴ SI	not interesting; doesn't make sense
沒意見	MEI² YI⁴ JIAN⁴	no objection, no comment

M14.1C Sample sentences:

我的意思是等他們來信。　　　　　　　　（意思：idea）
WO DE YI SI SHI DENG TA MEN LAI XIN.　（等 = 等候）
My idea is to wait for their letter.

"等候"是甚麼意思？　　　　　　　　　　（意思：meaning）
DENG HOU SHI SHEN MO YI SI?
What is the meaning of "wait"?

那個地方我去過了，沒(有)意思。　　　　（沒(有)意思：not interesting）
NEI GE DI FANG WO QU GUO LE, MEI YOU YI SI.
I had been there before, not interesting at all.

我沒有意思要去。　　　　　　　(沒有意思：no intention)

WO MEI YOU YI SI YAO QU.

I have no intention to go there.

他講了很多, 文不對題, 沒意思。　　(沒意思：doesn't make sense)

TA JIANG LE HEN DUO, WEN BU DUI TI, MEI YI SI.

He talked a lot away from the theme. It just doesn't make sense.

ANNOTATIONS ———

沒意思 = 沒有意思. The short form is often used to mean "doesn't make sense".

我的意見是：做得好。　　　　　(意見：opinion)

WO DI YI JIAN SHI: ZUO DE HAO.

My opinion is: well done.

請大家提意見。　　　　　　　(意見：feedback; input)

QING DA JIA TI YI JIAN.

Your feedback (comment, criticism, suggestion, input) would be appreciated.

大家有沒有意見?　　　　　　(意見：objection; comment)

DA JIA YOU MEI YOU YI JIAN?

Any objection or comment?

他對你有意見。　　　　　　　(意見：complaint)

TA DUI NI YOU YI JIAN.

He has complaints against you.

———

意見、意思 are commonly used. Compare the different usage in the above sample sentences. Notice the different applications.

請等一等。　QING DENG YI DENG.

Just a minute, please.

他來的時候, 你不在, 等了一下。　　　　　(等 = 等候)

TA LAI DE SHI HOD, NI BU ZAI, DENG LE YI XIA.

When he came, you were not here and he waited for a while.

當 (DANG$_1$: when) can be added in front of the above sentence. The meaning of the two sentences is the same.

他有時候來的。　TA YOU SHI HOU LAI DE.

He sometimes comes. (He comes once in a while.)

有時候你來, 有時候我來。

YOU SHI HOU NI LAI, YOU SHI HOU WO LAI.

Sometimes you come and other times I come.

In the above last two sentences, it is fine to use 有時 instead of 有時候. In Mandarin, stick with 有時候; in Cantonese, 有時 is used more often. No difference in meaning.

我相信他說的。　　　　　　　　(相信: believe)

WO XIANG XIN TA SHUO DE.

I believe in what he said.

---

cf. M9.3C second NOTE.

我相信她。　　　　　　　　　　　　(相信：trust)

WO XIANG XIN TA.

I trust her.

他是好心好意，一心要辦好，沒想到辦不好，完全想不到。

TA SHI HAO XIN HAO YI, YI XIN YAO BAN HAO, MEI XIANG DAO BAN BU HAO, WAN QUAN XIANG BU DAO.

He was determined to do a good job with all his good intention and good will. It is totally unexpected that it wasn't done well.

學習英、法、中、日文等等，都很有用。

XUE XI YING, FA, ZHONG, RI WEN DENG DENG, DOU HEN YOU YONG.

It is very useful to learn English, French, Chinese, Japanese, etc.

(NOTE: 英、法、中、日文：languages of English, French, Chinese, and Japanese) (cf. M10.2C last NOTE)

———

MODULE 14

M14.2 SECOND GROUP OF 5 NEW CHARACTERS:

情₂	況₄	寫₃	清₁	楚₃
QING	KUANG	XIE	QING	CHU
feeling	condition	write	clear	neat

M14.2A Build vocabulary and expressions with these five characters:

情況	QING KUANG (2 4)	situation; circumstances
清楚	QING CHU (1 3)	clear
情況寫清楚。	QING KUANG XIE QING CHU (2 4 3 1 3)	Write down the situation clearly.

M14.2B Expand vocabulary and expressions by using all the 205 characters learned:

情人	QING REN (2 2)	sweetheart; lover
情信	QING XIN (2 4)	love letter
情理	QING LI (2 3)	reasoning
情面	QING MIAN (2 4)	feelings
人情	REN QING (2 2)	human feelings; human touch
心情	XIN QING (1 2)	mood; state of mind
寫信	XIE XIN (3 4)	write a letter
清理	QING LI (1 3)	clear up; clean up
清清楚楚	QING QING CHU CHU (1 1 3 3)	clearly and explicitly

M14.2C Sample sentences:

1. 請把情況用信寫清楚。　　　　　　（情況：situation)
   QING BA QING KUANG YONG XIN XIE QING CHU.
   Please state the situation clearly in a letter.

2. 情況在信裡寫得清清楚楚。
   QING KUANG ZAI XIN LI XIE DE QING QING CHU CHU.
   The situation is clearly written in the letter.

ANNOTATIONS ———

(1) The above two sample sentences demonstrate Voice of a Verb in Chinese. Sentence 1 is in active voice while 2 is in passive voice.

(2) 清清楚楚 = 清楚 with emphasis.

有甚麼情況？　　　　　　　　　　　（情況：situation)
YOU SHEN MO QING KUANG?
How is the situation?

情況不明，說不清楚。
QING KUANG BU MING, SHUO BU QING CHU.
The situation is unclear and nothing can be said with certainty.

你不來, 他不來, 叫我自己完成, 這情況下我不做。（情況：circumstances)
NI BU LAI, TA BU LAI, JIAO WO ZI JI WAN CHENG, ZHE QING KUANG XIA WO BU ZUO.
You are not coming, he is not coming, and I am asked to finish it all by myself. Under such circumstances, I am not going to do it.

她說得不合情理。

TA SHUO DE BU HE QING LI.

What she said is beyond reasoning.

心情不好, 寫不出來。

XIN QING BU HAO, XIE BU CHU LAI.

Not in the right mood, nothing is written.

請把投資的情況寫一寫。

QING BA TOU ZI DE QING KUANG XIE YI XIE.

Please write something about the investment.

請把投資的情況寫出來。

QING BA TOU ZI DE QING KUANG XIE CHU LAI.

Please state the investment situation in writing.

---

(1) 寫一寫、寫出來、寫下來: all carry the similar meaning -- write it down; put it in writing.

(2) 寫一寫 is a more casual expression.

Q: "你在做甚麼?"

   "NI ZAI ZUO SHEN MO? "

   "What are you doing? "

A: "給家裡寫信。" / "寫信給家裡。"

   "GEI JIA LI XIE XIN." / "XIE XIN GEI JIA LI."

   "Writing my letter home."

給家裡寫信 = 寫信給家裡: the former expression tends to be northern usage as in Mandarin while the latter tends to be southern usage as in Cantonese. Both are Chinese expressions, (cf. NOTE in M9.3C.)

他說的不合情理, 我才不信。　　　　　　(不信 = 不相信)

TA SHUO DE BU HE QING LI, WO CAI BU XIN.

What he said is beyond reasoning. I wouldn't believe it at all. (.... I don't buy it.)

---

(1) The relative pronoun 'what' does not occur in the above Chinese sentence. By context, 他說的 (what he said) is a noun clause used as subject of 不合情理 (is beyond reasoning).

(2) 他說的不合情理 = 他說的是不合情理的

我才不信 = 我才不相信 = 我才不會相信。

Conciseness is always valued in Chinese, especially in writing.

(3) The Chinese sentence actually says: Since what he said is beyond reasoning, I wouldn't believe it at all. Therefore, in Chinese expression, it is in one sentence with conjunctive word omitted, and a comma is used between the two segments.

(4) Conciseness is always valued. Even in speaking, 我才不信 is more often used than 我才不相信.

MODULE 14

M14.3 THIRD GROUP OF 5 NEW CHARACTERS:

其 ²	餘 ²	交 ²	開 ¹	會 ⁴
QI	YU	JIAO	KAI	HUI
that	remaining	hand over	open	meeting
which	balance			would could

M14.3A Build vocabulary and expressions with these five characters:

其餘	QÍ YÚ	the remaining; the rest; the balance
開會	KAI HUÌ	meeting
其餘交開會。	QÍ YÚ JIAO KAI HUÌ	The rest will be turned over to the meeting.

M14.3B Expand vocabulary and expressions by using all the 210 characters learned:

其他	QÍ TA	others
其他人	QÍ TA REN	other people
其中	QÍ ZHONG	in which; among which (其中=當中, cf. M12.2B)
餘下的	YÚ XIÀ DE	the rest; the balance (餘下的 = 其餘)
多餘	DUO YÚ	extra
開工	KAI GONG	work starts; working
開心	KAI XIN	happy (More often used in Cantonese.)
開年	KAI NIAN	celebrate the beginning of the Lunar New Year

年會	NIÁN HUÌ	annual meeting
大會	DÀ HUÌ	conference
國會	GUÓ HUÌ	Congress
工會	GŌNG HUÌ	labor union
入會	RÙ HUÌ	join as member (in a club, association, union)
理事會	LǏ SHÌ HUÌ	council
交心	JIĀO XĪN	open one's heart to
交情	JIĀO QÍNG	friendship; rapport
交朋友	JIĀO PÉNG YOU	make friends
交會點	JIĀO HUÌ DIǍN	point of intersection

M14.3C Sample sentences:

這個項目,我們已經談了這些方面,其餘的就等交給開會討論。

ZHE GE XIANG MU, WO MEN YI JING TAN LE ZHE XIE FANG MIAN, QI YU DE JIU DENG JIAO GEI KAI HUI TAO LUN.

On this project, we have talked about these aspects already. The rest are to be turned over to the meeting for discussion.

來開會的人很多,可以交很多朋友。　　(開會: meeting)

LAI KAI HUI DE REN HEN DUO, KE YI JIAO HEN DUO PENG YOU.

There are many people coming to attend the meeting. (We, …) can make a lot of friends.

你會不會講中文?　　(會: can, being able to)

NI HUI BU HUI JIANG ZHONG WEN?

Can you speak Chinese?

我學是學過中文,可是學不會。　　(不會: did not master (some knowledge))
WO XUE SHI XUE GUO ZHONG WEN, KE SHI XUE BU HUI.
I did learn Chinese, but I didn't make it.

她明天會不會來?　　　　　　　　　(會不會: would)
TA MING TIAN HUI BU HUI LAI?
Would she come tomorrow?
COMPARE: 她明天來不來?
TA MING TIAN LAI BU LAI?
 Is she coming tomorrow?

已經遲了,他還不來,會不會是有甚麼事?　　(會不會: could)
YI JING CHI LE, TA HAI BU LAI, HUI BU HUI SHI YOU SHEN ME SHI?
It's late already and he hasn't come yet. Could it be something happened?

MODULE 15

M15.1 FIRST GROUP OF 5 NEW CHARACTERS:

向	公	司	報	告
XIANG⁴	GONG¹	SI¹	BAO⁴	GAO⁴
to	public	take charge	report	tell

M15.1A Build vocabulary and expressions with these five characters:

公司	GŌNG SĪ	company (business)
報告	BÀO GÀO	report
公報	GŌNG BÀO	communique; government bulletin
公告	GŌNG GÀO	announcement; proclamation
向公司報告。	XIÀNG GŌNG SĪ BÀO GÀO.	Report to the Company.

(Notice that the verb is the first word in English while it is the last one in Chinese.)

M15.1B Expand vocabulary and expressions by using all the 215 characters learned:

向上	XIÀNG SHÀNG	upward
向下	XIÀNG XIÀ	downward
向來	XIÀNG LÁI	always
一向	YĪ XIÀNG	always
意向	YÌ XIÀNG	intent
方向	FĀNG XIÀNG	direction
面向	MIÀN XIÀNG	face (toward)
定向	DÌNG XIÀNG	fixed direction

去向	QÙ XIÀNG	whereabouts
公文	GŌNG WÉN	official document
公事	GŌNG SHÌ	official matter
公共	GŌNG GÒNG	public (public nature)
公有	GŌNG YǑU	publicly owned
公用	GŌNG YÒNG	for public use
公道	GŌNG DÀO	fair, just; reasonable
公法	GŌNG FǍ	public laws
公理	GŌNG LǏ	generally acknowledged truth/rule
公論	GŌNG LÙN	public opinion
公家	GŌNG JIA	belong to an organization (of any size)
公立	GŌNG LÌ	established for public (e.g. public school)
公開	GŌNG KĀI	disclose; exposed; open to public
司法	SĪ FǍ	administration of justice
報應	BÀO YÌNG	retribution
報時	BÀO SHÍ	report the correct time
上報	SHÀNG BÀO	report to upper level
日報	RÌ BÀO	daily newspaper
時報	SHÍ BÀO	daily newspaper (times)
商報	SHĀNG BÀO	business (commercial) newspaper
小報	XIǍO BÀO	tabloid

情報	QING² BAO⁴	intelligence; information
告別	GAO⁴ BIE²	leave; say good-bye to
原告	YUAN² GAO⁴	plaintiff
廣告	GUANG³ GAO⁴	advertisement; commercial
告發	GAO⁴ FA¹	report (an offender)

M15.1C Sample Sentences:

這裡有個問題, 相當大, 不得不向公司報告, 把情況寫清楚。

ZHE LI YOU GE WEN TI, XIANG DANG DA, BU DE BU XIANG GONG SI BAO GAO, BA QING KUANG XIE QING CHU.

There is a problem here, pretty big. (We, you,..) have to state the situation clearly in writing and report to the Company.

ANNOTATIONS

Indefinite person in a sentence is commonly used in Chinese.

情況是上報了, 就等公司開會決定了。

QING KUANG SHI SHANG BAO LE, JIU DENG GONG SI KAI HUI JUE DING LE.

The situation has already been reported. Just wait for the Company to make decisions at the meeting.

你當時為甚麼不及時向上面報告?

NI DANG SHI WEI SHEN ME BU JI SHI XIANG SHANG MIAN BAO GAO?

At that time, why didn't you report to the upper level (the authority) timely?

這家公立中學管理得很好。

ZHE JIA GONG LI ZHONG XUE GUAN LI DE HEN HAO.

This public high school (secondary school) is well managed.

ANNOTATIONS ────

Passive voice in Chinese is expressed as if it is in active voice in the above example. This is a common feature.

這地方是公用的，人人都可以來。

ZHE DI FANG SHI GONG YONG DE, REN REN DOU KE YI LAI.

This place is for public use. Everybody can come.

說話辦事要講道理。

SHUO HUA BAN SHI YAO JIANG DAO LI.

What one says and does has to be sensible.

ANNOTATIONS ────

Sentences with indefinite person are commonly used in Chinese, especially in scientific research paper, survey and business reports. Instead of beginning with "*I/WE discovered that ...* " in a sentence, "*It is discovered that ...* " is more often used. Even in conversation, people often try to avoid using too many "I" or "We" as a respect to the other party.

他的事，見不得人的多，怕(給)人家公開出來。

TA DE SHI, JIAN BU DE REN DE DUO, PA (GEI) REN JIA GONG KAI CHU LAI. (The character 給 is often omitted.)

Many of his affairs are shameful and he is afraid of being exposed.

MODULE 15

M15.2 SECOND GROUP OF 5 NEW CHARACTERS:

而₂	且₃	打₃	傳₂	眞₁
ER	QIE	DA	CHUAN	ZHEN
but	also	hit, make	pass on	real

M15.2A Build vocabulary and expressions with these five characters:

而且	ER₂ QIE₃	and also; furthermore
傳眞	CHUAN₂ ZHEN₁	facsimile (FAX)
而且打傳眞。	ER₂ QIE₃ DA₃ CHUAN₂ ZHEN₁.	And also send FAX.

M15.2B Expand vocabulary and expressions by using all the 220 characters learned:

而今	ER₂ JIN₁	and now (in writing)
而現在	ER₂ XIAN₄ ZAI₄	and now
而後	ER₂ HOU₄	after that; and then (而後 = 然後 RAN₂ HOU₄, cf. M12.3B)
而已	ER₂ YI₃	no more than that
打人	DA₃ REN₂	throw into; battery
打工	DA₃ GONG₁	being employed
打手	DA₃ SHOU₃	hired hit-man
傳說	CHUAN₂ SHUO₁	it is said; hearsay
傳話	CHUAN₂ HUA₂	pass on a message
家傳	JIA₁ CHUAN₂	passed on from family generations

真人	ZHEN¹ REN²	real person
真事	ZHEN¹ SHI⁴	real event; fact
真心	ZHEN¹ XIN¹	whole-hearted
真理	ZHEN¹ LI³	truth
真是!	ZHEN¹ SHI⁴!	oh, gosh! (followed by an exclamation mark)
天真	TIAN¹ ZHEN¹	innocent and artless (children); naive (adults)

M15.2C Sample Sentences;

(真是: really)

過去並沒有傳真, 而今有了, 真是方便。

GUO QU BING MEI YOU CHUAN ZHEN, ER JIN YOU LE, ZHEN SHI FANG BIAN.

There wasn't any Fax in the past. It is now available, really convenient.

(真是!: oh, gosh)

太遲了, 他還沒來, 真是![沒來 = 沒有來]

TAI CHI LE, TA HAI MEI LAI, ZHEN SHI!

Oh, gosh. He is not here yet. It's too late.

他真好, 經常來幫我。   (真好 == 真是好)

TA ZHEN HAO, JING CHANG LAI BANG WO.

He is really nice. He often comes to help me.

我在學的不是日文,而是中文。　　　　（而是）

WO ZAI XUE DE BU SHI RI WEN, ER SHI ZHONG WEN.

What I am studying now is not Japanese. It is Chinese.

他學中文不多,幾個月而已。　　　　（而已）

TA XUE ZHONG WEN BU DUO, JI GE YUE ER YI.

He didn't learn much Chinese, no more than a few months.

　　　　　　　　　　　　　（才....而已）

他學中文,才幾個月而已,已經會說好些了。

TA XUE ZHONG WEN, CAI JI GE YUE ER YI, YI JING HUI SHUO HAO XIE LE.

He has been learning Chinese for only a few months and he can speak quite a bit already.

他說的這些話,我相信是眞心話。　　（眞心話）

TA SHUO DE ZHE XIE HUA, WO XIANG XIN SHI ZHEN XIN HUA.

我相信他說的這些話是眞心話。

WO XIANG XIN TA SHUO DE ZHE XIE HUA SHI ZHEN XIN HUA.

I believe what he said was from his heart.

ANNOTATIONS ———

Both expressions are fine; the first better. (cf. M12.3C last NOTE.)

請對他說眞話。(眞話)

QING DUI TA SHUO ZHEN HUA.

Please, tell him the truth.

———

MODULE 15

M15.3 THIRD GROUP OF 5 NEW CHARACTERS:

電 4	腦 3	內 4	外 4	通 1
DIAN	NAO	NEI	WAI	TONG
electricity	brain	inside	outside	connect

M15.3A Build vocabulary and expressions with these five characters:

電腦	DIAN⁴ NAO³	computer
內外	NEI⁴ WAI⁴	inside and outside
電腦內外通。	DIAN⁴ NAO³ NEI⁴ WAI⁴ TONG¹.	Computer connects inside and outside.

ANNOTATIONS ────────

電腦 literally means 'electronic brain'. In China (mainland), computer is translated as 計算機 JI₄ SUAN₄ JI₁ which literally means 'computing machine'; or in its full name '電子計算機' DIAN₄ ZI₃ JI₄ SUAN₄ JI₁ which literal-ly means "electronic computing machine'.

────────

M15.3B Expand vocabulary and expressions by using all the 225 characters learned:

電力	DIAN⁴ LI⁴	electric power
電報	DIAN⁴ BAO⁴	telegram
電話	DIAN⁴ HUA⁴	telephone
電傳	DIAN⁴ CHUAN²	telex
人腦	REN² NAO³	human brain
腦力	NAO³ LI⁴	mental
內力	NEI⁴ LI⁴	internal force

內面	NEI⁴ MIAN⁴	inside
內地	NEI⁴ DI⁴	inland
內因	NEI⁴ YIN¹	internal cause
內定	NEI⁴ DING⁴	officially pre-deter-mined but not announced
內在	NEI⁴ ZAI⁴	inherent
內行	NEI⁴ HANG²	expertise; expert (casual)
內心	NEI⁴ XIN¹	deep in one's heart
內應	NEI⁴ YING⁴	planted agent; undercover agent
年內	NIAN² NEI⁴	within the year
國內	GUO² NEI⁴	domestic (of a nation)
國外	GUO² WAI⁴	foreign (countries)
題外	TI² WAI⁴	away from theme/topic
裡外	LI³ WAI⁴	inside and outside (裡外 = 內外; 內外 is more often used in Cantonese in speaking)
外人	WAI⁴ REN²	outsider
外力	WAI⁴ LI⁴	external force
外國	WAI⁴ GUO²	foreign country
外因	WAI⁴ YIN¹	external cause
外行	WAI⁴ HANG²	layman; non-professional
通天	TONG¹ TIAN¹	exceedingly high or great (capability)
通力 (通力 = 全力 QUAN² LI⁴)	TONG¹ LI⁴	full effort; concerted effort

通才	TŌNG CÁI	versatile person
(通才 = 全才 QUAN₂ CAI₂)		
通商	TŌNG SHĀNG	having trade relation (between nations)
通話	TŌNG HUÀ	converse over the phone; phone line connected
通知	TŌNG ZHĪ	notice
通報	TŌNG BÀO	notice circulation
通告	TŌNG GÀO	public notice
通電	TŌNG DIÀN	connect electric power
通信	TŌNG XÌN	correspondence
通向	TŌNG XIÀNG	leading to
通道	TŌNG DÀO	passage
通到	TŌNG DÀO	reaching; leading to
通行	TŌNG XÍNG	pass through
通通	TŌNG TŌNG	all; entirely; completely
中國通	ZHŌNG GUÓ TŌNG	expert of China affairs
想通	XIǍNG TŌNG	straighten up one's thinking; convinced

M15.3C Sample Sentences:

家裡有電腦,通過電話,就可以通到公司、外地、外國。

JIA LI YOU DIAN NAO, TONG GUO DIAN HUA, JIU KE YI TONG DAO GONG SI, WAI DI, WAI GUO.

A computer at home, via telephone, can connect to the company, outside area and to foreign countries.

ANNOTATIONS ──────

There is no plural form of nouns or Articles (a, an, the) in Chinese. By context, it is clear enough to tell that it means 'a computer', 'the company' and 'foreign countries'. (cf. NOTE of M12.2C: the second and third sample sentences from the end.)

他對公司裡裡外外的事都很清楚。

(裡裡外外=內內外外 NEI₁ NEI₁ WAI₁ WAI₁)

TA DUI GONG SI LI LI WAI WAI DE SHI DOU HEN QING CHU.

He knows very well about the company, from inside to outside matters.

──────

ANNOTATIONS ──────

裡裡外外 tends to be northern China oral usage.

叫他通過朋友請些人來幫工。

JIAO TA TONG GUO PENG YOU QING XIE REN LAI BANG GONG.

Tell him to hire some helpers through his friends.

──────

ANNOTATIONS ──────

(1) Another example of plural forms by context in Chinese.

   請些人 = 請一些人 --- Here "some" is specified.

   通過朋友 --- Here "through friends" :plural by context.

(2) 請：invite, hire, please. Here by context, it means "hire". (cf. M3.1)

   他說得沒有道理，哪裡講得通？

   TA SHUO DE MEI YOU DAO LI, NA LI JIANG DE TONG?

   What he said is beyond reasoning. How can it be convincing?

這個電話很難打，你打通了叫我。
ZHE GE DIAN HUA HEN NAN DA, NI DA TONG LE JIAO WO.
This phone is hard to get through. Call me when you get connected.

這些通通都不是我的。　　　(通通=全=全部 QUAN₂ BU₄)
ZHE XIE TONG TONG DOU BU SHI WO DE.　(通通)
All of these are not mine.

我通常都不到那些地方去的。(通常)
WO TONG CHANG DOU BU DAO NA/NEI XIE DI FANG QU DE.
I usually don't go to those places.

不論我說得多麼清楚，他還是想不通。
BU LUN WO SHUO DE DUO ME QING CHU, TA HAI SHI XIANG BU TONG.
No matter how clearly I explained, he was still not convinced.

他到國外以後，和我們有通信。
TA DAO GUO WAI YI HOU, HE WO MEN YOU TONG XIN.
After he went abroad, he had correspondence with us.

他知道內情，不便對外人說就是了。
TA ZHI DAO NEI QING, BU BIAN DUI WAI REN SHUO JIU SHI LE.
He has some insider information but is not supposed to tell outsiders.

他們在外面等你。
TA MEN ZAI WAI MIAN DENG NI.
They are waiting for you outside.

MODULE 16

M16.1 FIRST GROUP OF 5 NEW CHARACTERS:

但 [4]	求 [2]	從 [2]	此 [3]	忙 [2]
DAN	QIU	CONG	CI	MANG
but	beg	from	here this	busy

M16.1A Build vocabulary and expressions with these five characters:

但求	DÀN QIÚ	wish; hope
從此	CÓNG CǏ	from now on

ANNOTATIONS ─────

從此	= 從此以後	CÓNG CǏ YǏ HÒU
	= 此後	CǏ HÒU (written style)
	= 以後	YǏ HÒU
	= 從今以後	CÓNG JIN YǏ HÒU
	= 今後	JIN HÒU
但求從此忙。		DÀN QIÚ CÓNG CǏ MÁNG.
		(I, We,...) Hope it stays busy from now on.

───────

M16.1B Expand vocabulary and expressions by using all the 230 characters learned:

但是	DÀN SHÌ	but
不但	BÙ DÀN	not only
不但...而且...	BÙ DÀN ... ÉR QIĚ ...	not only...; but also ...
從來	CÓNG LÁI	always; at all times

194   Mastering Mandarin: Your Path to Proficiency

從不 (從不 = 從來不)	CÓNG BÙ	never ever
從前	CÓNG QIÁN	once upon a time; formerly; in the past
從而	CÓNG ÉR	thus; thereby
從事	CÓNG SHÌ	be engaged in; work on
自從	ZÌ CÓNG	since; ever since
自…到…	ZÌ …DÀO …	from…to …
從…到…	CÓNG … DÀO …	from…to …
因此	YĪN CǏ	therefore; that's why
爲此	WÈI CǏ	for this reason/purpose
求人	QIÚ RÉN	ask for help
求助	QIÚ ZHÙ	ask for help

ANNOTATIONS

1. 求人 = 求助 = 求人幫助 QIU REN BANG ZHU;

2. In writing or oral, the shorter forms are often used. (But not 求幫.)

求見	QIÚ JIÀN	request to see; request for an interview

求見 = 要求見面 = 請求見面

求學	QIÚ XUÉ	pursue studies; attend school or college
求情	QIÚ QÍNG	plead; beg for favor or leniency
求和	QIÚ HÉ	sue for peace; seek to stop fighting

要求	YÃO QIŪ (1,2)	require; demand
請求	QĬNG QIŪ (3,2)	beg; request
忙人	MÁNG RÉN (2,2)	busy person
幫忙	BĀNG MÁNG (1,2)	help (幫忙 = 幫助)

M16.1C Sample sentences:

今年不是好年，不求加工資，但求有工作。

JIN NIAN BU SHI HAO NIAN, BU QIU JIA GONG ZI, DAN QIU YOU GONG ZUO.

This year is not a good year. Don't expect to have a raise. Only hope to keep the job.

從去年到今年，我沒有見過他。

CONG QU NIAN DAO JIN NIAN, WO MEI YOU JIAN GUO TA.

From last year to this year, I have not seen him.
(I have not seen him since last year.)

我從來沒有見過他，因此那天有人來，要求見面，我不知道就是他。

WO CONG LAI MEI YOU JIAN GUO TA, YIN CI NEI TIAN YOU REN LAI, YAO QIU JIAN MIAN, WO BU ZHI DAO JIU SHI TA.

I never met him before. That's why the other day when somebody came and asked to see me, I didn't know it was him.

ANNOTATIONS

The above sentence in Chinese indicates past tense from the context.

公司要我今年到中國去工作,爲此我要下決心學好中文。

GONG SI YAO WO JIN NIAN DAO ZHONG GUO QU GONG ZUO, YIN CI WO YAO XIA JUE XIN XUE HAO ZHONG WEN.

The Company is going to send me to work in China this year. For this reason, I must make up my mind to learn and master Chinese.

學好 means to learn and do well in learning: master it.

他是個忙人,可他還是很肯幫助別人,一叫就到。

TA SHI GE MANG REN, KE TA HAI SHI HEN KEN BANG ZHU BIE REN, YI JIAO JIU DAO.

He is a busy man; however, he is still very willing to help other people whenever called for.

可 = 可是 = 但 = 但是

他學英文,不但在美國學了幾年,而且還到英國去學了幾年。

TA XUE YING WEN, BU DAN ZAI MEI GUO XUE LE JI NIAN, ER QIE HAI DAO YING GUO QU XUE LE JI NIAN.

He not only studied English in America for a few years, he also studied in the U.K. for a few years.

他以前從來沒想過要學中文,但是自從到中國去過之後,就下決心學了。

TA YI QIAN CONG LAI MEI XIANG GUO YAO XUE ZHONG WEN, DAN SHI ZI CONG DAO ZHONG GUO QU GUO ZHI HOU, JIU XIA JUE XIN XUE LE.

In the past he never thought about learning Chinese. However, he made up his mind to learn after he visited China.

(1) 沒想過 = 沒有想過:never thought about it. A related expression meaning unexpected, not prepared: 沒想到 = 沒有想到 = 想不到

(2) 自從到中國去過之後 = 到中國去過之後 . = 去過中國之後

   自從… 之後 = … 之後 = … 以後;

   自從 is often used to add emphasis.

(3) 以前 = 從前:In actual application, 從前 is often used in fairy tales similar to: "Once upon a time … " in English.

他經常忙不過來, (但是)從來不要求幫忙。

TA JING CHANG MANG BU GUO LAI, (DAN SHI) CONG LAI BU YAO QIU BANG MANG. (但是 but --- very often omitted.)

He is often busier than he can handle, but he never asks for help.

MODULE 16

M16.2 SECOND GROUP OF 5 NEW CHARACTERS:

早₃	至₄	晚₃	平₂	安₁
ZAO	ZHI	WAN	PING	AN
morning	to	evening	flat	peaceful
early	until	late	level	calm

M16.2A Build vocabulary and expressions with these five characters:

早晚	ZǍO WĂN	morning and/to evening; sooner or later
平安	PÍNG ĀN	safe and sound
早安	ZǍO ĀN	good morning
晚安	WĂN ĀN	good night
早至晚平安。	ZǍO ZHÌ WĂN PÍNG ĀN.	

(早至晚 = 從早到晚 CÓNG₂ ZǍO₃ DÀO₄ WĂN₃)

From morning to evening, safe and sound.

M16.2B Expand vocabulary and expressions by using all the 235 characters learned:

早上	ZǍO SHÀNG	morning (早上 = 上午)
早日	ZǍO RÌ	soon
早已	ZǍO YǏ	long ago
早年	ZǍO NIÁN	in the early years
早報	ZǍO BÀO	morning newspaper
早點	ZǍO DIǍN	breakfast (light meal)

早一點	ZAO³ YI⁴ DIAN³	a little early/earlier
早知道	ZAO³ ZHI¹ DAO⁴	know long ago; had it been known beforehand
及早	JI² ZAO³	as soon as possible; before it is too late
清早	QING¹ ZAO³	early in the morning
遲早	CHI² ZAO³	sooner or later
(遲早=早晚)		
晚上	WAN³ SHANG⁴	evening
晚年	WAN³ NIAN²	one's later years; old age
晚會	WAN³ HUI⁴	evening party
晚點	WAN³ DIAN³	behind schedule (of bus, train, plane)
至上	ZHI⁴ SHANG⁴	supreme; top priority
至少	ZHI⁴ SHAO³	at least
至多	ZHI⁴ DUO¹	at the most
至今	ZHI⁴ JIN¹	to this day; so far
至於	ZHI⁴ YU²	as to
甚至	SHEN⁴ ZHI⁴	even; so much so that
平白	PING² BAI²	for no reason
平手	PING² SHOU³	tie; draw
(平手 = 打平 DA³ PING² = 打和 DA³ HE²)		
平常	PING² CHANG²	ordinary; common
平等	PING² DENG³	equality; equal
平地	PING² DI⁴	flat/level ground
平定	PING² DING⁴	calm down; put down (such as a riot)

平方	PING² FANG¹	square (maths)
平分	PING² FEN¹	equally shared/split
平和	PING² HE²	gentle; mild
平面	PING² MIAN⁴	plane; face
平時	PING² SHI²	ordinary times
平行	PING² XING²	parallel
平信	PING² XIN⁴	surface mail
平平	PING² PING²	average; mediocre
太平	TAI⁴ PING²	peace (casual use)

(太平 = 和平 HE₂ PING₂)

和平	HE² PING²	peace
安家	AN¹ JIA¹	settle down; set up a home
安定	AN¹ DING⁴	stable; settled
安心	AN¹ XIN¹	relieved; at ease
安全	AN¹ QUAN²	safe; secure
安然	AN¹ RAN²	quietly; calmly

M16.2C Sample sentences:

早知道他不來,我就不會來了。

ZAO ZHI DAO TA BU LAI, WO JIU BU HUI LAI LE.

Had I known that he would not come, I wouldn't have come.

ANNOTATIONS ─────

The subjunctive mood of the sentence in Chinese is based on the context without particular grammatical rules.

MODULE 16

他每天清早就起來學中文,當然學得快。

TA MEI TIAN QING ZAO JIU QI LAI XUE ZHONG WEN, DANG RAN XUE DE KUAI.

Everyday he gets up early in the morning to study Chinese. Certainly, he learns fast.

清早 = 一早 (一早：more often used in Cantonese)

　　　= 大清早 more often used in Northern China

明天有個晚會,大家都會早一點去,想多和一些人談談。

MING TIAN YOU GE WAN HUI, DA JIA DOU HUI ZAO YI DIAN QU, XIANG DUO HE YI XIE REN TAN TAN.

There is an evening party tomorrow. Everybody would get there earlier, hoping to chat with more people.

至於我自己,我要及早學中文,要不然下一次公司要人到中國去工作,我又不合要求,去不了。

ZHI YU WO ZI JI, WO YAO JI ZAO XUE ZHONG WEN, YAO BU RAN XIA YI CI GONG SI YAO REN DAO ZHONG GUO QU GONG ZUO, WO YOU BU HE YAO QIU, QU BU LIAO.

As to myself, I've got to learn Chinese before it's too late. Otherwise, next time when the Company needs someone to work in China, I would fail to qualify again and can't go.

他不肯學,遲早要出問題。

TA BU KEN XUE, CHI ZAO YAO CHU WEN TI.

He is not willing to learn. Sooner or later he is going to run into trouble.

In northern China, people tend to say 早晚 For 遲早 in speaking to mean the same.

MODULE 16

M16.3 THIRD GROUP OF 5 NEW CHARACTERS:

使 	初	步	比	較
3	1	4	3	4
SHI	CHU	BU	BI	JIAO
send / cause	beginning	step	compare	compare

M16.3A Build vocabulary and expressions with these five characters:

初步	CHU¹ BU⁴	initial; preliminary
比較	BI³ JIAO⁴	compare
使初步比較。	SHI³ CHU¹ BU⁴ BI³ JIAO⁴.	Make a preliminary comparison.

M16.3B Expand vocabulary and expressions by using all the 240 characters learned:

起初	QI³ CHU¹	at the beginning; at first; initially
初時	CHU¹ SHI²	(ditto)
初初	CHU¹ CHU¹	(ditto)

ANNOTATIONS ———

The above three terms have the same meaning. The last two tend to be used more often in Cantonese.

當初	DANG¹ CHU¹	initially; originally; in the first place
使用	SHI³ YONG⁴	use
天使	TIAN¹ SHI³	angel

大使	DÀ SHǏ	ambassador
即使	JÍ SHǏ	even if; even though
(即使 = 即便 (cf. M13.2))		
一步步	YĪ BÙ BÙ	step by step
步行	BÙ XÍNG	on foot (cf. 不行 BU₄ XING₂) (cf. M5.1C)
比方	BǏ FĀNG	for instance
對比	DUÌ BǏ	compare; contrast
較好	JIÀO HǍO	better
較快	JIÀO KUÀI	faster
較量	JIÀO LIÀNG	have a contest with; square-off; face off

(1) 較好 = 比較好;較 or 比較 is the comparative of adjectives and adverbs such as: 多、少、大、小、快、慢 to lean lore, less, bigger, smaller, faster and slower.

(2) 較 is the short form and is often matched with one character such as: 較快.(較快=比較快)

M16.3C Sample sentences:

這方法學中文好得多,使大家學得快很多。　　　　(使)

ZHE FANG FA XUE ZHONG WEN HAO DE DUO, SHI DA JIA XUE DE KUAI HEN DUO.

This method of learning Chinese is much better. It helps everybody learn much faster.

他這麼說,使我覺得很不好意思。　　　　　　(使)

TA ZHE ME SHUO, SHI WO JUE DE HEN BU HAO YI SI.

What he said made me feel very embarrassed.

通知了我們去開會,你不去,叫我一個人去,使我很爲難。　(使)

TONG ZHI LE WO MEN QU KAI HUI, NI BU QU, JIAO WO YI GE REN QU, SHI WO HEN WEI NAN.

We are notified to attend the meeting. You are not going and ask me to go alone. This puts me in a very difficult position.

你肯幫助他,這使他非常高興。　　　　　　(使)

NI KEN BANG ZHU TA, ZHE SHI TA FEI CHANG GAO XING.

You are willing to help him. It makes him very happy.

即使你自己忙,也該放下一天去幫人家,使大家對你有信心。(即使)

JI SHI NI ZI JI MANG. YE GAI FANG XIA YI TIAN QU BANG REN JIA, SHI DA JIA DUI NI YOU XIN XIN.

Even if you are busy, you ought to set aside one day to help people. This will help everybody have confidence in you.

ANNOTATIONS

(1) 使 is a character commonly used. The above sample sentences give an idea of its flexibility in meaning.
(2) In the last sentence above: 也該 = 也應該.

叫我學中文,起初我心想很難。眞的學起來,用這方法,一點也不難。

JIAO WO XUE ZHONG WEN, QI CHU WO XIN XIANG HEN NAN. ZHEN DE XUE QI LAI, YONG ZHE FANG FA, YI DIAN YE BU NAN.

At the beginning, I thought it would be very difficult when I was asked to learn Chinese. After really started, it wasn't difficult at all by applying this method.

使用過這方法學中文的人都說好。

SHI YONG GUO ZHE FANG FA XUE ZHONG WEN DI REN DOU SHUO HAO.

這方法學中文,使用過的人都說好。

ZHE FANG FA XUE ZHONG WEN, SHI YONG GUO DI REN DOU SHUO HAO.

Everybody who has used it says that this method of learning Chinese is good.

---

(1) 使用 = 用: use, utilize, apply.
(2) The above two sentences in Chinese mean the same and both are perfect Chinese sentences. However, the second one, with a comma and the sentence becomes two segments, is used more often. In Chinese expression, shorter segments of sentences are preferred, (cf. NOTE in M15.2C).

早知道今天要用中文,當初兩年前我就該學中文了。

ZAO ZHI DAO JIN TIAN YAO YONG ZHONG WEN, DANG CHU LIANG NIAN QIAN WO JIU GAI XUE ZHONG WEN LE.

Had I known that I need to use Chinese today, I should have learned Chinese two years ago in the first place.

這方法很有意思,邊學邊用,一步步學下去。　　　(很有意思)

ZHE FANG FA HEN YOU YI SI, BIAN XUE BIAN YONG, YI BU BU XUE XIA QU.

This method is very interesting; use it as we learn, step by step.

學了幾天中文,初步覺得很有意思,並不比英文難學。　　(很有意思)

XUE LE JI TIAN ZHONG WEN, CHU BU JUE DE HEN YOU YI SI, BING BU BI YING WEN NAN XUE.

After learning Chinese for a few days, my initial feeling is that it is pretty interesting, not really harder than learning English.

這裡有個初步報告，提出了五個項目，要對這五個項目做比較，作出決定。

ZHE LI YOU GE CHU BU BAO GAO, TI CHU LE WU GE XIANG MU, YAO DUI ZHE WU GE XIANG MU ZUO BI JIAO, ZUO CHU JUE DING.

Here's a preliminary report with five projects proposed. Need to compare these five projects and make a decision.

這個項目很好，即使現在做不來，也不要放過，等看看明年的情況再說。

ZHE GE XIANG MU HEN HAO, JI SHI XIAN ZAI ZUO BU LAI, YE BU YAO FANG GUO, DENG KAN KAN MING NIAN DE QING KUANG ZAI SHUO.

This project is very good. Even if it can't be done now, don't give up. Wait and see the situation next year.

初步看來，這個項目是比較好的一個。　　　　　（比較好）

CHU BU KAN LAI, ZHE GE XIANG MU SHI BI JIAO HAO DE YI GE.

(My) preliminary impression is that this project is a better one. (比較好 = 較好)

他們兩個的力量都不相上下，今天大可較量較量。　　　　　（較量）

TA MEN LIANG GE DE LI LIANG DOU BU XIANG SHANG XIA, JIN TIAN DA KE JIAO LIANG JIAO LIANG.

The strength of the two is pretty much equal. Today both of them can have a nice square-off.

---

1. 不相上下: about equal; pretty close.
2. 較量 in this sample sentence is used as a verb. 較量較量 means 較量 with emphasis.
3. 大可=大可以=完全可以.

他比我學得快很多。

TA BI WO XUE DE KUAI HEN DUO.

He learns much faster than I do.

他比我大。

TA BI WO DA.

He is older than I am.

比起來, 他學得多一些。

BI QI LAI, TA XUE DE DUO YI XIE.

In comparison, he learned more.

MODULE 17

M17.1 FIRST GROUP OF 5 NEW CHARACTERS:

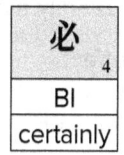    

BI	XU	SHI	BIAO	XIAN
certainly	must	see / depend on	surface	now / show

M17.1A Build vocabulary and expressions with these five characters:

必須	BI XU	must; required
表現	BIAO XIAN	performance, behavior
必須視表現。	BI XU SHI BIAO XIAN.	Must see performance.
視 = 看 = 看見	(SHI = KAN = KAN JIAN)	

M17.1B Expand vocabulary and expressions by using all the 245 characters learned:

必定	BI DING	bound to
必然	BI RAN	inevitable (必定=必然)
必要	BI YAO	essential; necessary
必需	BI XU	necessity; must
電視	DIAN SHI	television
表面	BIAO MIAN	surface; superficial
外表	WAI BIAO	outside surface; appearance
時間表	SHI JIAN BIAO	timetable; schedule
現在	XIAN ZAI	now; at present
現時	XIAN SHI	currently; at present
現今	XIAN JIN	nowadays (in writing)

MODULE 17

現有	XIAN⁴ YOU³	existing; now available
現成	XIAN⁴ CHENG²	ready-made; readily available
現行	XIAN⁴ XING²	currently in effect (laws, regulations, ...); active (criminal,...)

M17.1C Sample Sentences:

這就要看他的表現才決定得了。

ZHE JIU YAO KAN TA DE BIAO XIAN CAI JUE DING DE LIAO.

This depends on his performance before a decision can be made.

需視其表現而定。

XU SHI QI BIAO XIAN ER DING.

Decision depends on checking performance.

ANNOTATIONS ———

(cf. M11.3C)

(1) The above two sentences in Chinese express the same content. The same holds true in English.

(2) The first sentence is longer (13 characters) and the second one is shorter (7 characters). The longer one is in vernacular style while the short one is close to classical style writing.

(3) Orally spoken is often longer than written in terms of expressing a content. It is more so in Chinese. Furthermore, the shorter form in writing also reflects one's education level and language skill: precise and concise.

(4) The character 其 (QI) is a pronoun which could be his, her, its or their depending on context.

做這工作必須懂中文。

ZUO ZHE GONG ZUO BI XU DONG ZHONG WEN.

Knowledge of Chinese is a must to do this job.

現有五個人,都懂中文,現成的,可以立即到中國去。

XIAN YOU WU GE REN, DOU DONG ZHONG WEN, XIAN CHENG DE, KE YI LI JI DAO ZHONG GUO QU.

There are five people who understand Chinese. They are readily available and can go to China right away.

只從表面上看,看不出問題。

ZHI CONG BIAO MIAN SHANG KAN, KAN BU CHU WEN TI.

No problems discovered by just looking at it superficially.

現今學中文的人多起來了。〔現今=現時=現在〕

XIAN JIN XUE ZHONG WEN DI REN DUO QI LAI LE.

Nowadays more and more people learn Chinese.

MODULE 17

M17.2 SECOND GROUP OF 5 NEW CHARACTERS:

注	重	字	拼	音
ZHU⁴	ZHONG⁴	ZI⁴	PIN¹	YIN¹
pour	heavy	word	put together	sound

M17.2A Build vocabulary and expressions with these five characters:

注重	ZHÙ ZHÒNG	pay attention to; emphasize
字	ZÌ	word; character
拼音	PĪN YĪN	spell; phoneticize
注音	ZHÙ YĪN	phonetic notation
重音	ZHÒNG YĪN	accent (on a syllabic)
注重字拼音。	ZHÙ ZHÒNG ZÌ PĪN YĪN.	Pay attention to the spelling of a word.

M17.2B Expand vocabulary and expressions by using all the 250 characters learned:

注意	ZHÙ YÌ	attention; pay attention
注定	ZHÙ DÌNG	bound to
下注	XIÀ ZHÙ	make a bet
重大	ZHÒNG DÀ	important; major
重點	ZHÒNG DIĂN	focus; emphasis
重要	ZHÒNG YÀO	important
重視	ZHÒNG SHÌ	value highly; pay high attention to
重力	ZHÒNG LÌ	gravity

重心	ZHONG XIN (4,1)	center of gravity
重量	ZHONG LIANG (4,4)	weight
重	ZHONG (4)	heavy
文字	WEN ZI (2,4)	writing; character
寫字	XIE ZI (3,4)	write a word/character
美國之音	MEI GUO ZHI YIN (3,2,1,1)	Voice of America

M17.2C Sample Sentences:

(當中 = 其中)

這八個項目, 公司很重視, 當中有兩個是今年的重點。

ZHE BA GE XIANG MU, GONG SI HEN ZHONG SHI, DANG ZHONG YOU LIANG GE SHI JIN NIAN DE ZHONG DIAN.

These eight projects receive high attention from the Company. Two of them are the focus of this year. (Two of them are top priorities this year.)

請大家注意, 時間到了。

QING DA JIA ZHU YI, SHI JIAN DAO LE.

Your attention, please. Time's up.

我不清楚他來了沒有, 沒注意到。

WO BU QING CHU TA LAI LE MEI YOU, MEI ZHU YI DAO.

I'm not sure if he has come yet. I didn't pay attention.

我只看到一大件, 沒有注意重不重。

WO ZHI KAN DAO YI DA JIAN, MEI YOU ZHU YI ZHONG BU ZHONG.

I only saw a big piece. I didn't notice heavy or not.

中文字有拼音，學起來方便多了。

ZHONG WEN ZI YOU PIN YIN, XUE QI LAI FANG BIAN DUO LE.

With phonetic spelling, it is much easier to learn Chinese characters.

他很注重天天學中文。

TA HEN ZHU ZHONG TIAN TIAN XUE ZHONG WEN.

He pays high attention to learning Chinese everyday.

你會寫幾個中文字？　　　　　　　　　(幾個：how many)

NI HUI XIE JI GE ZHONG WEN ZI? (幾個?=多少個?)

How many Chinese characters can you write?

你會寫幾個中文字嗎？　　　　　　　　(幾個：some)

NI HUI XIE JI GE ZHONG WEN ZI MA? (幾個 = 一些)

Can you write some Chinese characters?

ANNOTATIONS ———

Both expressions are fine; the first better. (cf. M12.3C last NOTE.)

請對他說真話。(真話)

QING DUI TA SHUO ZHEN HUA.

Please, tell him the truth.

MODULE 17

M17.3 THIRD GROUP OF 5 NEW CHARACTERS:

M17.3A Build vocabulary and expressions with these five characters:

錯誤	CUO⁴ WU⁴	mistake; error; wrong
未	WEI⁴	not yet
除	CHU²	eliminate, get rid of
除光	CHU² GUANG¹	totally eliminated
錯誤未除光。	CUO⁴ WU⁴ WEI⁴ CHU² GUANG¹.	Errors are not yet totally eliminated.

M17.3B Expand vocabulary and expressions by using all the 255 characters learned:

錯開	CUO⁴ KAI¹	stagger (alternating)
錯過	CUO⁴ GUO⁴	miss (such as time, opportunity)
錯覺	CUO⁴ JUE²	misconception; illusion
誤會	WU⁴ HUI⁴	misunderstanding
誤點	WU⁴ DIAN³	not on schedule (bus, train, airplane)
	(cf. M16.2: 晚點 WAN₃ DIAN₃ behind schedule)	
除非	CHU² FEI¹	only if; unless
除了	CHU² LE²	except; other than

除此以外	CHÚ CǏ YǏ WÀI	in addition
開除	KĀI CHÚ	expel; fire
清除	QĪNG CHÚ	clear away
未來	WÈI LÁI	future
未必	WÈI BÌ	not necessarily
未定	WÈI DÌNG	not yet decided
光明	GUĀNG MÍNG	bright
光學	GUĀNG XUÉ	optics
光管	GUĀNG GUǍN	fluorescent light
光電	GUĀNG DIÀN	photoelectricity
光年	GUĀNG NIÁN	light-year (Astronomy)
日光	RÌ GUĀNG	sun light
月光	YUÈ GUĀNG	moon light

M17.3C Sample Sentences:

他做了很多錯事,公司不得不把他給開除了。

TA ZUO LE HEN DUO CUO SHI, GONG SI BU DE BU BA TA GEI KAI CHU LE.

He made a lot of mistakes and the Company had no choice but to discharge (fire) him.

ANNOTATIONS ───────

把他給開除了 = 把他開除了。The former expression 把他給開除了 is typical in Mandarin especially spoken by people from Northern part of China. The second expression 把他開除了 is perfectly fine. There is a third way of expressing this phrase: 開除了他, no difference in meaning.

你來得晚,會開完了,除了我還在,沒有其他人了。

NI LAI DE WAN, HUI KAI WAN LE, CHU LE WO HAI ZAI, MEI YOU QI TA REN LE.

You are late. The meeting is over. Nobody is here except me.

明天一定要早一點來,別誤了。

MING TIAN YI DING YAO ZAO YI DIAN LAI, BIE WU LE.

Be sure to come earlier tomorrow. Don't miss it.

不是你的錯,提出來討論就是了。不要搞錯,我不是對你有意見。

BU SHI NI DE CUO, TI CHU LAI TAO LUN JIU SHI LE, BU YAO GAO CUO, WO BU SHI DUI NI YOU YI JIAN.

It's not your fault. It is brought up for discussion only. Don't get me wrong; I'm not against you.

他錯了,這裡可能有些誤會。

TA CUO LE, ZHE LI KE NENG YOU XIE WU HUI.

He is wrong. There could be some misunderstanding.

ANNOTATIONS

Notice the use of the character 錯 in the above sentences. 你的錯: your fault. 錯 = 錯誤; but, the short form is fine. (But not 你的誤).

搞錯　　: get confused, make a mistake; But not 搞錯誤.

他錯了　: He is wrong. (But not 他錯誤了.)

他誤了　: He missed it. / He caused it. (time)

他未來到, 我們等一等。

TA WEI LAI DAO, WO MEN DENG YI DENG.

He hasn't come yet. Let's wait.

(He isn't here yet. Let's wait.)

他還沒有來到, 我們等一等。

TA HAI MEI YOU LAI DAO, WO MEN DENG YI DENG.

He hasn't come yet. Let's wait.

ANNOTATIONS ───

Expression variations:

(1) 未 = 還沒有 : not yet. The above two sentences express the same meaning.

(2) The first sentence is a typical southern China usage as in Cantonese. The second sentence is a typical northern China usage as in Mandarin. Both sentences are perfect Chinese expressions.

我們的未來一定是光明的。

WO MEN DI WEI LAI YI DING SHI GUANG MING DE.

Our future is definitely bright.

ANNOTATIONS ───

未來 in this sentence is used as a noun and it means future. In the previous sentence, 未來到 WEI LAI DAO: 未 is used separately as an adverb while 來 is a verb. This example shows one difficulty in learning Chinese: for beginners it is often hard to tell where the break-line of a term or word is. In Romanized Chinese, it can be written like this: WEILAI (未來 future) as one word with two syllables while WEI LAI DAO must be separately written.

That's why in this book, focus is on:

character --> word --> expression.

光你一個人不行, 要兩個人。

GUANG NI YI GE REN BU XING, YAO LIANG GE REN.

Only you alone are not enough. Need two people.

(除非: unless)

除非你明天八點之前來到, 要不, 我們就不等了。

CHU FEI NI MING TIAN BA DIAN ZHI QIAN LAI DAO, YAO BU, WO MEN JIU BU DENG LE.

Unless you arrive before eight tomorrow, otherwise we are not going to wait.

除了你, 還有人嗎?

CHU LE NI, HAI YOU REN MA?

Anybody else, other than you?

除此以外, 不可再多。

CHU CI YI WAI, BU KE ZAI DUO.

No more, other than this (these).

MODULE 18

M18.1 FIRST GROUP OF 5 NEW CHARACTERS:

假³	如²	怕⁴	麻²	煩²
JIA	RU	PA	MA	FAN
false	if similar	fear	jute	trouble

M18.1A Build vocabulary and expressions with these five characters:

假如	JIĀ RÚ (3 2)	if; in case
怕	PÀ (4)	fear; afraid of
麻煩	MÁ FÁN (2 2)	trouble; bother
怕麻煩	PÀ MÁ FÁN (4 2 2)	afraid of being bothered; reluctant to take the trouble or put in effort
假如怕麻煩,..	JIĀ RÚ PÀ MÁ FÁN,.. (3 2 4 2 2)	If (you) don't want to take the trouble to ...,

M18.1B Expand vocabulary and expressions by using all the 260 characters learned:

假使	JIĀ SHǏ (3 3)	if; in case	假如=假使
假人	JIĀ RÉN (3 2)	mannequin	
眞假	ZHĒN JIĂ (1 3)	true or false	
假名	JIĂ MÍNG (3 2)	pseudonym	
說假話	SHUŌ JIĂ HUÀ (1 3 4)	lie	(假: JIA₃)
作假	ZUÒ JIĂ (4 3)	counterfeit; falsify	
放假	FÀNG JIÀ (4 4)	holiday; day off	(假: JIA₄)

不怕	BU⁴ PA⁴	not afraid of
怕事	PA⁴ SHI⁴	overly cautious
大麻	DA⁴ MA²	hemp; marijuana
煩請	FAN² QING³	could you please

M18.1C Sample sentences:

是真是假，分不清楚。SHI ZHEN SHI JIA, FEN BU QING CHU.
Whether it's true or false (genuine or fake), hard to tell.

假如我是你，我就不會同意。　　　（假如：if）
JIA RU WO SHI NI, WO JIU BU HUI TONG YI.
If I were you, I wouldn't agree. If I were you, I wouldn't have agreed.

ANNOTATIONS ———

假如 JIA₃ RU₂ , 假使 JIA₃ SHI₃ , 要是 YAO₄ SHI₄ :
all mean the same and can be used interchangeably.

學外文，如中文、日文，也不是太難的事。
XUE WAI WEN, RU ZHONG WEN, RI WEN, YE BU SHI TAI NAN DI SHI.
Learning a foreign language, such as Chinese or Japanese, isn't too difficult.

學甚麼外文都要不怕麻煩，經常學，習慣了就不難了。
XUE SHEN ME WAI WEN DOU YAO BU PA MA FAN, JING CHANG XUE, XI GUAN LE JIU BU NAN LE.
In learning any foreign language, one must take the trouble to practice often. Once you get used to it, it isn't hard.

麻煩你來一下,好嗎?　　　　　　　　(麻煩: please)

MA FAN NI LAI YI XIA, HAO MA?

Could you come over, please. (Literally: May I trouble you to come over, please?)

這次麻煩了。　　　　　　　　　　　(麻煩: trouble)

ZHE CI MA FAN LE.

This time (we, you,...) get into trouble.

他又來煩我,搞得我心都煩了。　　　　(煩: bother)

TA YOU LAI FAN WO, GAO DE WO XIN DOU FAN LE.

He came to bother me again. It made me upset.

麻煩您,這是甚麼地方?　　　　　　　(麻煩: excuse)

MA FAN NIN, ZHE SHI SHEN MO DI FANG?

Excuse me, what is this place?

煩請來信或傳真。　　　　　　　　　(煩請: appreciate)

FAN QING LAI XIN HUO CHUAN ZHEN.　(Written)

Your letter or fax would be appreciated.

他說的假話就多了,我才不信,搞怕了。

TA SHUO DE JIA HUA JIU DUO LE, WO CAI BU XIN, GAO PA LE.

He has been lying a lot. I wouldn't believe it. I'm scared.

這個人,我才不怕他。

ZHE GE REN, WO CAI BU PA TA.

This guy (fellow)? I'm not afraid of him at all.

假如怕這怕那,那你甚麼事也辦不成。

JIA RU PA ZHE PA NA, NA NI SHEN ME SHI YE BAN BU CHENG.

If you are afraid of everything, then you wouldn't be able to have anything accomplished.

快放假了,有甚麼地方好去?

KUAI FANG JIA LE, YOU SHEN MO DI FANG HAO QU?

Holiday is coming soon. Is there any place worth going?

Q:

"我們公司過年放兩天假,你們放幾天?"

"WO MEN GONG SI GUO NIAN FANG LIANG TIAN JIA, NI MEN FANG JI TIAN?"

"Our Company gives us two days off for New Year. How many days off do you get?"

A:

"我們才放一天。"

"WO MEN CAI FANG YI TIAN."

"We get only one day off."

―――――

MODULE 18

M18.2 SECOND GROUP OF 5 NEW CHARACTERS:

樣⁴	子³	無²	所³	謂⁴
YANG	ZI	WU	SUO	WEI
appearance	son	nil	place	say

M18.2A Build vocabulary and expressions with these five characters:

樣子	YÁNG ZI	appearance; the look; the behavior
所謂	SUǑ WÈI	so called
謂	WÈI	say; call
無	WÚ	nil; nothing

ANNOTATIONS ———

| 無 | = 沒有 | MÉI YǑU | in many applications. |
| | = 無謂 | WÚ WÈI | senseless; not necessary |

無謂	= 沒(有)意思	MÉI (YǑU) YÌ SI.	
	= 沒有必要	MÉI YǑU BÌ YÀO.	
無所謂		WÚ SUǑ WÈI	take it easy; it doesn't matter
樣子無所謂。		YÀNG ZI WÚ SUǑ WÈI.	(He ..) Doesn't seem to care about.

M18.2B Expand vocabulary and expressions by using all the 265 characters learned:

這樣	ZHE⁴ YANG⁴	so; such; this way
這樣子	ZHE⁴ YANG⁴ ZI	so; such; this way
那樣	NA⁴ YANG⁴	then; that way
那樣子	NA⁴ YANG⁴ ZI	then; that way

ANNOTATIONS ———

這樣、那樣 are perfect expressions in oral or written form in Mandarin or Cantonese; 這樣子、那樣子 tend to be Northern oral usage in Mandarin. It's a matter of individual habit.

日子	RI⁴ ZI³	days; the period of time
面子	MIAN⁴ ZI³	face (physical part as well as one's respect)
電子	DIAN⁴ ZI³	electron; electronic
無人	WU² REN²	vacant; not occupied
無心	WU² XIN¹	not intentional; not paying attention
無理	WU² LI³	unreasonable
無能	WU² NENG²	incompetent; incapable
無力	WU² LI⁴	lack of strength; weak
無情	WU² QING²	merciless; ruthless
無非	WU² FEI²	nothing but (無非=只不過) (M11.1C)
所以	SUO³ YI³	therefore; thus
所有	SUO³ YOU³	possession; all

謂之　　　　WEI⁴ ZHI¹　　　　　called; known as

M18.2C Sample sentences:

〔無謂〕

看他那個樣子,天天遲到,無心向學,無謂要他學下去了。

KAN TA NEI GE YANG ZI, TIAN TIAN CHI DAO, WU XIN XIANG XUE, WU WEI YAO TA XUE XIA QU LE.

Look at his behavior, being late everyday and paying no attention to studies. It doesn't make sense to require him to go on with his studies.

Q: ˝麻煩你幫個忙,好嗎?˝/ ˝麻煩你,幫個忙好嗎?

"MA FAN NI BANG GE MANG, HAO MA?"

"May I trouble you to give a hand? " /

"Excuse me, could you give a hand?

A: ˝無所謂。˝　　　(無所謂)

"WU SUO WEI."

"Fine with me." ("No problem.")

ANNOTATIONS ———

The above sentence Q in Chinese can also be:

"我可以麻煩你幫個忙嗎?" -- Such a sentence is correct in Chinese, and is pretty much similar to the English sentence. In writing or speaking alike, the other 2 expressions are more natural expressions in Chinese. (cf. M15.2C).

學外文,要每天學。這樣,學起來就不會難。　　(這樣)

XUE WAI WEN, YAO MEI TIAN XUE. ZHE YANG, XUE QI LAI JIU BU HUI NAN.

In learning a foreign language, one needs to study everyday. This way, it shouldn't be hard.

之所以要你來，是因爲你會講中文。　　(之所以)

ZHI SUO YI YAO NI LAI, SHI YIN WEI NI HUI JIANG ZHONG WEN.

The reason you are asked to come is that you can speak Chinese.

　　　　　　　　　　　　　　(無非)
所謂開會，無非就是請大家一起來商量。　(所謂)

SUO WEI KAI HUI, WU FEI JIU SHI QING DA JIA YI QI LAI SHANG LIANG.

The so-called meeting is nothing more than getting everybody together to have a discussion.

無非=只不過 ZHI$_3$ BU$_4$ GUO$_4$ (cf. M11.1B);

cf. M11.1C: 4th sample sentence from the end.

你看他那個樣子，無所用心，哪裡會做好工作？

NI KAN TA NEI GE YANG ZI, WU SUO YONG XIN, NA LI HUI ZUO HAO GONG ZUO?

You just look at his performance. He doesn't care about anything. How can he do a good job?

他的要求太過了，完全不合理，看樣子公司不會同意。

TA DE YAO QIU TAI GUO LE, WAN QUAN BU HE LI, KAN YANG ZI GONG SI BU HUI TONG YI.

His demand is asking for too much, totally unreasonable. It appears (to me) that the Company wouldn't agree to it.

MODULE 18

M18.3 THIRD GROUP OF 5 NEW CHARACTERS:

怎	能	建	功	績
3	2	4	1	1
ZEN	NENG	JIAN	GONG	JI
how	can	build	merit	accomplishment

M18.3A Build vocabulary and expressions with these five characters:

怎能	ZEN³ NENG²	how can
怎 = 怎麼	ZEN³ ME	how; how come
能 = 能夠	NENG² GOU⁴	can
怎能 = 怎麼能夠	ZEN³ ME NENG² GOU⁴.	
建	JIAN⁴	build; establish
建 = 建立	JIAN⁴ LI⁴	build; establish
功績	GONG¹ JI¹	merit and accomplishment
怎能建功績?	ZEN³ NENG² JIAN⁴ GONG¹ JI¹?	
(怎麼能夠建立功績?	ZEN³ ME NENG² GOU⁴ JIAN⁴ LI⁴ GONG¹ JI¹?)	

How can merit and accomplishment be established?

M18.3B Expand vocabulary and expressions by using all the 270 characters learned:

怎麼	ZEN³ ME	how; why
怎樣	ZEN³ YANG⁴	how; why (怎樣=怎麼樣)
能夠	NENG² GOU⁴	can; being able to
能力	NENG² LI⁴	capability; ability
無能	WU² NENG²	incompetent

才能	CÁI NÉNG	ability; talent
才能 (夠)	CÁI NÉNG GÒU	so that; before it can be done
電能	DIÀN NÉNG	electric energy
建立	JIÀN LÌ	establish; build
成功	CHÉNG GŌNG	success; succeed
立功	LÌ GŌNG	render meritorious service; win honor
記功	JÌ GŌNG	record merit; record a meritorious service
用功	YÒNG GŌNG	diligent; work hard
成績	CHÉNG JĪ	accomplishment; result

M18.3C Sample sentences:

怎麼?你明天就要到中國去?　　　　(怎麼: what)

ZEN ME? NI MING TIAN JIU YAO DAO ZHONG GUO QU?

What? You are leaving for China tomorrow?

你怎麼這麼遲才到?　　　　(怎麼: why)

NI ZEN ME ZHE ME CHI CAI DAO?

Why are you so late? (遲 = 晚 WAN₃)

怎麼辦?　　(怎辦? ZEN BAN?)　　(怎麼辦)

ZEN ME BAN?

What's to be done? / What should (I/we) do?

怎麼搞的, 成了甚麼樣子!　　　　(怎麼搞的)

ZEN ME GAO DE, CHENG LE SHEN ME YANG ZI?

What's going on? What a mess.

一起去, 怎麼樣?   (怎麼樣: how about)

YI QI QU, ZEN ME YANG?

Let's go together. How about that?

成功的功字怎樣拼音?   (怎樣: how)

CHENG GONG DI GONG ZI ZEN YANG PIN YIN?

How to spell the character "GONG" as in CHENG GONG?

Q: "叫你到中國去工作一年, 你能去嗎?"

"JIAO NI DAO ZHONG GUO QU GONG ZUO YI NIAN, NI NENG QU MA?"

"If you are asked to work in China for one year, can you do that?"

A: "當然能去, 不想去就是了。"

"DANG RAN NENG QU, BU XIANG QU JIU SHI LE."

"I certainly can go, but I just don't want to."

他學中文快, 成績很好, 非常成功。

TA XUE ZHONG WEN KUAI, CHENG JI HEN HAO, FEI CHANG CHENG GONG.

He studies Chinese fast with very good results, very successful.

(1) 你要學點中文, 公司才能給你到中國去工作。 (才能 = 才能夠)

NI YAO XUE DIAN ZHONG WEN, GONG SI CAI NENG GEI NI DAO ZHONG GUO QU GONG ZUO.

You have to learn some Chinese before the Company can let you go and work in China.

(2) 他是真的很有才能。　　　　　　　(才能：talent)

TA SHI ZHEN DE HEN YOU CAI NENG.

He is really very talented.

ANNOTATIONS ──────

In the last two sentences above, notice the two characters 才能 CAI$_2$ NENG$_2$ are used differently:

(1) 才能夠 is used in short form 才能. It is used like an adverb of condition followed by a verb.

(2) 才能 is used as a noun in the Chinese sentence. In Romanized Chinese, it can be printed as CAINENG which is definitely a term (word) with 2 syllables. (cf. M17.3C third NOTE.) However, the foundation of Chinese is on the characters. You must focus on the characters and know how each character is used. Romanized spelling is only a tool to pronounce the character.

──────

MODULE 19

M19.1 FIRST GROUP OF 5 NEW CHARACTERS:

買³	東¹	西¹	帶⁴	錢²
MAI	DONG	XI	DAI	QIAN
buy	east	west	bring	money

M19.1A Build vocabulary and expressions with these five characters:

東西	DŌNG XĪ	thing, object; east and west (direction)
帶	DÀI	bring; carry
帶錢	DÀI QIÁN	bring money
買	MĀI	buy
買東西帶錢。	MĀI DŌNG XĪ DÀI QIÁN.	To go shopping, bring money.

M19.1B Expand vocabulary and expressions by using all the 275 characters learned:

買方	MĀI FĀNG	purchasing party
買家	MĀI JIĀ	buyer
東方	DŌNG FĀNG	eastern; oriental
西方	XĪ FĀNG	western; occidental
東面	DŌNG MIÀN	east, east side
(東面=東邊 DŌNG₁ BIĀN₁)		(西面=西邊 XĪ₁ BIĀN₁)
西面	XĪ MIÀN	west, west side
向東	XIÀNG DŌNG	facing east; heading east; eastbound

向西	XIÀNG XĪ	facing west; heading west; westbound
地帶	DÌ DÀI	strip of land; area
白帶	BÁI DÀI	leucorrhea; whites

M19.1C Sample sentences:

文字方面，東方完全不同於西方。

WEN ZI FANG MIAN, DONG FANG WAN QUAN BU TONG YU XI FANG.

In terms of written language, the East is totally different from the West.

我們晚上到，東西方向也分不清。　　　　　(東西: east, west)

WO MEN WAN SHANG DAO, DONG XI FANG XIANG YE FEN BU QING.

We arrived at night. We couldn't even tell the direction east or west.
(東西 DONG₁ XI₁)

這是甚麼東西？　　　　　　　　　(東西: stuff)

ZHE SHI SHEN ME DONG XI?　　　(東西 DONG₁ XI. XI: Light Tone)

What is this stuff?

"到哪裡去？"　　　　　　　　　　"買東西去。"

"DAO NA LI QU?"　　　　　　　　"MAI DONG XI QU."

"Where are you going?"　　　　　　"Shopping."

"去哪裡？"　　　　　　　　　　　"去買東西。"

"QU NA LI?"　　　　　　　　　　"QU MAI DONG XI."

"Where are you going?"　　　　　　"Shopping."

ANNOTATIONS ———

The above two colloquial expressions demonstrate a difference among Chinese dialects. The second expression is more of a southern usage (Cantonese) while the first one is a typical northern usage (Mandarin). There is even another expression per Northern China oral usage.
("上哪兒?" SHMG₄ NA₃R?)

今天開會,要把這兩個文件帶去。

JIN TIAN KAI HUI, YAO BA ZHE LIANG GE WEN JIAN DAI QU.

These two documents need to be brought to the meeting today.

多少錢?　　　　　　　　　　　多少人?

DUO SHAO QIAN?　　　　　　　DUO SHAO REN?

How much?　　　　　　　　　　How many people?

那裡東西很多,不過,我沒買甚麼。　　(沒=沒有)

NA LI DONG XI HEN DUO, BU GUO, WO MEI MAI SHEN ME.

There were lots of things there, but I didn't buy anything.

他是買家,他定要求。

TA SHI MAI JIA, TA DING YAO QIU.

He is the buyer and he sets the requirements.

還要帶甚麼沒有?

HAI YAO DAI SHEN ME MEI YOU?

Need to bring anything else?

MODULE 19

M19.2 SECOND GROUP OF 5 NEW CHARACTERS:

賣 ₄	則 ₂	走 ₃	南 ₂	北 ₃
MAI	ZE	ZOU	NAN	BEI
sell	then	go; run	south	north

M19.2A Build vocabulary and expressions with these five characters:

| 南北 | NÁN BĚI | north and south |
| 賣則走南北。 | MÀI ZÉ ZŎU NÁN BĚI. | To sell, one has to go north and south. |

M19.2B Expand vocabulary and expressions by using all the 280 characters learned:

賣方	MÀI FĀNG	selling party
賣家	MÀI JIĀ	seller
買賣	MĂI MÀI	buy and sell; business
外賣	WÀI MÀI	take out order (food to go)
出賣	CHŪ MÀI	offer for sale; betray
東南	DŌNG NÁN	southeast
東北	DŌNG BĚI	northeast
西南	XĪ NÁN	southwest
西北	XĪ BĚI	northwest
東南西北	DŌNG NÁN XĪ BĚI	north, south, east and west
四面八方	SÌ MIÀN BĀ FĀNG	all directions

MODULE 19

ANNOTATIONS ────────

The expression of the cardinal directions reflects a cultural difference between Chinese and English. The Chinese way is based on east and west while in English it is north and south.

────────

M19.2C Sample sentences:

買不太難, 賣則非常難, 從南走到北, 也不一定賣得出去。
MAI BU TAI NAN, MAI ZE FEI CHANG NAN, CONG NAN ZOU DAO BEI, YE BU YI DING MAI DE CHU QU.
To buy isn't too hard, but to sell is very tough, going from north to south and still may not be able to make a sale.

時間不早, 該走了, 要不然又要遲到了。
SHI JIAN BU ZAO, GAI ZOU LE, YAO BU RAN YOU YAO CHI DAO LE.
It's about time. Need to get going, otherwise it'll be late again.

"走開！我不要你。"
"ZOU KAI! WO BU YAO NI."
"Get out! I don't want you."

賣出了沒有？   (賣出: sold)
MAI CHU LE MEI YOU?
Is it sold?

這件東西要出賣。   (出賣: for sale)
ZHE JIAN DONG XI YAO CHU MAI.   (東西 $DONG_1$ XI_1)
This object is to be put up for sale.

ANNOTATIONS

There is another formal expression for "for sale" (出售 CHU₁ SHOU₄)

他出賣朋友。　　　　　　　　　　(出賣: betray)
TA CHU MAI PENG YOU.　　　　　(出賣: verb; 朋友: object)
He betrays his friend.

向哪個方向走?
XIAN NA GE FANG XIANG ZOU?
Which direction to go?

向東走, 然後向北。
XIANG DONG ZOU, RAN HOU XIANG BEI.
Go east and then north.

做買賣的, 東南西北四面八方都要去。
ZUO MAI MAI DE, DONG NAN XI BEI SI MIAN BA FANG DOU YAO QU.
People in buying and selling have to travel north, south, east, west in all directions.

日出東方。
RI CHU DONG FANG.
The sun rises from the East.

MODULE 19

M19.3 THIRD GROUP OF 5 NEW CHARACTERS:

言 ₂	語 ₃	極 ₂	客 ₄	氣 ₄
YAN	YU	JI	KE	QI
speech	language	extremely	guest visitor	gas air

M19.3A Build vocabulary and expressions with these five characters:

言語	YAN YU	spoken language; talk
語言	YU YAN	language
客氣	KE QI	polite; courteous
語氣	YU QI	tone / manner of speaking
極	JI	extreme; extremely
言語極客氣。	YAN YU JI KE QI.	Extremely courteous speaking.

(The 氣 in 客氣: light tone.)

M19.3B Expand vocabulary and expressions by using all the 285 characters learned:

英語	YING YU	English (language)

ANNOTATIONS ───────

(1) 英語 = 英文

   (英語: Tends to be northern China usage;

   英文: Tends to be southern China usage.)

(2) 英語 = 英國語 = 英國語言
    英文 = 英國文 = 英國文字

語言文字	YU³ YAN² WEN² ZI⁴	spoken and written language
語言學	YU³ YAN² XUE²	linguistics; philology
語言學家	YU³ YAN² XUE² JIA¹	linguist; philologist
語音	YU³ YIN¹	pronunciation
語音學	YU³ YIN¹ XUE²	phonetics
語音學家	YU³ YIN¹ XUE² JIA¹	phonetician
言論	YAN² LUN⁴	words and view points
語法	YU³ FA³	grammar
客人	KE⁴ REN²	guest; visitor
來客	LAI² KE⁴	visitor; visiting guest
請客	QING³ KE⁴	entertain a guest; stand treat

---

cf. M3.1: "我請" WO₃ QING₃ "Be my guest."

我請 = 我請客 WO₃ QING₃ KE₄

客家話	KE⁴ JIA¹ HUA⁴	Hakka (Karkah) (A Southern Chinese dialect)

'Hakka' is the sound of the first two characters in Cantonese; 'Karkah' is the sound based on that dialect.

氣力	QI⁴ LI⁴	strength; effort
氣量	QI⁴ LIANG⁴	mind tolerance (large minded or narrow minded)
氣人	QI⁴ REN²	outrageous

和氣	HÉ QÌ (2 4)	polite; amiable
不客氣	BÙ KE QÌ (4 4)	you're welcome; don't mention; no mercy
極力	JÍ LÌ (2 4)	do one's utmost
南極	NÁN JÍ (2 2)	South Pole
北極	BĚI JÍ (3 2)	North Pole

M19.3C Sample sentences:

1. "謝謝。"   "XIE XIE."   "Thank you."

   "謝謝你。"   "XIE XIE NI."   "Thank you."

   "謝謝您。"   "XIE XIE NIN."   "Thank you."

   NOTE: (cf. M3.3A: 您 --- Often used in northern China, Beijing in particular, to show respect.)

2. "不客氣。"   (不客氣)

   "BU KE QI."

   "You're welcome." / "Don't mention."

你天天遲到,這樣下去,我就不客氣了。　(不客氣)

NI TIAN TIAN CHI DAO, ZHE YANG XIA QU, WO JIU BU KE QI LE.

You are late everyday. If you keep on like this, I wouldn't be so easy.

他不客氣的,說開除就開除。　　　　(不客氣)

TA BU KE QI DE, SHUO KAI CHU JIU KAI CHU.

No mercy. When he says fire someone he means it.

賣東西的人, 說話極爲客氣。　　　（客氣）
MAI DONG XI DI REN, SHUO HUA JI WEI KE QI.
People in sales are extremely courteous when they speak.

"那是客氣話而已。"　　　（客氣話）
"NA SHI KE QI HUA ER YI."
"Those words are only out of courtesy."

"請提意見, 不要客氣, 有甚麼, 說甚麼。"　（不要客氣）
"QING TI YI JIAN, BU YAO KE QI, YOU SHEN ME, SHUO SHEN ME."
Please give your suggestion and feedback without reservation. Shoot.

不要客客氣氣的。
BU YAO KE KE QI QI DE.
Don't be standing on ceremony.

不要客氣, 請大家自便。
BU YAO KE QI, QING DA JIA ZI BIAN.
Make yourself at home. Help yourselves, please.

MODULE 20

M20.1 FIRST GROUP OF 5 NEW CHARACTERS:

男 ₂	女 ₃	老 ₃	師 ₁	樂 ₄
NAN	NU	LAO	SHI	LE
male	female	old	teacher	happy

M20.1A Build vocabulary and expressions with these five characters.

男女	NAN NÜ (2 3)	man and woman

女 NÜ (cf.p.426) (Ü: computer typing: NV (MS) to draw the character, some programs: NYU)

老師	LAO SHI (3 1)	teacher (respectful)
男老師	NAN LAO SHI (2 3 1)	male teacher
女老師	NÜ LAO SHI (3 3 1)	female teacher
樂 = 快樂	KUAI LE (4 4)	happy
男女老師樂。	NAN NÜ LAO SHI LE. (2 3 3 1 4)	Male and female teachers are happy.

M20.1B Expand vocabulary and expressions by using all the 290 characters learned:

音樂	YIN YUE (1 4)	music
老人	LAO REN (3 2)	old person; senior
老人家	LAO REN JIA (3 2 3)	Senior; elderly person
老家	LAO JIA (3 1)	homeland
老年	LAO NIAN (3 2)	old age
老成	LAO CHENG (3 2)	old head on young shoulders
老手	LAO SHOU (3 3)	old hand; experienced in trade

老子	LAO ZI (3,3)	father (casual)
男人	NAN REN (2,2)	man （男=男人=男子）
女人	NÜ REN (3,2)	woman （女=女人=女子）

ANNOTATIONS ———

男子、女子 are often used as courteous expressions for 男人、女人.

M20.1C Sample Sentences:

男女老少, 都在一起, 高高興興, 還有音樂, 十分快樂。

NAN NU LAO SHAO, DOU ZAI YI QI, GAO GAO XING XING, HAI YOU YIN YUE, SHI FEN KUAI LE.

Men and women, old and young, get together, and there is music too, cheerful and very happy.

不是他不同意, 是他老子不同意。 （老子: father）

BU SHI TA BU TONG YI, SHI TA LAO ZI BU TONG YI.

It isn't that he disagrees. It is his father (the old man) who doesn't agree.

他這個人自高自大, 老子才不要他在一起。(老子: I)

TA ZHE GE REN ZI GAO ZI DA, LAO ZI CAI BU YAO TA ZAI YI QI.

He is an arrogant guy. I wouldn't bother to take him with me.

ANNOTATIONS ———

老子 when used to mean 'I', is a kind of derog-gatory expression to the party in question.

Sometimes used in speaking for fun or when being outraged.

The tone of voice and manner of speaking make the difference in meaning. Use with caution.

他老說人家的是非,真氣人。　　(老: always)

TA LAO SHUO REN JIA DI SHI FEI, ZHEN QI REN.

He keeps talking about other's right and wrong. It's outrageous.

他老是在說些不三不四的話,沒人埋他。　(老是: always)

TA LAO SHI ZAI SHUO XIE BU SAN BU SI DI HUA, MEI REN LI TA.

He always talks indecent words. Nobody cares to listen.

ANNOTATIONS

(1) 老 or 老是 is typical northern China usage in speaking. (Similar to 常常 CHANG CHANG, 經常 JING CHANG.)

(2) A similar expression is 成天 CHENG₂ TIAN₁ or 成日 CHENG₂ RI₄ which literally means all day long. 成日 tends to be southern China usage as in Cantonese.

"您老人家多加小心。"

"NIN LAO REN JIA DUO JIA XIAO XIN."

"Take care, my Senior."

他老人家老在想你。

TA LAO REN JIA LAO ZAI XIANG NI.

The old senior missed you.

ANNOTATIONS ————

(1) 老人家 is a courteous and respectful expression in addressing elderly people. 您老人家 is a courteous and respectful salutation when speaking to a Senior. 他老人家 is used when speaking about a senior.

(2) In English, 您老人家 is "my Senior" rather than 'you Senior'. This demonstrates another example of cultural difference in expressions.

(3) '老 + Verb' or '老是 + Verb' is used as an adverb to mean 'always': keep doing something.

(4) '老 + (last name)': addressing an acquaintance in casual daily use. Here 老=老友=老朋友: 老友 LAO YOU is used in Cantonese while 老朋友 LAO PENG YOU is used in Mandarin.

(5) '(surname name) + 老': addressing or speaking about a senior with respect, here 老=老人家.

他是當老師的, 很會講話, 也很會寫。

TA SHI DANG LAO SHI DE, HEN HUI JIANG HUA, YE HEN HUI XIE.

He is a teacher, good in speaking and writing.

她很友好, 無論男女老少都合得來。

TA HEN YOU HAO, WU LUN NAN NYU LAO SHAO DOU HE DE LAI.

She is very friendly and gets along well with everybody, man or woman, old or young.

MODULE 20

M20.2 SECOND GROUP OF 5 NEW CHARACTERS:

XIAN (1)
early

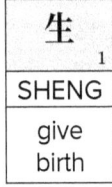
SHENG (1)
give birth

TE (4)
special

XI (3)
like joy

HUAN (1)
joy

M20.2A Build vocabulary and expressions with these five characters:

| 先生 | XIAN SHENG (1,1) | Mr. ; teacher |

ANNOTATIONS ⎯⎯⎯⎯

先生 used as teacher is the same as 老師. Both are used to address a teacher in respectful salutation. 先生 is more often used in Southern China such as in Cantonese to address a teacher.

| 喜歡 | XI HUAN (3,1) | like; fond of |
| 特 | TE (4) | especially; in particular |

(特=特別 TE BIE₂) (特 TE is an example of some spellings (syllables) which have only one tone.)

先生特喜歡。 XIAN SHENG TE XI HUAN (1,1,4,3,1). The teacher especially likes (it,..).

⎯⎯⎯⎯

M20.2B Expand vocabulary and expressions by using all the 295 characters learned:

先人	XIAN REN (1,2)	ancestor
先天	XIAN TIAN (1,1)	congenital
先後	XIAN HOU (1,4)	one after the other
先前	XIAN QIAN (1,2)	previously; previous
原先	YUAN XIAN (2,1)	originally; initially

起先	QI XIAN (3,1)	at first
生日	SHENG RI (1,4)	birthday
生人	SHENG REN (1,2)	stranger
生字	SHENG ZI (1,4)	new word
生意	SHENG YI (1,4)	business
生前	SHENG QIAN (1,2)	during one's life time
生手	SHENG SHOU (1,3)	new hand; new at a job
生理	SHENG LI (1,3)	physiology
天生	TIAN SHENG (1,1)	natural; born with it
前生	QIAN SHENG (2,1)	previous life
此生	CI SHENG (3,1)	current life
今生	JIN SHENG (1,1)	current life
特地	TE DI (4,4)	specially

M20.2C Sample Sentences:

他的生意不錯, 起先他自己一個人搞起來, 現在成爲大 公司了。(起先 = 起初 = 原先 = 開始)

TA DE SHENG YI BU CUO, QI XIAN TA ZI JI YI GE REN GAO QI LAI, XIAN ZAI CHENG WEI DA GONG SI LE.

His business is pretty good. At first it was started all by himself and now it has become a big company.

他一生幫助過很多人。

TA YI SHENG BANG ZHU GUO HEN DUO REN.

He had helped many people in his lifetime.

他生前我只見過一次。

TA SHENG QIAN WO ZHI JIAN GUO YI CI.

I only met him once in his life.

他喜歡音樂，樂於助人。(音樂 YIN₁ YUE₄ , 樂於 LE₄ YU₂)

TA XI HUAN YIN YUE, LE YU ZHU REN.

He likes music and is happy to help others.

他特別喜歡音樂。

TA TE BIE XI HUAN YIN YUE.

He especially likes music.

這是特地爲你做的。

ZHE SHI TE DI WEI NI ZUO DE.

This is specially prepared for you.

"您老人家好。我特地看您來了。"

"NIN LAO REN JIA HAO. WO TE DI KAN NIN LAI LE."

"How are you, my Senior? I've specially come to see you."

MODULE 20

M20.3 THIRD GROUP OF 5 NEW CHARACTERS:

祝 ₄	路 ₄	途 ₂	順 ₄	利 ₄
ZHU	LU	TU	SHUN	LI
wish	road	trip	along	benefit

M20.3A Build vocabulary and expressions with these five characters:

祝	ZHU$_4$	wish
路途	LU$_4$ TU$_2$	trip
順利	SHUN$_4$ LI$_4$	smooth; successful
祝路途順利。	ZHU$_4$ LU$_4$ TU$_2$ SHUN$_4$ LI$_4$.	Wish you a smooth trip.

ANNOTATIONS ⎯⎯⎯

There is a different formal expression for *"Bon voyage"* .(一帆風順 YI$_1$ FAN$_1$ FENG$_1$ SHUN$_4$.)

⎯⎯⎯

M20.3B Expand vocabulary and expressions by using all the 300 characters learned:

道路	DAO$_4$ LU$_4$	road
電路	DIAN$_4$ LU$_4$	electric circuit
半路	BAN$_4$ LU$_4$	half way
後路	HOU$_4$ LU$_4$	a way out; route of retreat
前途	QIAN$_2$ TU$_2$	future; prospect
中途	ZHONG$_1$ TU$_2$	mid-way
途中	TU$_2$ ZHONG$_1$	on the way

順便	SHÙN BIÀN	conveniently; in passing
順手	SHÙN SHǑU	smoothly; without difficulty
順心	SHÙN XĪN	satisfactory; as hoped for
有利	YǑU LÌ	advantageous; favorable
不利	BÙ LÌ	disadvantageous; unfavorable

M20.3C Sample Sentences:

他學習非常用心,學得也順心,前途一定很好。

TA XUE XI FEI CHANG YONG XIN, XUE DE YE SHUN XIN, QIAN TU YI DING HEN HAO.

He studies very attentively and is happy with his studies. It is certain that he will have a very bright future.

他明天要到這裡來,叫他順便把文件帶來。

TA MING TIAN YAO DAO ZHE LI LAI, JIAO TA SHUN BIAN BA WEN JIAN DAI LAI.

He is coming here tomorrow. Ask him to bring the document with him in passing.

祝你快樂。(Often used at the end of a letter.)

ZHU NI KUAI LE.

Wish you happy.

祝你萬事如意。

ZHU NI WAN SHI RU YI. (Wish you a golden touch.)

Wish you smooth and fine in everything.

祝您成功。

ZHU NIN CHENG GONG.

Wish you success.

現在學中文有利, 很需要。

XIAN ZAI XUE ZHONG WEN YOU LI, HEN XU YAO.

Chinese is in high demand. It is favorable to learn now.

學了一半, 放下不學, 對你不利。

XUE LE YI BAN, FANG XIA BU XUE, DUI NI BU LI.

It's half-way and you give up your studies. That's not in your favor.

學習中文, 此法特好, 大有幫助, 學習順利, 得心應手。

XUE XI ZHONG WEN, CI FA TE HAO, DA YOU BANG ZHU, XUE XI SHUN LI, DE XIN YING SHOD.

This method is especially good for learning Chinese, very helpful, smooth and like a golden touch. (cf. M12.2C: 10th sample sentence and NOTE.)

MODULE 20

PART 3
VOCABULARY AND EXPRESSIONS

1. VOCABULARY: 1,800+

2. IDIOMS AND EXPRESSIONS: 300+

PART 3

VOCABULARY AND EXPRESSIONS

FROM THE 300 CHINESE CHARACTERS IN SEQUENTIAL ORDER OF THE MODULES

Each character is matched with the other 299 characters to form a word, term or expression wherever applicable. Most words are composed of two characters, and can be viewed as words with two syllables. Some are already explained in the relevant Modules and others are new. Also included is a particular group of expressions, very often in four characters each. They are Idioms or phrases commonly used. These words and expressions can be found in a **CHINESE-ENGLISH DICTIONARY** by looking up the first character. PART 2 demonstrates the power and potential of learning these 300 very common characters in building words and expressions.

一 (M1.1)	YI$_1$	one
一半	YI^1 BAN^4	half
一邊	YI^1 BIAN^1	one side; one edge
一面	YI^1 MIAN^4	one side; one face
一邊..一邊..	YI^1 BIAN^1..YI^1 BIAN^1..	...while (as)...
一面..一面..	YI^1 MIAN^4..YI^1 MIAN^4..	...while (as)...
一等	YI^1 DENG^3	first class; first rate
一定	YI^1 DING^4	certainly; must
一共	YI^1 GONG^4	altogether; total
一經	YI^1 JING^1	as soon as; once
一起	YI^1 QI^3	together
一道	YI^1 DAO^4	together
一同	YI^1 TONG^2	together

一日	YĪ RÌ (1,4)	one day
一天	YĪ TIAN (1,1)	one day
一下(子)	YĪ XIA (ZI) (1,4)	all of a sudden
一向	YĪ XIANG (1,4)	consistently; all along
一一	YĪ YĪ (1,1)	individually; one by one
一月	YĪ YUE (1,4)	January
一個月	YĪ GE YUE (1,4,4)	one month
一再	YĪ ZAI (1,4)	time and again
一而再, 再而三	YĪ ER ZAI, ZAI ER SAN (1,2,4,4,2,1)	time and again; repeatedly
一錯再錯	YĪ CUO ZAI CUO (1,4,4,4)	making one mistake after another
一…再…	YĪ…ZAI… (1,4)	repeatedly
一看就明	YĪ KAN JIU MING (1,4,4,2)	understand at a glance
一..就..	YĪ..JIU.. (1,4)	…as soon as.,.
一了百了	YĪ LIAO BAI LIAO (1,3,3,3)	settle once and for all
一目十行	YĪ MU SHI HANG (1,4,2,2)	read ten lines at a glance (fast reading)
一目了然	YĪ MU LIAO RAN (1,4,3,2)	clear at a glance
一天到晚	YĪ TIAN DAO WAN (1,1,4,3)	all day long
一清二楚	YĪ QING ER CHU (1,1,4,3)	clearly and explicitly
一時一事	YĪ SHI YI SHI (1,2,1,4)	isolated act or a short period of time
一事無成	YĪ SHI WU CHENG (1,4,2,2)	nothing accomplished
一言爲定	YĪ YAN WEI DING (1,2,2,4)	the word is the deal
一言一行	YĪ YAN YI XING (1,2,1,2)	every word and every act
一五一十	YĪ WU YI SHI (1,3,1,2)	(telling) in full details

一無所有　　　　YI₁ WU₂ SUO₃ YOU₃　　　own nothing
(Brief as compared to: 甚麼都沒有 SHEN₂ ME DOU₁ MEI₂ YOU₃.)
一心一意　　　　YI₁ XIN₁ YI₁ YI₄　　　　whole-heartedly
一問三不知　　　YI₁ WEN₄ SAN₁ BU₄ ZHI₁　absolutely ignorant
(Literally: Say 3 times "I don't know" to every question.)

二　(M1.2)　　　 ER₄　　　　　　　　　　two
二十　　　　　　ER₄ SHI₂　　　　　　　　twenty
二百　　　　　　ER₄ BAI₃　　　　　　　　(=兩百 LIANG₃ BAI₃)
　　　　　　　　　　　　　　　　　　　　two hundred (cf. M12.1 兩)
二千　　　　　　ER₄ QIAN₁ (=兩千)　　　 two thousand
二萬　　　　　　ER₄ WAN₄ (=兩萬)　　　　twenty thousand
二月　　　　　　ER₄ YUE₄　　　　　　　　February
二元論　　　　　ER₄ YUAN₂ LUN₄　　　　　dualism
二話不說　　　　ER₄ HUA₄ BU₄ SHUO₁　　　without demur

三　(M1.1)　　　 SAN₁　　　　　　　　　 three
三月　　　　　　SAN₁ YUE₄　　　　　　　 March
三心兩意　　　　SAN₁ XIN₁ LIANG₃ YI₄　　shilly-shally
(Opposite of 一心一意 YI₁ XIN₁ YI₁ YI₄: whole-hearted)
三言兩語　　　　SAN₁ YAN₂ LIANG₃ YU₃　　in just a few words; curt
三思而行　　　　SAN₁ SI₁ ER₂ XING₂　　　think before you leap
(Literally: Think three times before you act.)
(Note: Same as 三思而後行 SAN SI ER HOU₄ XING)
三人同行, 必有我師。　　SAN₁ REN₂ TONG₂ XING₂, BI₄ YOU₃ WO₃ SHI₁.
Among the three of us together, there must be one who can be my teacher.

VOCABULARY: 1,800+

ANNOTATIONS ───────

The last sentence above is one of the teachings from Confucius, a respected scholar and educator in China, approximately (551-479 B.C.)

───────

十 (M1.1)	SHI²	ten
十月	SHI² YUE⁴	October
十一月	SHI² YI¹ YUE⁴	November
十二月	SHI² ER⁴ YUE⁴	December
十分	SHI² FEN¹	very; ten points
十之八九	SHI² ZHI¹ BA¹ JIU³	eight, nine out of ten (very likely)
十全十美	SHI² QUAN² SHI² MEI³	absolutely perfect
人 (M1.1)	REN²	person; human
人人	REN² REN²	people; everybody
人手	REN² SHOU³	helping hand
人力	REN² LI⁴	manpower
人日	REN² RI⁴	man-day
人家	REN² JIA¹	families; other people
人事	REN² SHI⁴	personnel
人們	REN² MEN²	people; the public
人情	REN² QING²	human feeling
人間	REN² JIAN¹	human world; human society
人工	REN² GONG¹	manually (wage; casual)
人才	REN² CAI²	talent; capable person
人道	REN² DAO⁴	humanity

VOCABULARY: 1,800+

人為	RÉN WÉI	caused by human
人心	RÉN XĪN	human heart; public trend
人所共知	RÉN SUǑ GÒNG ZHĪ	everybody knows; publicly known
人心所向	RÉN XĪN SUǑ XIÀNG	people's choice; public trend
人為錯誤	RÉN WÉI CUÒ WÙ	human error
人之常情	RÉN ZHĪ CHÁNG QÍNG	natural by human nature
日 (M1.2)	RÌ	day; sun
日出	RÌ CHŪ	sunrise
日間	RÌ JIĀN	daytime
日常	RÌ CHÁNG	day-to-day
日用	RÌ YÒNG	daily use; household use
日前	RÌ QIÁN	the other day
日後	RÌ HÒU	in future
日子	RÌ ZǏ	the days
日記	RÌ JÌ	diary
日文	RÌ WÉN	Japanese (Language)
日元	RÌ YUÁN	Japanese Yen (dollar)
日日如是	RÌ RÌ RÚ SHÌ	day in and day out
(cf. 天天如此	TIĀN TIĀN RÚ CǏ	day in and day out)
月 (M1.2)	YUÈ	month; moon
月中	YUÈ ZHŌNG	middle of the month
月經	YUÈ JĪNG	menstruation; monthly period
月光	YUÈ GUĀNG	moon light

月大	YUE⁴ DA⁴	a long month
月小	YUE⁴ XIAO³	a short month

(NOTE: A long month has 31 days: a short month 30 or less.)

大 (M1.2)	DA⁴	big; large
大小	DA⁴ XIAO³	size
大人	DA⁴ REN²	adult
大事	DA⁴ SHI⁴	major event or issue
大家	DA⁴ JIA¹	all of us (you, them) everybody
大地	DA⁴ DI⁴	the Earth
大學	DA⁴ XUE²	university, college
大學生	DA⁴ XUE² SHENG¹	college student
大寫	DA⁴ XIE³	capital letter
大便	DA⁴ BIAN⁴	bowel movement; stool
大腦	DA⁴ NAO³	cerebrum
大方	DA⁴ FANG¹	generous; elegant
大難	DA⁴ NAN²	very difficult
大難	DA⁴ NAN⁴	disaster (Note: tone 4)
大白天	DA⁴ BAI² TIAN¹	bright day light
大半天	DA⁴ BAN⁴ TIAN¹	a long while; longer than half day
大不了	DA⁴ BU⁴ LIAO³	at the worst; at the most
大大小小	DA⁴ DA⁴ XIAO³ XIAO³	all sizes; people of all ages
大材小用	DA⁴ CAI² XIAO³ YONG⁴	put fine timber to petty use; waste one's talent on a petty job

大不相同	DÀ BÙ XIĀNG TÓNG	very different
大而無當	DÀ ÉR WÚ DÀNG	large but impractical
大功告成	DÀ GŌNG GÀO CHÉNG	mission accomplished; crowned with success
大快人心	DÀ KUÀI RÉN XĪN	win public satisfaction and support (on punishing evil acts)
大有見地	DÀ YǑU JIÀN DÌ	with good vision
大有人在	DÀ YǑU RÉN ZÀI	plenty of such people
大有可爲	DÀ YǑU KĚ WÉI	good potential to work on
大有作爲	DÀ YǑU ZUÒ WÉI	plenty of room for a talent to work on
大是大非	DÀ SHÌ DÀ FĒI	major issues of principle
小 (M1.2)	XIĂO	little; small
小人	XIĂO RÉN	villain; vile character
小子	XIĂO ZI	fellow; guy
小看	XIĂO KÀN	look down upon, belittle; underestimate (casual)
小事	XIĂO SHÌ	trivial; minor matter
小說	XIĂO SHUŌ	novel
小心	XIĂO XĪN	look out; be careful
小氣	XIĂO QÌ	stingy; mean
小寫	XIĂO XIĚ	small letter (non-capital)
小腦	XIĂO NĂO	cerebellum
小便	XIĂO BIÀN	urine; pass water
小學	XIĂO XUÉ	elementary school

小學生	XIAO³ XUE² SHENG¹	pupil
小朋友	XIAO³ PENG² YOU³	honey (Literally: Little Friend.) (an adult addressing a child or children)
小時	XIAO³ SHI²	hour
小時候	XIAO³ SHI² HOU⁴	childhood
小意思	XIAO³ YI⁴ SI	small token of kindly feeling; e.g."This is a little keepsake for you."
小小意思	XIAO³ XIAO³ YI⁴ SI	same as 小意思
小題大作	XIAO³ TI² DA⁴ ZUO⁴	make a fuss over a trifling matter; make a mountain out of a molehill
天 (M1.2)	TIAN₁	sky; day
天天	TIAN¹ TIAN¹	daily; every day
天上	TIAN¹ SHANG⁴	in the sky
天下	TIAN¹ XIA⁴	under the sky; the land under heaven
天才	TIAN¹ CAI²	genius
天意	TIAN¹ YI⁴	act of Nature; God's will
天明	TIAN¹ MING²	sunrise; daybreak
天然	TIAN¹ RAN²	natural
天生	TIAN¹ SHENG	born; inborn; innate
天平	TIAN¹ PING²	balance (weight scale)
天眞	TIAN¹ ZHEN¹	innocent and artless
天時	TIAN¹ SHI²	weather (casual use)
天氣	TIAN¹ QI⁴	weather (formal use)

天南地北	TIAN¹ NAN² DI⁴ BEI³	a world apart
天文地理	TIAN¹ WEN² DI⁴ LI³	astronomy to geography (very knowledgeable)
天時地利	TIAN¹ SHI² DI⁴ LI⁴	good weather and fertile soil; at the right time and at the right place
天公地道	TIAN¹ GONG¹ DI⁴ DAO⁴	absolutely fair (Literally: Fair in Heaven and fair on Earth.) (公道 GONG₁ DAO₄; fair.)
天地人和	TIAN¹ DI⁴ REN² HE²	The Heaven, the Earth and Human all in harmony
天時地利人和	TIAN¹ SHI² DI⁴ LI⁴ REN² HE²	at the right time, at the right place and with the right people
天不怕, 地不怕。	TIAN¹ BU⁴ PA⁴, DI⁴ BU⁴ PA⁴.	fearless (Literally: Fear neither Heaven nor Earth)

天下無難事, 只怕有心人。
TIAN¹ XIA⁴ WU² NAN² SHI⁴, ZHI³ PA⁴ YOU³ XIN¹ REN². It's dogged that does it.

不 (M1.3)	BU₄	not; no
不是	BU⁴ SHI⁴	not, no
不好	BU⁴ HAO³	not fine; no good
不大	BU⁴ DA⁴	not big; not quite
不小	BU⁴ XIAO³	not small; pretty big
不少	BU⁴ SHAO³	quite a bit; not too less
不成	BU⁴ CHENG²	no; not OK
不行	BU⁴ XING²	no; not OK

不可	BÙ KĚ	not allowed
不同	BÙ TÓNG	different; not the same
不夠	BÙ GÒU	not enough; insufficient
不難	BÙ NÁN	not difficult
不便	BÙ BIÀN	inconvenient (=不方便)
不必	BÙ BÌ	not necessary
不合	BÙ HÉ	not conforming to; not suitable; not fit
不和	BÙ HÉ	not getting along well
不安	BÙ ĀN	uneasy
不定	BÙ DÌNG	not certain; indefinite
不得	BÙ DÉ	not permitted
不通	BÙ TŌNG	not through; blocked
不對	BÙ DUÌ	incorrect; wrong
不當	BÙ DÀNG	improper; inappropriate
不錯	BÙ CUÒ	it's true; pretty good (Literally: not wrong--not bad)
不利	BÙ LÌ	not favorable; disadvantageous
不會	BÙ HUÌ	not being able to; it would not
不外	BÙ WÀI	nothing more than
不日	BÙ RÌ	in a few days; coming soon
不法	BÙ FǍ	unlawful; illegal
不比	BÙ BǏ	unlike
不論	BÙ LÙN	regardless

不理	BU⁴ LI³	ignore; disregard
不信	BU⁴ XIN⁴	disbelieve
不忙	BU⁴ MANG²	wait; no hurry; not busy
不只	BU⁴ ZHI³	not only; more than
不光	BU⁴ GUANG¹	not only
不但	BU⁴ DAN⁴	not only
不時	BU⁴ SHI²	from time to time
不然	BU⁴ RAN²	otherwise; not true
不過	BU⁴ GUO⁴	however; not more than
不大於	BU⁴ DA⁴ YU²	not bigger than
不小於	BU⁴ XIAO³ YU²	not smaller than
不少於	BU⁴ SHAO³ YU²	not less than
不遲於	BU⁴ CHI² YU²	no later than
不完全	BU⁴ WAN² QUAN²	not entirely
不公平	BU⁴ GONG¹ PING²	unfair
不中用	BU⁴ ZHONG¹ YONG⁴	good for nothing
不得不	BU⁴ DE² BU⁴	no choice but to
不得已	BU⁴ DE² YI³	reluctantly
不得了	BU⁴ DE² LIAO³	extremely; very serious
不由得	BU⁴ YOU² DE²	can't help
不見得	BU⁴ JIAN⁴ DE²	not really
不怎麼	BU⁴ ZEN³ ME	not very; not quite
不大不小	BU⁴ DA⁴ BU⁴ XIAO³	just right; doesn't fit
不上不下	BU⁴ SHANG⁴ BU⁴ XIA⁴	hung up in the air; in a dilemma

VOCABULARY: 1,800+

不三不四	BÙ SĀN BÙ SÌ (4 1 4 4)	unpopular; indecent
不明不白	BÙ MÍNG BÙ BÁI (4 2 4 2)	without knowing why; unaccounted for
不清不楚	BÙ QĪNG BÙ CHǓ (4 1 4 3)	unclear; ambiguous
不知不覺	BÙ ZHĪ BÙ JUÉ (4 1 4 2)	unconsciously; without knowing it
不知所謂	BÙ ZHĪ SUǑ WÈI (4 1 3 4)	unintelligible
不了了之	BÙ LIǍO LIǍO ZHĪ (4 3 3 1)	without an end; being left unresolved
不得而知	BÙ DÉ ÉR ZHĪ (4 2 2 1)	no way to find out
不相上下	BÙ XIĀNG SHÀNG XIÀ (4 1 4 4)	pretty close; very similar
不在話下	BÙ ZÀI HUÀ XIÀ (4 4 4 4)	nothing difficult; a piece of cake
不問不說	BÙ WÈN BÙ SHUŌ (4 4 4 1)	don't ask don't tell; don't say if not asked
不由分說	BÙ YÓU FĒN SHUŌ (4 2 1 1)	without listening; not given a chance to speak
不問情由	BÙ WÈN QÍNG YÓU (4 4 4 2)	without consideration; without asking why
不可多得	BÙ KĚ DUŌ DÉ (4 3 1 2)	hard to come by
不可告人	BÙ KĚ GÀO RÉN (4 3 4 2)	don't want to be known (evil motive,...)
不好意思	BÙ HǍO YÌ SI (4 3 4)	embarrassed; hesitate
不以爲然	BÙ YǏ WÉI RÁN (4 3 2 2)	not convinced; holding a different view
不自量力	BÙ ZÌ LIÀNG LÌ (4 4 4 4)	over-estimate oneself
不怎麼樣	BÙ ZĚN ME YÀNG (4 3 4)	not impressed; so so

Mastering Mandarin: Your Path to Proficiency

是 (M1.3)	SHI₄	is (verb 'to be'); yes
是日	SHI₄ RI₄	on this day

(NOTE: written form, old style)
(是日=當天 DANG₁ TIAN₁ = 在這一天 ZAI₄ ZHE₄ YI₁ TIAN₁)

是的	SHI₄ DE (DI)	yes, that's correct
是非	SHI₄ FEI₁	right and wrong; gossip
是是非非	SHI₄ SHI₄ FEI₁ FEI₁	the right and wrong; gossips
是真是假	SHI₁ ZHEN₁ SHI₁ JIA₂	true or false; truth or lie; genuine or fake
很 (M1.3)	HEN₃	very
好 (M1.3)	HAO₃ good	HAO₄ like; love

ANNOTATIONS ———

(1) 好 when used as an adverb, it is pretty much like the character 很 and is more often used orally, e.g. 好快 HAO₃ KUAI₄ = 很快 HEN₃ KUAI₄.

(2) 好 when used as an adjective and adverb, it is pronounced as HAO₃ ; when used as a verb, it is pronounced HAO₄.

———

好人	HAO₃ REN₂	nice person
好天	HAO₃ TIAN₁	fine weather
好在	HAO₃ ZAI₄	fortunately (casual)
好用	HAO₃ YONG₄	handy
好說	HAO₃ SHUO₁	oh, you're so kind; OK, I'll do it; fine
好話	HAO₃ HUA₄	good words (about somebody or something)

好手	HAO³ SHOU³	good hand
好過	HAO³ GUO⁴	better than; better off
好辦	HAO³ BAN⁴	that's easy; that helps
好買	HAO³ MAI³	easy to buy
好賣	HAO³ MAI⁴	selling fast
好比	HAO³ BI³	similar to; such as
好心	HAO³ XIN¹	good intention
好意	HAO³ YI⁴	good intention
好心人	HAO³ XIN¹ REN²	Samaritan
好日子	HAO³ RI⁴ ZI	good days
好商量	HAO³ SHANG¹ LIANG²	open for negotiation
好好先生	HAO³ HAO³ XIAN¹ SHENG¹	"a nice guy" (one who for his own sake doesn't want to criticize anybody)
好自爲之	HAO³ ZI⁴ WEI² ZHI¹	better know how to behave oneself
好心好意	HAO³ XIN¹ HAO³ YI⁴	out of good faith and good intention
好客	HAO⁴ KE⁴	hospitable; hospitality
好學	HAO⁴ XUE³	strong desire to learn
好大喜功	HAO⁴ DA⁴ XI³ GONG¹	like to exaggerate and claim credit
嗎 (M1.3)	MA	(question indicator)
上 (M2.1)	SHANG4	up
上午	SHANG⁴ WU³	morning; a.m.

VOCABULARY: 1,800+

上工	SHANG⁴ GONG¹	go to work
上學	SHANG⁴ XUE²	go to school/class
上天	SHANG⁴ TIAN¹	Heaven; go to Heaven
上文	SHANG⁴ WEN²	above said
上下文	SHANG⁴ XIA⁴ WEN²	context
上年	SHANG⁴ NIAN²	previous year
上等	SHANG⁴ DENG³	first class
上司	SHANG⁴ SI¹	supervisor; boss
上面	SHANG⁴ MIAN⁴	upper level; up there
上邊	SHANG⁴ BIAN¹	upper level; up there
上報	SHANG⁴ BAO⁴	report to the authority; publish on the newspaper
上告	SHANG⁴ GAO⁴	complain to authority
上交	SHANG⁴ JIAO⁴	submit to authority
上當	SHANG⁴ DANG⁴	be taken in; being duped
上光	SHANG⁴ GUANG⁴	polishing
上路	SHANG⁴ LU⁴	take off for a trip
上個月	SHANG⁴ GE⁴ YUE⁴	last month
上上下下	SHANG⁴ SHANG⁴ XIA⁴ XIA⁴	all levels of staff; from leaders to subordinates
下 (M2.1)	XIA⁴	down
下午	XIA⁴ WU³	afternoon, p.m.
下等	XIA⁴ DENG³	lower level; lower class
下放	XIA⁴ FANG⁴	assign to lower level
下面	XIA⁴ MIAN⁴	down below

下邊	XIA$_4$ BIAN$_1$	down below
下一年	XIA$_4$ YI$_1$ NIAN$_2$	the following year; next year
下個月	XIA$_4$ GE$_4$ YUE$_4$	next month

(cf. 明) MING$_2$ TIAN$_1$ tomorrow, 明年 MING$_2$ NIAN$_2$ next year)

下定決心	XIA$_4$ DING$_4$ JUE$_2$ XIN$_1$	determined to
午 (M2.1)	WU$_3$	noon
午前	WU$_3$ QIAN$_2$	before noon
午後	WU$_3$ HOU$_4$	after noon
午間	WU$_3$ JIAN$_1$	noon time
工 (M2.1)	GONG$_1$	work
工人	GONG$_1$ REN$_2$	worker
工時	GONG$_1$ SHI$_1$	work hour; man hour
工資	GONG$_1$ ZI$_1$	salary; wage
工錢	GONG$_1$ QIAN$_2$	wage (casual)
工作	GONG$_1$ ZUO$_4$	work
工地	GONG$_1$ DI$_4$	site (construction,...)
工作日	GONG$_1$ ZUO$_4$ RI$_4$	workday
工會	GONG$_1$ HUI$_4$	labor union
工事	GONG$_1$ SHI$_4$	work related projects, tasks, or events.
工友	GONG$_1$ YOU$_3$	fellow worker (in a plant or shop)
作 (M2.1)	ZUO$_4$	do
作文	ZUO$_4$ WEN$_2$	composition; essay
作用	ZUO$_4$ YONG$_4$	affect; function

作法	ZUO⁴ FA³	way of doing things
作假	ZUO⁴ JIA³	falsify
作對	ZUO⁴ DUI⁴	oppose; against
作爲	ZUO⁴ WEI²	conduct; as
作者	ZUO⁴ ZHE³	author; writer
作家	ZUO⁴ JIA¹	writer
作客	ZUO⁴ KE⁴	being a guest
左 (M2.2)	ZUO₃	left
左手	ZUO³ SHOU³	left hand
左邊	ZUO³ BIAN¹	left side
左面	ZUO³ MIAN⁴	left side
左右	ZUO³ YOU⁴	left and right; approximately; influence (as a verb)
左右手	ZUO³ YOU⁴ SHOU³	left hand and right hand; key assistant
左右爲難	ZUO³ YOU⁴ WEI² NAN²	in a dilemma; in an awkward predicament
右 (M2.2)	YOU₄	right
右手	YOU⁴ SHOU³	right hand
右邊	YOU⁴ BIAN¹	right side
右面	YOU⁴ MIAN⁴	right side
手 (M2.2)	SHOU₃	hand
手力	SHOU³ LI⁴	hand force
手工	SHOU³ GONG¹	hand craft; craftmanship

手提	SHOU³ TI²	portable; hand-carry
手上	SHOU³ SHANG⁴	in hand
手下	SHOU³ XIA⁴	subordinates; under one's leadership
手法	SHOU³ FA³	skill; ploy
手提電話	SHOU³ TI² DIAN⁴ HUA⁴	portable/cellular phone.

Often as 手機 SHOU₃ JI₁ (手提電話機) orally

用 (M2.2)	YONG₄	use
用力	YONG⁴ LI⁴	apply strength; use force
用人	YONG⁴ REN²	use human resource
用心	YONG⁴ XIN¹	attentively; diligently
用功	YONG⁴ GONG¹	diligently
用意	YONG⁴ YI⁴	intention
用以	YONG⁴ YI³	in order to; so as to
用不了	YONG⁴ BU⁴ LIAO³	more than enough; in less than
用力不當	YONG⁴ LI⁴ BU⁴ DANG⁴	force applied incorrectly
用人不當	YONG⁴ REN² BU⁴ DANG⁴	inappropriate use of people

力 (M2.2)	LI₄	force; strength
力學	LI⁴ XUE⁴	Mechanics (science)
力量	LI⁴ LIANG⁴	physical strength; force
力氣	LI⁴ QI⁴	physical strength
力求	LI⁴ QIU²	strive to
力求成功	LI⁴ QIU² CHENG² GONG¹	do the best to succeed

VOCABULARY: 1,800+

力不從心	LÌ BÙ CÓNG XĪN (4 4 2 1)	beyond one's ability and effort
力所能及	LÌ SUǑ NÉNG JÍ (4 3 2 2)	within one's ability
肯 (M2.3)	KEN₃	willing; agree
肯定	KEN DING (3 4)	affirm; positively
肯學	KEN XUE (3 2)	willing/eager to learn
肯定成績	KEN DING CHENG JI (3 4 2 1)	affirm accomplishment
自 (M2.3)	ZÌ₄	self; from
自己	ZÌ JǏ (4 3)	self
自從	ZÌ CÓNG (4 2)	since; ever since
自然	ZÌ RÁN (4 2)	natural; naturally
自學	ZÌ XUÉ (4 2)	self-study; self-help
自由	ZÌ YÓU (4 2)	freedom; liberty
自用	ZÌ YÒNG (4 4)	private use
自問	ZÌ WÈN (4 4)	ask oneself
自便	ZÌ BIÀN (4 4)	do as one pleases
自大	ZÌ DÀ (4 4)	arrogant
自助	ZÌ ZHÙ (4 4)	self-service; self-help
自傳	ZÌ ZHUÀN (4 4)	autobiography

(NOTE: cf. M15.2 傳真 CHUAN₂ ZHEN₁ fax; 傳 in 自傳 is pronounced ZHUAN₄)

自信	ZÌ XÌN (4 4)	self-confident
自己人	ZÌ JǏ RÉN (4 3 2)	one of us; belong to the group
自上而下	ZÌ SHÀNG ÉR XIÀ (4 4 2 4)	from top/above down

VOCABULARY: 1,800+

自下而上	ZI⁴ XIA⁴ ER² SHANG⁴	from bottom/lower up
自成一家	ZI⁴ CHENG² YI¹ JIA¹	one's unique style
自由自在	ZI⁴ YOU² ZI⁴ ZAI⁴	freely and leisurely
自言自語	ZI⁴ YAN² ZI⁴ YU³	talking to oneself
自然而然	ZI⁴ RAN² ER² RAN²	naturally; spontaneously
自以爲是	ZI⁴ YI³ WEI² SHI⁴	considers oneself always correct
自得其樂	ZI⁴ DE² QI² LE⁴	be content with one's lot
自行其是	ZI⁴ XING² QI² SHI⁴	go one's own way
自行其道	ZI⁴ XING² QI² DAO⁴	go one's own way
自力更生	ZI⁴ LI⁴ GENG¹ SHENG¹	self-effort and self-support
自不量力	ZI⁴ BU⁴ LIANG⁴ LI⁴	overestimate one's ability

(NOTE: 力量 LI₄ LIANG₄ strength; force; 量 is used as a noun; while in 量力 LIANG LI, 量 is used as a verb; measure strength.)

自知之明	ZI⁴ ZHI¹ ZHI¹ MING²	know thyself
己 (M2.3)	JI₃	self (己 JI₃) (已 YI₃) (M7.1)
出 (M2.3)	CHU₁	out
出入	CHU¹ RU⁴	in and out; discrepancy
出現	CHU¹ XIAN⁴	occur
出去	CHU¹ QU⁴	go out
出於	CHU¹ YU²	with the intention of
出生	CHU¹ SHENG¹	birth; born
出賣	CHU¹ MAI⁴	for sale; betray

Mastering Mandarin: Your Path to Proficiency

出事	CHU¹ SHI⁴	accident; something happened
出事地點	CHU¹ SHI⁴ DI⁴ DIAN³	place of accident; site of accident
出手大方	CHU¹ SHOU³ DA⁴ FANG¹	spend generously (such as in gifts, gratuity,..)
出其不意	CHU¹ QI² BU⁴ YI⁴	to people's surprise; catch somebody off-guard
出沒無常 (cf. M5.2 沒 MEI₂)	CHU¹ MO⁴ WU² CHANG²	appear and disappear irregularly
出以公心	CHU¹ YI³ GONG¹ XIN¹	without selfish intention
出入平安	CHU¹ RU⁴ PING² AN¹	in and out safe and well

(NOTE: This is a well wish expression often posted on the header of an entry door in Chinese villages on Lunar New Year.)

入 (M2.3)	RU⁴	in
入學	RU⁴ XUE²	enroll in school
入會	RU⁴ HUI⁴	join membership
我 (M3.1)	WO³	I, me
我的	WO³ DE	my; mine
我們	WO³ MEN²	we; us
我等	WO³ DENG³	we; us (written style)
我方	WO³ FANG¹	our side; our party; we
請 (M3.1)	QING³	invite; please
請人	QING³ REN²	hire helpers; employ
請客	QING³ KE⁴	entertain a guest

請問	QĬNG WÈN	Excuse me, please. (To ask a question.)
請說	QĬNG SHUŌ	go ahead, please
請求	QĬNG QIÚ	request; ask
請便	QĬNG BIÀN	do as you please; it's up to you
請假	QĬNG JIÀ	asking for time off work
請功	QĬNG GŌNG	request credit for a merit
你 (M3.1)	NĬ	you (singular)
你們	NĬ MÉN	you (plural)
你的	NĬ DE	your (singular)
你們的	NĬ MÉN DE	your (plural)
來 (M3.1)	LÁI	come
來信	LÁI XÌN	write to us; letter received
來文	LÁI WÉN	document received
來電	LÁI DIÀN	telegram received
來件	LÁI JIÀN	parcel/mail received
來人	LÁI RÉN	bearer; messenger; order an attendant to come in
來者	LÁI ZHĚ	visitor
來客	LÁI KÈ	visiting guest
來意	LÁI YÌ	intention of visit
來年	LÁI NIÁN	coming year; next year
來得及	LÁI DÉ JÍ	time still allows
來不及	LÁI BÙ JÍ	running out of time

來不得	LAI² BU⁴ DE²	not supposed to; not allowed to
來路不明	LAI² LU⁴ BU⁴ MING²	unidentified; source unknown
來文要點	LAI² WEN² YAO⁴ DIAN³	key points of document received

看 (M3.1)	KAN⁴	see
看見	KAN⁴ JIAN⁴	see

(NOTE: 看見、看到 KAN DAO、見到 JIAN DAO、看、見 --- all mean the same; 看見 is the formal word in vocabulary.)

看看	KAN⁴ KAN	take a look; let's see
看來	KAN⁴ LAI²	it appears; it looks like
看出	KAN⁴ CHU¹	see and discover
看中	KAN⁴ ZHONG⁴	take a fancy to: settle on
看上	KAN⁴ SHANG⁴	take a fancy to
看法	KAN⁴ FA³	point of view
看慣了	KAN⁴ GUAN⁴ LE	often seen and get used to it
看不慣	KAN⁴ BU⁴ GUAN⁴	can't bear the sight of
看不見	KAN⁴ BU⁴ JIAN⁴	can't see
看不起	KAN⁴ BU⁴ QI³	look down upon (cf.小看) (M1.2)
看得起	KAN⁴ DE² QI³	have a good opinion on
看樣子	KAN⁴ YANG⁴ ZI	seem; it looks like
看上去	KAN⁴ SHANG⁴ QU⁴	seem; it looks like

他 (M3.2)	TA¹	he; him
他人	TA¹ REN²	other people

VOCABULARY: 1,800+

| 他日 | TA¹ RI⁴ | in future; some day |
| 他們 | TA¹ MEN² | they, them |

和 (M3.2)	HE²	and
和平	HE² PING²	peace
和好	HE² HAO³	become reconciled
和氣	HE² QI⁴	friendly

她 (M3.2)	TA¹	she; her
她們	TA¹ MEN²	they; them (female)
她們的	TA¹ MEN² DE	their; theirs (female)

| 們 (M3.2) | MEN² | (plural form for pronouns) |

問 (M3.2)	WEN⁴	ask
問好	WEN⁴ HAO³	greeting; say hello to
問安	WEN⁴ AN¹	extend well wishes to (usually to elderly)
問候	WEN⁴ HOU⁴	extend greetings to
問題	WEN⁴ TI²	question; problem; issue

說 (3.3)	SHUO¹	say
說話	SHUO¹ HUA⁴	say; speak
說道	SHUO¹ DAO⁴	say; speak
說到	SHUO¹ DAO⁴	mention
說成	SHUO¹ CHENG²	call it; describe as
說明	SHUO¹ MING²	explain

VOCABULARY: 1,800+

說好	SHUO¹ HAO³	with the understanding or consent
說法	SHUO¹ FA³	the way it is said
說情	SHUO¹ QING²	plead for mercy; asking for a favor
說理	SHUO¹ LI³	argue; reason things out
說不通	SHUO¹ BU⁴ TONG¹	not convincing
說不定	SHUO¹ BU⁴ DING⁴	maybe
說不上	SHUO¹ BU⁴ SHANG⁴	can't be treated as
說得上	SHUO¹ DE² SHANG⁴	can be treated as
說大話	SHUO¹ DA⁴ HUA⁴	boast; brag
說不清楚	SHUO¹ BU⁴ QING¹ CHU³	cannot be explained
說得清楚	SHUO¹ DE² QING¹ CHU³	can be clearly explained
說完又說	SHUO¹ WAN² YOU⁴ SHUO¹	keep repeating
說到做到	SHUO¹ DAO⁴ ZUO⁴ DAO⁴	do as one says
說一不二	SHUO¹ YI¹ BU⁴ ER⁴	stand by one's words
說不過去	SHUO¹ BU⁴ GUO⁴ QU⁴	not convincing
說得過去	SHUO¹ DE² GUO⁴ QU⁴	passable
您 (M3.3)	NIN²	you
(singular; respect to senior, elderly, visitor …)		
您好	NIN² HAO³	Hello. How do you do?; Hi. How are you?
還 (M3.3)	HAI²	still; (還)
	HUAN²	return
還是	HAI² SHI⁴	still; nonetheless

還有	HÁI YǑU	further; and
還說	HÁI SHUŌ	further said
還給	HUÁN GĚI	return (something) to
還原	HUÁN YUÁN	reduction (chemical)

在 (M3.3)	ZÀI	at; on
在家	ZÀI JIĀ	at home
在學	ZÀI XUÉ	enrolled at school
在行	ZÀI HÁNG	experienced in trade
在商言商	ZÀI SHĀNG YÁN SHĀNG	business is business

家 (M3.3)	JIĀ	home
家常	JIĀ CHÁNG	family talk; small talk
家人	JIĀ RÉN	family member
家法	JIĀ FǍ	family rules
家信	JIĀ XÌN	family letter
家和萬事興	JIĀ HÉ WÀN SHÌ XĪNG	Family harmony brings in prosperity.

(Literally: Family harmony helps thousands of things bloom.)

學 (M4.1)	XUÉ	learn; study
學習	XUÉ XÍ	learn; study
學問	XUÉ WÈN	knowledge
學力	XUÉ LÌ	level of education
學者	XUÉ ZHĚ	scholar
學年	XUÉ NIÁN	school year; academic year
學會	XUÉ HUÌ	academic society, institution

學報	XUE² BAO⁴	academic gazette
學說	XUE² SHUO¹	theory; doctrine
學生	XUE² SHENG¹	student; pupil
學時	XUE² SHI²	credit hour
學分	XUE² FEN¹	credit

習 (M4.1)	XI²	practice; exercise
習慣	XI² GUAN⁴	get used to
習作	XI² ZUO⁴	exercise (schoolwork)
習題	XI² TI²	question in an exercise
習以爲常	XI² YI³ WEI² CHANG²	accustomed to it and it becomes the norm
習非成是	XI² FEI¹ CHENG² SHI⁴	accustomed to it and wrong becomes right

中 (M4.1)	ZHONG¹	center; middle; medium
中國	ZHONG¹ GUO²	China
中文	ZHONG¹ WEN²	Chinese (language)
中國人	ZHONG¹ GUO² REN²	Chinese (person)
中間	ZHONG¹ JIAN¹	middle; between; among
中等	ZHONG¹ DENG³	medium; middle class
中立	ZHONG¹ LI⁴	neutrality; impartial
中點	ZHONG¹ DIAN³	midpoint
中心	ZHONG¹ XIN¹	center
中年	ZHONG¹ NIAN²	middle age
中途	ZHONG¹ TU²	midway

中午	ZHŌNG WǓ	noon
中子	ZHŌNG ZǏ	neutron
中原	ZHŌNG YUÁN	Middle China
中東	ZHŌNG DŌNG	Middle East
中方	ZHŌNG FĀNG	Chinese side
中共	ZHŌNG GÒNG	Chinese Communist Party (abbreviated)
中英	ZHŌNG YĪNG	China-Britain

(Sometimes Sino-Britain is used in which Sino is in Latin.)

中美	ZHŌNG MĚI	China-U.S.
中日	ZHŌNG RÌ	China-Japan
中法	ZHŌNG FǍ	China-France
中外	ZHŌNG WÀI	China and foreign countries
中外合資	ZHŌNG WÀI HÉ ZĪ	joint venture of Chinese and foreign capital

英 (M4.1)	YĪNG$_1$	English
英國	YĪNG GUÓ	United Kingdom
英國人	YĪNG GUÓ RÉN	British/English (person)
英文	YĪNG WÉN	English (language)
英語	YĪNG YǓ	English (language)
英明	YĪNG MÍNG	brilliant; wise
英才	YĪNG CÁI	person with outstanding ability

文 (M4.1)	WÉN$_2$	writing
文字	WÉN ZÌ	character; writing

VOCABULARY: 1,800+

文件	WEN² JIAN⁴	document
文明	WEN² MING²	civilization
文人	WEN² REN²	scholar; literati
文才	WEN² CAI²	literary talent
文法	WEN² FA³	grammar
文理	WEN² LI³	unity and coherence in writing
文言文	WEN² YAN² WEN²	classical style Chinese
文不對題	WEN² BU⁴ DUI⁴ TI²	content irrelevant to the topic
美 (M4.2)	MEI₃	beautiful; pretty
美人	MEI³ REN²	beauty
美好	MEI³ HAO³	happy; glorious
美國	MEI³ GUO²	U.S.A.
美元	MEI³ YUAN²	U.S. Dollar
美國人	MEI³ GUO² REN²	American (person)
美國之音	MEI³ GUO² ZHI¹ YIN¹	Voice of America (Radio)
國 (M4.2)	GUO₂	country; nation; state
國家	GUO² JIA¹	nation; country; state
國力	GUO² LI⁴	national strength (國力=國家(的)力量)
國立	GUO² LI⁴	national/state run
國都	GUO² DU¹	capital of a nation (Note: not GUO₂ DOU₁)
國會	GUO² HUI⁴	Congress; Parliament; Diet

國法	GUO² FA³	national laws and regulation
國手	GUO² SHOU³	national champion/team
國人	GUO² REN²	countrymen
國內	GUO² NEI⁴	domestic/internal of a nation
國外	GUO² WAI⁴	foreign
國事	GUO² SHI⁴	national affairs
國家大事	GUO² JIA¹ DA⁴ SHI⁴	major issues of a nation
國家之間	GUO² JIA¹ ZHI¹ JIAN¹	between/among countries
國家投資	GUO² JIA¹ TOU² ZI¹	national investment
國立大學	GUO² LI⁴ DA⁴ XUE²	national university

都 (M4.2)	DOU₁	all; already
	DU₁	capitol
去 (M4.2)	QU₄	go
去年	QU⁴ NIAN²	last year
去向	QU⁴ XIANG⁴	direction of going; whereabouts
去路	QU⁴ LU⁴	way out; outlet
了 (M4.2)	LIAO₃ ; LE	end; already
了事	LIAO³ SHI⁴	get it over; put an end
了一件事	LIAO³ YI¹ JIAN⁴ SHI⁴	get it over; put an end to a matter
叫 (M4.3)	JIAO₄	call; greet; shout
叫好	JIAO⁴ HAO³	excited and happy

叫做	JIAO⁴ ZUO⁴	known as; called
叫人	JIAO⁴ REN²	greet people
叫人生氣	JIAO⁴ REN² SHENG¹ QI⁴	make people upset/ outraged
叫人喜歡	JIAO⁴ REN² XI³ HUAN¹	delightful
叫人高興	JIAO⁴ REN² GAO¹ XING⁴	make people happy
謝 (M4.3)	XIE⁴	thank
謝謝	XIE⁴ XIE⁴	thank you

(NOTE: 謝謝 is the usual expression in Mandarin; southern usage as in Cantonese, 多謝 DUO₁ XIE₄ is more often used.)

謝意	XIE⁴ YI⁴	gratitude; thankfulness
謝天謝地	XIE⁴ TIAN¹ XIE⁴ DI⁴	thank goodness; thank God (Literally: Thank Heaven and Earth.)
又 (M4.3)	YOU⁴	again; also
再 (M4.3)	ZAI⁴	again
再見	ZAI⁴ JIAN⁴	goodbye; see you again (Daily use)
再會	ZAI⁴ HUI⁴	goodbye; see you again (written); (=再見)
再現	ZAI⁴ XIAN⁴	reappear
再次	ZAI⁴ CI⁴	once again
再三	ZAI⁴ SAN¹	over and over again
再說	ZAI⁴ SHUO¹	furthermore (再說, ...); wait until (....再說。)
再者	ZAI⁴ ZHE³	postscript (P.S.); furthermore

再生	ZAI⁴ SHENG¹	renewable; reproduce
再不	ZAI⁴ BU⁴	or else; otherwise

見 (M4.3)	JIAN⁴	see
見面	JIAN⁴ MIAN⁴	meet face to face
見習	JIAN⁴ XI²	practice; training
見外	JIAN⁴ WAI⁴	not treating somebody as one of the group
見地	JIAN⁴ DI⁴	knowledgeable; knowledge
見報	JIAN⁴ BAO⁴	publish on the newspaper
見不得人	JIAN⁴ BU⁴ DE² REN²	can't afford to be exposed; behind the closet

常 (M5.1)	CHANG2	ordinary; often
常常	CHANG2 CHANG2	often; frequent
常年	CHANG2 NIAN2	year-long; year after year
常見	CHANG2 JIAN4	of common occurrence
常有	CHANG2 YOU3	often happens
常人	CHANG2 REN2	ordinary person
常事	CHANG2 SHI4	ordinary matter
(常事 = 平常事 PING2 CHANG2 SHI4)		
常會	CHANG2 HUI4	regular meeting; session
("常會+Verb" ; (action) would often happen; e.g. 常會遲到=常常會遲到 CHANG2 CHANG2 HUI4 CHI2 DAO4 often being late.)		
常客	CHANG2 KE4	frequent visitor; regular guest; patron
常用	CHANG2 YONG4	in common use

常說	CHÁNG SHUŌ	saying
常言道	CHÁNG YÁN DÀO	as the saying goes
常情常理	CHÁNG QÍNG CHÁNG LǏ	common sense and reasoning
做 (M5.1)	ZUÒ	do; act
做工	ZUÒ GŌNG	work; labor
做人	ZUÒ RÉN	behave (being a human)
做事	ZUÒ SHÌ	handle things
做作	ZUÒ ZUÒ	unnatural acts; no sincere acts; acting
慣 (M5.1)	GUÀN	get used to; habitual
慣用	GUÀN YÒNG	habitually practiced
就 (M5.1)	JIÙ	exactly; only; near
就地	JIÙ DÌ	on the site
就學	JIÙ XUÉ	study at
就是	JIÙ SHÌ	exactly; it is
就是說	JIÙ SHÌ SHUŌ	that is to say
就事論事	JIÙ SHÌ LÙN SHÌ	just talk about the matter per se
就此了事	JIÙ CǏ LIǍO SHÌ	this puts an end to it
行 (M5.1)	XÍNG	fine, okay; move
	HÁNG	trade
行好	XÍNG HǍO	be merciful
行爲	XÍNG WÉI	behavior

行使	XÍNG SHǏ	exercise (power or authority)
行事	XÍNG SHÌ	handle things
行文	XÍNG WÉN	style of writing in documents
行走	XÍNG ZǑU	walk; walk around
行人	XÍNG RÉN	pedestrian
行人道	XÍNG RÉN DÀO	pavement/sidewalk; pedestrian crossing
行不行?	XÍNG BÙ XÍNG?	Is that all right? Is that OK?
行	XÍNG	fine; all right
行家	HÁNG JIĀ	expert in trade; pro of a trade
行話	HÁNG HUÀ	trade jargon
今 (M5.2)	JIN₁	this; now
今天	JĪN TIĀN	today
今日	JĪN RÌ	today
今晚	JĪN WǍN	this evening; tonight
今年	JĪN NIÁN	this year; current year
今後	JĪN HÒU	from now on
今生	JĪN SHĒNG	this life; current life cycle
年 (M5.2)	NIAN₂	year
年年	NIÁN NIÁN	every year; year after year
年月	NIÁN YUÈ	year and month; during that period of time
年間	NIÁN JIĀN	during those years
年成	NIÁN CHÉNG	harvest of the year

年報	NIAN² BAO⁴	annual report
年表	NIAN² BIAO³	chronological table
年假	NIAN² JIA⁴	annual holiday; vacation
年會	NIAN² HUI⁴	annual meeting
年利	NIAN² LI⁴	annual interest rate
年少有為	NIAN² SHAO⁴ YOU³ WEI²	young and promising
年過半百	NIAN² GUO⁴ BAN⁴ BAI⁵	pass fifty years old
並 (M5.2)	BING⁴	just; combine; side by side
並非	BING⁴ FEI¹	it is not
並且	BING⁴ QIE³	moreover
並重	BING⁴ ZHONG⁴	equally important
並行	BING⁴ XING²	concurrent; run parallel
沒 (M5.2)	MEI²	without
沒有	MEI² YOU³	no; without; do not
沒錯	MEI² CUO⁴	nothing wrong
(沒錯 = 沒有錯 MEI² YOU³ CUO⁴)		
沒法	MEI² FA³	no way; no choice
(沒法 = 沒有辦法 MEI² YOU³ BAN⁴ FA³)		
沒事	MEI² SHI⁴	nothing serious; nothing happened
沒甚麼	MEI² SHEN² ME⁴	nothing
沒完沒了	MEI² WAN² MEI² LIAO³	never ends; drag on and on
有 (M5.2)	YOU³	possess; exist; have
有人	YOU³ REN²	occupied (e.g. rest room door sign); somebody

有力	YOU³ LI⁴	strong; effective
有利	YOU³ LI⁴	advantageous; beneficial
有理	YOU³ LI³	reasonable
有錢	YOU³ QIAN³	rich; wealthy
有心	YOU³ XIN¹	have a mind to
有意	YOU³ YI⁴	intentionally
有爲	YOU³ WEI²	promising; capable
有事	YOU³ SHI⁴	problem occurs; busy
有功	YOU³ GONG¹	having credit/merit
有喜	YOU³ XI³	pregnant (casual)
有喜事	YOU³ XI³ SHI⁴	happy event (wedding,..)
有一些	YOU³ YI¹ XIE¹	some (有些 = 有一些)
有一點 (有點 = 有一點)	YOU³ YI¹ DIAN³	somewhat; a little
有時候	YOU³ SHI² HOU	sometimes (有時 = 有時候)
有意思	YOU³ YI⁴ SI	interesting; having the intention of
有助於	YOU³ ZHU⁴ YU²	helpful to
有能力	YOU³ NENG² LI⁴	capable
有學問	YOU³ XUE² WEN⁴	knowledgeable
有心無力	YOU³ XIN¹ WU² LI⁴	out of reach; willing but not capable
有生力量	YOU³ SHENG¹ LI⁴ LIANG⁴	strong and effective force
有言在先	YOU³ YAN² ZAI⁴ XIAN¹	warned beforehand
有兩下子	YOU³ LIANG³ XIA⁴ ZI	very skillful; know one's stuff
有過之而無不及	YOU³ GUO⁴ ZHI¹ ER² WU² BU⁴ JI²	go even further than (when comparing acts or persons)

要 (M5.3)	YAO₄	essential; need; want
(cf.重要 ZHONG₄ YAO₄ (M17.2))		
要人	YAO⁴ REN⁴	very important person (VIP)
要事	YAO⁴ SHI⁴	important event
(要事=重要的事)(cf. 要是)		
要地	YAO⁴ DI⁴	important place
要道	YAO⁴ DAO⁴	important path
要件	YAO⁴ JIAN⁴	important document
要點	YAO⁴ DIAN³	key points
要是	YAO⁴ SHI⁴	if; in case (cf.要事)
要就	YAO⁴ JIU⁴	or else
要不	YAO⁴ BU⁴	otherwise
要不然	YAO⁴ BU⁴ RAN²	otherwise
要不得	YAO⁴ BU⁴ DE²	no good; intolerable
要不要?	YAO⁴ BU⁴ YAO⁴?	Do you want it ? Is it necessary to ...?
要面子	YAO⁴ MIAN⁴ ZI³	concern about losing face
要人有人	YAO⁴ REN² YOU³ REN²	people are ready when called for
要錢有錢	YAO⁴ QIAN² YOU³ QIAN²	money is ready when needed
要言不煩	YAO⁴ YAN² BU⁴ FAN²	terse (Important speeches are concise.)
多 (M5.3)	DUO₁	many; much
多多	DUO¹ DUO¹	a lot

VOCABULARY: 1,800+

多少	DUO¹ SHAO³	more or less
多少?	DUO¹ SHAO³?	how many? how much?
多半	DUO¹ BAN	most; more likely
多邊	DUO¹ BIAN¹	multilateral
多次	DUO¹ CI⁴	many times
多事	DUO¹ SHI⁴	meddlesome
多心	DUO¹ XIN¹	oversensitive; without a focus
多面手	DUO MIAN⁴ SHOU⁴	a versatile person
多方	DUO¹ FANG	in different ways
(多方=多方面	DUO₁ FANG₁ MIAN₄)	
多面	DUO¹ MIAN⁴	in different ways
多方面	DUO¹ FANG¹ MIAN⁴	in different ways
多麼	DUO¹ ME	how; what; so...
多年生	DUO¹ NIAN² SHENG¹	perennial (plants)
多國公司	DUO¹ GUO² GONG¹ SI¹	multinational company
多邊會談	DUO¹ BIAN¹ HUI⁴ TAN²	multilateral talks

少 (M5.3)	SHAO₃	less; little;
	SHAO₄	young
少量	SHAO³ LIANG	small amount; a little
少不得	SHAO³ BU⁴ DE²	cannot be without
少不了	SHAO³ BU⁴ LIAO³	cannot be without
少年	SHAO⁴ NIAN²	early youth; teenager
少女	SHAO⁴ NÜ³ (NV/NYU)	young girl (NÜ: 2 dots on U)
少年老成	SHAO⁴ NIAN² LAO³ CHENG²	an old head on young shoulders

才 (M5.3)	CAI₂	talent; just; only
才能	CAI₂ NENG₂	ability; talent (noun)
才學	CAI₂ XUE₂	talent and learning
才子	CAI₂ ZI₃	a talent
才能夠	CAI₂ NENG₂ GOU₄	before it can be

('才能夠 + Verb' = '才能 + Verb')
(e.g. 才能夠買 = 才夠買 before it can be purchased)

才可以	CAI₂ KE₃ YI₃	before it can be

e.g. 才可以 + verb: 才可以說/做/走

夠 (M5.3)	GOU₄	enough; sufficient
夠力	GOU₄ LI₄	strong enough
夠錢	GOU₄ QIAN₂	enough money
夠了	GOU₄ LE	enough (That's enough.)
夠不夠?	GOU₄ BU GOU₄?	Is it enough?
夠朋友	GOU₄ PENG₂ YOU₃	be friend indeed
夠意思	GOU₄ YI₄ SI	interesting enough
這 (M6.1)	ZHE₄	this; the
這個	ZHE₄ GE	this one; this
這裡	ZHE₄ LI₃	here
這邊	ZHE₄ BIAN₁	here; this side
這麼	ZHE₄ ME	so ...; such
這一點	ZHE₄ YI₁ DIAN₃	this; this issue
這些	ZHE₄ XIE₁	these
這樣	ZHE₄ YANG₄	this way; like this; so
這次	ZHE₄ CI₄	this time

這時	ZHE⁴ SHI⁴	at this time
這時候	ZHE⁴ SHI² HOU⁴	at this time
這個時候	ZHE⁴ GE SHI² HOU⁴	at this time
這下子	ZHE⁴ XIA⁴ ZI	and so; and then
這一下	ZHE⁴ YI¹ XIA⁴	and so; and then
這麼搞	ZHE⁴ ME GAO³	doing like this; this way
這件事	ZHE⁴ JIAN⁴ SHI⁴	this matter; this event
裡 (M6.1)	LI₃	in; interior
裡面	LI³ MIAN⁴	inside; interior
裡裡外外	LI³ LI³ WAI⁴ WAI⁴	inside and outside
裡通外國	LI³ TONG¹ WAI⁴ GUO²	illicit relationship with a foreign country (to become a traitor)
裡應外合	LI³ YING⁴ WAI⁴ HE²	collaborate with inside forces in a covert operation
非 (M6.1)	FEI₁	not; no; wrong
非常	FEI¹ CHANG²	extraordinary; very
非法	FEI¹ FA³	illegal
非得	FEI¹ DE²	must
非但..而且..	FEI¹ DAN⁴ ...ER² QIE³...	not only...; but also...
非..不可	FEI¹ .. BU⁴ KE³	must; bound to
非難	FEI¹ NAN⁴	blame
非人	FEI¹ REN²	inhumane

那 (M6.1)	NA₄	that; then
那裡	NA⁴ LI³	there
那邊	NA⁴ BIAN¹	there
那麼	NA⁴ ME	then; so ...
那時	NA⁴ SHI²	at that time; by that time
那時候	NA⁴ SHI² HOU⁴	at that time; in those days
那樣	NA⁴ YANG⁴	in that case
那還了得?	NA⁴ HAI² LIAO³ DE²	how terrible; how could that be?
那還得了?	NA⁴ HAI² DE² LIAO³	how terrible; how could that be?

ANNOTATIONS ───────

The first of the last 2 expressions tends to be northern China usage (the second one more often used in southern China such as in Cantonese.)

───────

邊 (M6.1)	BIAN₁	side; edge
邊走邊談	BIAN¹ ZOU³ BIAN¹ TAN²	talk while walking; talk as (they) walk
邊看邊說	BIAN¹ KAN⁴ BIAN¹ SHUO¹	speak while watching
哪 (M6.2)	NA₃	how; where; which
哪裡	NA³ LI³	where
哪有	NA³ YOU³	how come
哪邊	NA³ BIAN¹	which side

VOCABULARY: 1,800+

哪一個	NA³ YI¹ GE⁴	which one
哪個	NA³ GE⁴	which (singular)
哪些	NA³ XIE¹	which (plural)
哪能	NA³ NENG²	how can
哪肯	NA³ KEN³	how can
哪怕	NA³ PA⁴	even if
些 (M6.2)	XIE₁	some (e.g. 多一些, 好些) (plural of uncertain quantity); more (comparative degree)
相 (M6.2)	XIANG₁	each other; one another
相信	XIANG¹ XIN⁴	believe
相同	XIANG¹ TONG²	same
相好	XIANG¹ HAO³	intimate (friends, lovers)
相思	XIANG¹ SI¹	lovesick
相比	XIANG¹ BI¹	compare; in comparison
相當	XIANG¹ DANG¹	match; equivalent
相當於	XIANG¹ DANG¹ YU²	equivalent to
相等	XIANG¹ DENG³	equal
相對	XIANG¹ DUI⁴	opposite; relatively
相傳	XIANG¹ CHUAN²	by tradition; generation to generation
相見	XIANG¹ JIAN⁴	see each other; meet one another
相間	XIANG¹ JIAN⁴	alternating with
相應	XIANG¹ YING⁴	corresponding

Mastering Mandarin: Your Path to Proficiency

相通	XIANG¹ TONG¹	interlinked; through
相提並論	XIANG¹ TI² BING⁴ LUN⁴	mention in same breadth
同 (M6.2)	TONG₂	same
同日	TONG² RI⁴	the same day
同月	TONG² YUE⁴	the same month
同年	TONG² NIAN²	the same year
同一	TONG² YI¹	same; identical
同等	TONG² DENG³	same class; same rank; same status
同步	TONG² BU⁴	synchronism; synchronize
同學	TONG² XUE²	classmate; schoolmate
同事	TONG² SHI⁴	colleague; co-worker
同樣	TONG² YANG⁴	same
同時	TONG² SHI²	at the same time; meanwhile
同行	TONG² HANG²	same trade; same profession
同行	TONG² XING²	travel together
同路	TONG² LU⁴	going the same direction
同情	TONG² QING²	sympathy; sympathize
同意	TONG² YI⁴	agree; consent
同心合力	TONG² XIN¹ HE² LI⁴	together heart and soul
的 (M6.2)	DE, DI	of; target
爲 (M6.3)	WEI⁴ WEI₂	for; in order to
爲此	WEI⁴ CI³	for this reason; thus

爲了	WEI⁴ LE	for the sake of; in order to
爲甚麼	WEI⁴ SHEN² ME	why
爲的是	WEI⁴ DI⁴ SHI	for the sake of
爲人爲己	WEI⁴ REN² WEI⁴ JI³	for others and for ourselves (oneself)
爲難	WEI² NAN²	feel embarrassed; make it hard for (Note: WEI₂)
爲人	WEI² REN²	behave; conduct oneself
爲時過早	WEI² SHI² GUO⁴ ZAO³	premature; too soon
爲人師表	WEI² REN² SHI¹ BIAO³	being a teacher or role model

甚 (M6.3)   SHEN₄   very; what

甚爲	SHEN⁴ WEI²	very (written); (=很 HEN)
甚麼	SHEN² ME	what
甚至	SHEN⁴ ZHI⁴	even ...
甚而	SHEN⁴ ER²	even ... (written)

麼 (M6.3)   ME   (Some dictionaries: MO)
(follows other characters to mean why; how; what)

難 (M6.3)   NAN₂   hard; difficult

	NAN₄	disaster
難看	NAN² KAN⁴	ugly
難懂	NAN² DONG³	hard to comprehend
難得	NAN² DE²	hard to come by
難點	NAN² DIAN³	difficult point
難過	NAN² GUO⁴	have a hard time; feel sorry

難道	NAN² DAO⁴	isn't it; how can
難說	NAN² SHUO¹	hard to say
難爲	NAN² WEI²	embarrassed; make it hard
難以	NAN² YI³	hard to
難上難	NAN² SHANG⁴ NAN²	extremely difficult
難爲情	NAN² WEI² QING²	embarrassed
難以相信	NAN² YI³ XIANG¹ XIN¹	incredible

懂 (M6.3)	DONG³	understand
懂得	DONG³ DE²	understand; know
懂事	DONG³ SHI⁴	sensible

已 (M7.1)	YI³	already (已/己 JI³) (M2.3)
已經	YI³ JING¹	already
已知	YI³ ZHI¹	it is known; given the fact

經 (M7.1)	JING¹	pass through
經常	JING¹ CHANG²	often
經過	JING¹ GUO⁴	pass through; via
經年	JING¹ NIAN²	year round
經手	JING¹ SHOU³	handle; deal with
經辦	JING¹ BAN⁴	handle
經管	JING¹ GUAN³	manage
經理	JING¹ LI³	manage; manager
經得起	JING¹ DE² QI³	can stand (test of time)
經不起	JING¹ BU⁴ QI³	cannot stand (a test,..)

VOCABULARY: 1,800+

過 (M7.1)   GUO₄   pass; over; too

("Verb + 過" specifies past or perfect tense; e.g. 看過 KAN₄ GUO₄ saw, had seen)

過去	GUO₄ QU₄	in the past
過後	GUO₄ HOU₄	after that
過來	GUO₄ LAI₂	towards; come over
過分	GUO₄ FEN₄ (FEN₄, not FEN₁)	too; excessive
過目	GUO₄ MU₄	review (for approval)
過年	GUO₄ NIAN₂	celebrate New Year
過時	GUO₄ SHI₂	obsolete
過手	GUO₄ SHOU₃	change hands (e.g. money)
過重	GUO₄ ZHONG₄	too heavy; excessive weight
過半	GUO₄ BAN₄	more than half
過於	GUO₄ YU₂	too; excessively
過問	GUO₄ WEN₄	concern about; intervene
過錯	GUO₄ CUO₄	fault
過得去	GUO₄ DE QU₄	can get by; passable
過不去	GUO₄ BU₄ QU₄	cannot get through; not getting along
過來人	GUO₄ LAI₂ REN₂	person who had been through the situation
過意不去	GUO₄ YI₄ BU₄ QU₄	feel sorry; apologetic

各 (M7.1)   GE₄   each; every; various

各人	GE₄ REN₂	each one; every one
各地	GE₄ DI₄	different places

各方	GE⁴ FANG¹	different parties/sides
(Note: 各方 = 各方面 GE₄ FANG₁ MIAN₄)		
各自	GE⁴ ZI⁴	each; respective
各半	GE⁴ BAN⁴	half-half; fifty-fifty
各行其是	GE⁴ XING² QI² SHI⁴	each goes his own way
各得其所	GE⁴ DE² QI² SUO³	each has a role to play; each gets what he deserves
各有所好	GE⁴ YOU³ SUO³ HAO⁴	each has his likes and dislikes
(Note: 好 usually is pronounced HAO₃, here it is HAO₄; it is used as a verb here.)		
地 (M7.1)	DI₄	place
地方	DI⁴ FANG¹	place; local
地帶	DI⁴ DAI⁴	area; region; belt
地點	DI⁴ DIAN³	location
地面	DI⁴ MIAN⁴	on the ground
地理	DI⁴ LI³	geography
地表	DI⁴ BIAO³	land surface; earth surface
地道	DI⁴ DAO⁴	tunnel; genuine; typical
地下	DI⁴ XIA⁴	underground
地心	DI⁴ XIN¹	earth core
地少人多	DI⁴ SHAO³ REN² DUO¹	dense population on limited land
心 (M7.2)	XIN₁	heart; mind
心情	XIN¹ QING²	mood
心事	XIN¹ SHI⁴	worry; concern

心理	XĪN LĪ (1,3)	psychology; mentality
心裡	XĪN LĪ (1,3)	in one's mind; in one's heart
心力	XĪN LÌ (1,4)	mental & physical effort; function of the heart
心意	XĪN YÌ (1,4)	regard; kindly feeling
心思	XĪN SĪ (1,1)	thought; idea
心地	XĪN DÌ (1,4)	mind, moral nature
心得	XĪN DÉ (1,2)	learned from experience
心裡話	XĪN LĪ HUÀ (1,3,4)	words from one's heart
心上人	XĪN SHÀNG RÉN (1,4,2)	sweetheart; lover
心目中	XĪN MÙ ZHŌNG (1,4,1)	in one's eyes
心安理得	XĪN ĀN LĪ DÉ (1,1,3,2)	feel at ease and justified
心平氣和	XĪN PÍNG QÌ HÉ (1,2,4,2)	calm; stay calm
完 (M7.2)	WAN₂	intact; whole
完全	WÁN QUÁN (2,2)	completely; entirely
完成	WÁN CHÉNG (2,2)	accomplish; fulfill
完好	WÁN HĀO (2,3)	intact
完了	WÁN LE (2)	finished; it's over
完事	WÁN SHÌ (2,4)	end of the matter
完工	WÁN GŌNG (2,1)	complete (a project)
完人	WÁN RÉN (2,2)	perfect person
完全明白	WÁN QUÁN MÍNG BÁI (2,2,2,2)	fully understand
完全沒錯	WÁN QUÁN MÉI CUÒ (2,2,2,4)	nothing wrong at all

全 (M7.2)	QUAN₂	complete
全家	QUAN₂ JIA₁	whole family
全國	QUAN₂ GUO₂	entire nation
全年	QUAN₂ NIAN₂	whole year
全等	QUAN₂ DENG₂	congruent (triangle)
全面	QUAN₂ MIAN₄	overall
全都	QUAN₂ DOU₁	all without exception
全才	QUAN₂ CAI₂	a versatile person
全能	QUAN₂ NENG₂	all-round
全力	QUAN₂ LI₄	full effort
全文	QUAN₂ WEN₂	full text
全天候	QUAN₂ TIAN₁ HOU₄	all weather
全知全能	QUAN₂ ZHI₁ QUAN₂ NENG₂	omniscient and omnipotent
全心全意	QUAN₂ XIN₁ QUAN₂ YI₄	heart and soul; wholeheartedly
明 (M7.2)	MING₂	bright; understand; clear
明天	MING₂ TIAN₁	tomorrow
明年	MING₂ NIAN₂	next year
明月	MING₂ YUE₄	the bright moon
(Note: next month is 下個月 XIA₄ GE₄ YUE₄ (M2.1))		
明白	MING₂ BAI₂	understand
明明	MING₂ MING₂	obviously; undoubtedly
明文	MING₂ WEN₂	in writing; stipulate
明快	MING₂ KUAI₄	lucid and lively
明知	MING₂ ZHI₄	knowingly
明明白白	MING₂ MING₂ BAI₂ BAI₂	clearly and explicitly

明白無誤	MÍNG BÁI WÚ WÙ	understand clearly with no misunderstanding
白 (M7.2)	BÁI	white
白天	BÁI TIĀN	daytime
白人	BÁI RÉN	white person; Caucasian
白做	BÁI ZUÒ	done in vain
白白	BÁI BÁI	in vain
白字	BÁI ZÌ	wrongly written or mis-spelled word
白話	BÁI HUÀ	vernacular
白話文	BÁI HUÀ WÉN	vernacular writings
白手起家	BÁI SHǑU QǏ JIĀ	build up from nothing; start from scratch
知 (M7.3)	ZHĪ	know
知道	ZHĪ DÀO	know; aware of
知己	ZHĪ JǏ	intimate; intimate friend
知交	ZHĪ JIĀO	intimate friend
知覺	ZHĪ JUÉ	consciousness
知情不報	ZHĪ QÍNG BÙ BÀO	conceal what one knows of a case
知心朋友	ZHĪ XĪN PÉNG YǑU	intimate friend
知人之明	ZHĪ RÉN ZHĪ MÍNG	a keen insight into a person's character
知無不言	ZHĪ WÚ BÙ YÁN	tell everything without reservation
知其一不知其二	ZHĪ QÍ YĪ BÙ ZHĪ QÍ ÈR	know only one side of a story

知其然不知其所以然   ZHI¹ QI² RAN² BU⁴ ZHI¹ QI² SUO³ YI³ RAN²
know something but can't explain further

知人知面不知心   ZHI¹ REN² ZHI¹ MIAN⁴ BU⁴ ZHI¹ XIN¹
know a person's face but not his heart

道 (M7.3)	DAO⁴	road; way; say
道理	DAO⁴ LI³	principle; theory; truth
道路	DAO⁴ LU⁴	road; path
道謝	DAO⁴ XIE⁴	express thanks
道家	DAO⁴ JIA¹	Taoist School; a school of philosophy prevailed in China 770-221 B.C.

或 (M7.3)	HUO⁴	or
或者	HUO⁴ ZHE³	perhaps; maybe; or
或然	HUO⁴ RAN²	probable
或左或右	HUO⁴ ZUO³ HUO⁴ YOU⁴	either left or right

者 (M7.3)   ZHE3

(Used like a pronoun after an adjective, adverb, auxiliary verb or verb to mean the described person or thing or the doer. e.g. 學者 XUE2 ZHE3 scholar.)

對 (M7.3)	DUI⁴	correct; as to
對面	DUI⁴ MIAN⁴	opposite side; the other side across
對白	DUI⁴ BAI²	dialogue (e.g. opera)
對話	DUI⁴ HUA⁴	dialogue (e.g. between countries)
對半	DUI⁴ BAN⁴	half-half; fifty fifty

對比	DUI⁴ BI³	contrast; compare
對應	DUI⁴ YING⁴	correspond to
對等	DUI⁴ DENG³	reciprocal; equal
對方	DUI⁴ FANG¹	the counter party
對開	DUI⁴ KAI¹	divide into two halves; two routes to and from
對路	DUI⁴ LU⁴	on the right track
對手	DUI⁴ SHOU³	rival; opponent
對內	DUI⁴ NEI⁴	internally
對外	DUI⁴ WAI⁴	externally
對了	DUI⁴ LE	exactly; that's correct
對於	DUI⁴ YU²	to; as to
對得起	DUI⁴ DE QI³	fair enough
對不起	DUI⁴ BU⁴ QI³	sorry; excuse; pardon
對人對己	DUI⁴ REN² DUI⁴ JI³	to others and to oneself
對事不對人	DUI⁴ SHI⁴ BU⁴ DUI⁴ REN²	against the matter but not the person
每 (M8.1)	MEI₃	each; every
每次	MEI³ CI⁴	each time
每當	MEI³ DANG¹	whenever; every time
每每	MEI³ MEI³	often times
每天/月/年	MEI³ TIAN¹/YUE⁴/NIAN²	every day/month/year
次 (M8.1)	CI₄	time; order
次要	CI⁴ YAO⁴	secondary

次日	CI⁴ RI⁴	the next day
次等	CI⁴ DENG³	second class; lower grade
次子	CI⁴ ZI³	second son
前 (M8.1)	QIAN₂	front; before
前年	QIAN² NIAN²	the year before last
前天	QIAN² TIAN¹	day before yesterday
前一個月	QIAN² YI¹ GE⁴ YUE⁴	the month before last
(NOTE: Or 前個月, but not 前月)		
前人	QIAN² REN²	predecessor; forefathers
前途	QIAN² TU²	future; prospect
前提	QIAN² TI²	prerequisite; presupposition
前信	QIAN² XIN⁴	previous letter
前言	QIAN² YAN²	preface; introduction
前面	QIAN² MIAN⁴	the front; ahead
前者	QIAN² ZHE³	the former
前方	QIAN² FANG¹	ahead; the front
前後	QIAN² HOU⁴	altogether; around (time frame)
前前後後	QIAN² QIAN² HOU⁴ HOU⁴	altogether (within a period of time)
前所未有	QIAN² SUO³ WEI⁴ YOU³	unprecedented
前言後語	QIAN² YAN² HOU⁴ YU³	the entire context (of what one says)

(cf. 上下文 SHANG⁴ XIA⁴ WEN₂ context (in writing))

面 (M8.1)	MIAN₄	face; side
面對	MIAN⁴ DUI⁴	face; facing
面前	MIAN⁴ QIAN²	in front of
面商	MIAN⁴ SHANG¹	negotiate face to face
面向	MIAN⁴ XIANG⁴	facing
面談	MIAN⁴ TAN²	speak face to face; interview
面謝	MIAN⁴ XIE⁴	express thanks in person
面子	MIAN⁴ ZI	face; reputation
面目	MIAN⁴ MU⁴	face; features; look
面目全非	MIAN⁴ MU⁴ QUAN² FEI¹	changed or distorted beyond recognition
快 (M8.1)	KUAI₄	fast; quick
快快	KUAI⁴ KUAI⁴	hurry up
快慢	KUAI⁴ MAN⁴	speed (casual use)
快報	KUAI⁴ BAO⁴	bulletin
快件	KUAI⁴ JIAN⁴	express delivery
快信	KUAI⁴ XIN⁴	express mail
快活	KUAI⁴ HUO²	happy; cheerful
快樂	KUAI⁴ LE⁴	happy; joyful
快意	KUAI⁴ YI⁴	pleased
快走	KUAI⁴ ZOU³	hurry up; go faster
快中子	KUAI⁴ ZHONG¹ ZI³	high speed neutron
快慢由己	KUAI⁴ MAN⁴ YOU² JI³	at ones own pace

(Literally: Fast or slow, one decides for oneself.)

後 (M8.2)	HOU₄		behind; later; latter
後天	HOU₄ TIAN₁		day after tomorrow
後年	HOU₄ NIAN₁		year after next
後人	HOU₄ REN₂		future generations
後來	HOU₄ LAI₂		afterwards; thereafter
後面	HOU₄ MIAN₄		rear
後邊	HOU₄ BIAN₁		rear
後半	HOU₄ BAN₄		the rear half
後者	HOU₄ ZHE₃		the latter
後方	HOU₄ FANG₁		rear (of a battlefield)
後事	HOU₄ SHI₄		what happen next; funeral matter
後話	HOU₄ HUA₄		to be stated later
後生	HOU₄ SHENG₁		youngster
後記	HOU₄ JI₄		postscript
後進	HOU₄ JIN₄		lagging behind
後路	HOU₄ LU₄		route for retreat; fall back
後半生	HOU₄ BAN₄ SHENG₁		second half of life
半 (M8.2)	BAN₄		half
半天	BAN₄ TIAN₁		half day
半年	BAN₄ NIAN₂		half a year; 6 months
半個月	BAN₄ GE₄ YUE₄		half a month; fortnight
半邊	BAN₄ BIAN₄		half; one side
半公開	BAN₄ GONG₁ KAI₁		semi-overt

VOCABULARY: 1,800+

| 半路出家 | BÀN LÙ CHŪ JIĀ | change to a profession not trained for; change to a line of business not experienced in |

放 (M8.2)	FANG4	put; release
放假	FÀNG JIÀ	holiday; vacation
放心	FÀNG XĪN	at ease; rest assured
放大	FÀNG DÀ	enlarge; magnify
放出	FÀNG CHŪ	release
放在	FÀNG ZÀI	put at
放到	FÀNG DÀO	put onto
放人	FÀNG RÉN	release a person
放開	FÀNG KĀI	set free; release
放過	FÀNG GUÒ	let go
放手	FÀNG SHǑU	let go
放行	FÀNG XÍNG	let pass; release
放下	FÀNG XIÀ	put down
放工	FÀNG GŌNG	off work
放學	FÀNG XUÉ	off school
放光	FÀNG GUĀNG	illuminate
放電	FÀNG DIÀN	discharge (electricity)

慢 (M8.2)	MAN4	slow
慢慢來	MÀN MÀN LÁI	take it easy; take your time
慢走	MÀN ZǑU	wait a minute; good-bye
慢點	MÀN DIǍN	wait a minute; slow down

點 (M8.2)	DIAN₃	little bit; o' clock; pick
點心	DIAN₃ XIN₁	refreshments

(Note: It is often known as Dim Sum at Chinese restaurants in the U.S. DIM₂ SUM₁ is actually the sound of the two characters in Cantonese.)

點交	DIAN₃ JIAO₁	hand over item by item
原 (M8.3)	YUAN₂	original; former
原來	YUAN₂ LAI₂	originally; former
原告	YUAN₂ GAO₄	plaintiff
原文	YUAN₂ WEN₂	the original text; the original
原件	YUAN₂ JIAN₄	the original of a document
原意	YUAN₂ YI₄	original idea
原因	YUAN₂ YIN₁	reason; cause
原由	YUAN₂ YOU₂	cause; regarding
原先	YUAN₂ XIAN₁	former; originally
原作	YUAN₂ ZUO₄	original work; original
原理	YUAN₂ LI₂	principle; theory
原則	YUAN₂ ZE₂	principle; policy
原子	YUAN₂ ZI₃	atom
原來如此	YUAN₂ LAI₂ RU₂ CI₃	So, that's what it is! Oh, I see.
因 (M8.3)	YIN₁	because
因爲	YIN₁ WEI₄	because
因此	YIN₁ CI₃	therefore
因而	YIN₁ ER₂	as a result

因由	YIN¹ YOU²	reason; cause
因子	YIN¹ ZI³	factor

太 (M8.3)	TAI₄	too; excessive
太平	TAI⁴ PING²	peace and tranquility
太平間	TAI⁴ PING² JIAN¹	mortuary
太子	TAI⁴ ZI³	Crown Prince
太過分了。	TAI⁴ GUO⁴ FEN⁴ LE.	It has gone too far. (e.g. a wrongdoing)
太不成樣子了。	TAI⁴ BU⁴ CHENG² YANG⁴ ZI³ LE.	It is simply outrageous.

方 (M8.3)	FANG₁	square; direction; place
方面	FANG¹ MIAN⁴	aspect
方便	FANG¹ BIAN⁴	convenient
方法	FANG¹ FA³	method; way
方向	FANG¹ XIANG⁴	direction
方言	FANG¹ YAN²	dialect
方才	FANG¹ CAI²	just now; a while ago

便 (M8.3)	BIAN₄	convenient; handy
便於	BIAN⁴ YU²	easy to
便利	BIAN⁴ LI⁴	convenient for
便當	BIAN⁴ DANG⁴	convenient
(便當 =方便 FANG₁ BIAN₄) (M8.3)		
(便當 take-out lunch -- Taiwan usage)		
便道	BIAN⁴ DAO⁴	makeshift road

VOCABULARY: 1,800+

想 (M9.1)	XIANG₃	think
想想	XIANG₃ XIANG₃	think about it
想到	XIANG₃ DAO₄	think about
想不到	XIANG₃ BU₄ DAO₄	unexpected
想起	XIANG₃ QI₃	recall
想不起	XIANG₃ BU₄ QI₃	don't recall
想通	XIANG₃ TONG₁	straighten up one's thinking; being convinced
想不通	XIANG₃ BU₄ TONG₁	take a matter to heart
想不開	XIANG₃ BU₄ KAI₁	take things too hard
想法	XIANG₃ FA₃	thought; idea; opinion
想來	XIANG₃ LAI₂	presumably
想必	XIANG₃ BI₄	most likely
想家	XIANG₃ JIA₁	homesick
想當年	XIANG₃ DANG₁ NIAN₂	recall those years; during those days
想當然	XIANG₃ DANG₁ RAN₂	assume as a matter of course
想入非非	XIANG₃ RU₄ FEI₁ FEI₁	think wild; fantasy

起 (M9.1)	QI₃	up
起來	QI₃ LAI₂	get up

(Note: In *'Verb + 起來'*, 起來 becomes an adverb:
    看起來 KAN₄ QI₃ LAI₂: it looks; (看起來=看來)
    說起來 SHUO₁ QI₃ LAI₂: speaking about this
    問起來 WEN₄ QI₃ LAI₂: when asked
    做起來 ZUO₄ QI₃ LAI₂: doing it.)

起點	QI³ DIAN³	starting point
起先	QI³ XIAN¹	at first
起初	QI³ CHU¹	at first
起步	QI³ BU⁴	get started; get going
起行	QI³ XING²	start on a journey
起立	QI³ LI⁴	stand up
起家	QI³ JIA¹	grow and thrive
幾 (M9.1)	JI₃	several; how many
幾時	JI³ SHI²	when?

(幾時 = 甚麼時候 SHEN4 ME SHI2 HOU4)

(幾時 tends to be Cantonese or written form; 甚麼時候 is typical Mandarin.)

幾個	JI³ GE⁴	several; how many?
幾天	JI³ TIAN¹	several days; how many days? (added)
幾多	JI³ DUO¹	many; how many?

(NOTE: More often used in Cantonese expression; typical Mandarin is: 多少 DUO₁ SHAO₃?)

件 (M9.1)	JIAN₄	piece (of document, mail, clothing, ...)
事 (M9.1)	SHI₄	matter; affair
事件	SHI⁴ JIAN⁴	incident; event
事情	SHI⁴ QING⁴	matter; business; thing
事由	SHI⁴ YOU²	reference to

(In business letter topic, 事由: = Re:)

事先	SHI⁴ XIAN¹	in advance; prior to

事前	SHI⁴ QIAN²	before the incident; in advance; prior to
事後	SHI⁴ HOU⁴	after the incident/fact
事出有因	SHI⁴ CHU⁴ YOU³ YIN¹	it is by no means accidental
事在人爲	SHI⁴ ZAI⁴ REN² WEI²	it all depends on human effort

覺 (M9.2)	JUE²	sense; feel
覺得	JUE² DE²	feel

得 (M9.2)	DE₂	get; obtain
得出	DE² CHU¹	reach (a conclusion, result, ...)
得到	DE² DAO⁴	get; obtain
得以	DE² YI³	so that it is possible
得力	DE² LI²	helpful; effective
得意	DE² YI⁴	proud of oneself; pleased with oneself
得當	DE² DANG⁴	appropriate
得便	DE² BIAN⁴	at one's convenience
得分	DE² FEN¹	score
得法	DE² FA³	in the proper way; correctly
得手	DE² SHOU³	come off; succeed
得失相當	DE² SHI¹ XIANG¹ DANG¹	gain some and lose some; gain and loss even
得過且過	DE² GUO⁴ QIE³ GUO⁴	drift along
得心應手	DE² XIN¹ YING⁴ SHOU³	everything goes smooth; golden touch

VOCABULARY: 1,800+

可 (M9.2)	KE₃	may; can
可以	KE³ YI³	may; can; possible
可怕	KE³ PA⁴	terrible
可見	KE³ JIAN⁴	thus
可靠	KE³ KAO⁴	dependable
可能	KE³ NENG²	possible; maybe
可是	KE³ SHI⁴	however
可喜	KE³ XI³	gratifying
可可	KE³ KE³	cocoa
可行	KE³ XING²	feasible
可不行	KE³ BU⁴ XING²	no, can't do that
可有可無	KE³ YOU³ KE³ WU²	not indispensable
可大可小	KE³ DA⁴ KE³ XIAO³	It could be trivial or essential
可方便了	KE³ FANG¹ BIAN⁴ LE	it is so convenient
可不是嗎	KE³ BU⁴ SHI⁴ MA	Isn't that the case? Isn't that right?
以 (M9.2)	YI₃	use; take; with
以前	YI³ QIAN²	in the past
以後	YI³ HOU⁴	in future; from now on
以上	YI³ SHANG⁴	over; above; more than
以下	YI³ XIA⁴	under; less than; below
以內	YI³ NEI⁴	within; less than
以外	YI³ WAI⁴	beyond; more than
以來	YI³ LAI²	since

VOCABULARY: 1,800+

以求	YI³ QIU²	in order to
以爲	YI³ WEI²	think; consider
以...爲...	YI...WEI...	use...as...
以至	YI³ ZHI⁴	up to; down to; so much so that
以資	YI³ ZI¹	as a means of
以太	YI³ TAI⁴	ether
以一當十	YI³ YI¹ DANG⁴ SHI²	pit one against ten
以點帶面	YI³ DIAN³ DAI⁴ MIAN⁴	fan out from point to area

| 搞 (M9.2) | GAO₃ | do; carry out |
| 搞好 | GAO³ HAO³ | do a good job |

討 (M9.3)	TAO₃	demand; ask
討還	TAO³ HUAN²	demand return (of something loaned)
討論	TAO³ LUN⁴	discuss
討好	TAO³ HAO³	toady to

論 (M9.3)	LUN₄	discuss
論文	LUN⁴ WEN⁴	thesis; essay
論點	LUN⁴ DIAN³	point of debate or argument

| 給 (M9.3) | GEI₃ | give; being |

提 (M9.3)	TI₂	carry; lift; mention; propose
提出	TI² CHU¹	put forward; propose
提交	TI² JIAO¹	submit; turn in
提請	TI² QING³	draw the attention of
提問	TI² WEN⁴	raise questions; interrogate
提過	TI² GUO⁴	mentioned

(NOTE: 'verb + 過' --> verb past/perfect tens)

提到	TI² DAO⁴	mention
提起	TI² QI³	mention; lift
提成	TI² CHENG²	reserve (deduct) a portion from
提法	TI² FA³	wording; verbiage
提要	TI² YAO⁴	precis; synopsis
提前完成	TI² QIAN² WAN² CHENG²	complete ahead of schedule
提早放學	TI² ZAO³ FANG⁴ XUE²	school day ends ahead of schedule
提出問題	TI² CHU¹ WEN⁴ TI²	raise questions
到 (M9.3)	DAO₄	arrive; reach
到點	DAO⁴ DIAN³	time is up
到時	DAO⁴ SHI²	by that time
(到時=到時候	DAO₄ SHI₂ HOU₄)	
到家	DAO⁴ JIA¹	excellent skill
到來	DAO⁴ LAI²	arrival
到會	DAO⁴ HUI⁴	arriving at a meeting

到手	DAO⁴ SHOU³	in hand; in possession
五 (M10.1)	WU₃	five
五月	WU³ YUE⁴	May (the month of May)
六 (M10.1)	LIU₄	six
六月	LIU⁴ YUE⁴	June
六六六	LIU⁴ LIU⁴ LIU⁴	BHC (benzene hexachlor-ide) (a pesticide)
個 (M10.1)	GE₄	(unit)
個個	GE⁴ GE⁴	everyone; each
個人	GE⁴ REN²	individual; myself
個別	GE⁴ BIE²	isolated; individual
個子	GE⁴ ZI²	body build
項 (M10.1)	XIANG₄	item
項目	XIANG⁴ MU⁴	project; item
目 (M10.1)	MU₄	eye; target
目的	MU⁴ DI⁴	purpose; aim
目光	MU⁴ GUANG¹	vision
目前	MU⁴ QIAN⁴	at present; currently
目力	MU⁴ LI⁴	sight; view
目次	MU⁴ CI⁴	table of contents

目的地	MU⁴ DI⁴ DI⁴	destination
目中無人	MU⁴ ZHONG¹ WU² REN²	assuming oneself being above everyone else; supercilious
共 (M10.2)	GONG₄	total; common
共同	GONG⁴ TONG²	joint effort; common
共事	GONG⁴ SHI⁴	as co-workers
共生	GONG⁴ SHENG¹	intergrowth; symbiosis
共和	GONG⁴ HE²	republic
共和國	GONG⁴ HE² GUO²	republic (nation)
共同語言	GONG⁴ TONG² YU³ YAN²	common language
共同完成	GONG⁴ TONG² WAN² CHENG²	work together and complete it
七 (M10.2)	QI₁	seven
七月	QI¹ YUE⁴	July
七情	QI¹ QING²	the seven human emotions (joy, anger, sorrow, fear, love, hate and desire)
七十二行	QI¹ SHI² ER⁴ HANG²	all conceivable walks of life (Literally: 72 walks of life)
百 (M10.2)	BAI₃	hundred; numerous
百分比	BAI³ FEN³ BI³	percentage; percent
百年之後	BAI³ NIAN² ZHI¹ HOU⁴	after one passes away (Literally: one hundred years later)

萬 (M10.2)	WAN₄	ten thousand; numerous
萬萬	WAN₄ WAN₄	never ever; one hundred million
萬一	WAN₄ YI₁	in case; just in case
萬年	WAN₄ NIAN₄	ten thousand years; forever; eternity
萬難	WAN₄ NAN₂	extremely difficult
萬能	WAN₄ NENG₂	universal
萬萬不可	WAN₄ WAN₄ BU₄ KE₃	never ever (caution)
萬事如意	WAN₄ SHI₄ RU₂ YI₄	everything smooth and successful (wish)
元 (M10.2)	YUAN₂	dollar; unit; first; primary
元月	YUAN₂ YUE₄	January
(元月 = 一月	YI₁ YUE₄)	
元音	YUAN₂ YIN₁	vowel
元年	YUAN₂ NIAN₂	first year of an era; first year of the reign of an emperor or regime
元氣	YUAN₂ QI₄	vitality (of health, strength)
元老	YUAN₂ LAO₃	senior/ranking member
元	YUAN₂	dollar (monetary unit)
投 (M10.3)	TOU₂	throw; put in
投資	TOU₂ ZI₁	invest; investment
投放	TOU₂ FANG₄	put in

投入	TOU² RU⁴	put in
投下	TOU² XIA⁴	put in; throw down
投靠	TOU² KAO⁴	go and seek refuge
投合	TOU² HE²	cater to somebody's desire
資 (M10.3)	ZI₁	capital; money
資方	ZI¹ FANG¹	capital provider
資力	ZI¹ LI⁴	financial strength
資助	ZI¹ ZHU⁴	financial aid; subsidize
八 (M10.3)	BA₁	eight
八月	BA¹ YUE⁴	August
八成	BA¹ CHENG²	eighty percent
八開	BA¹ KAI¹	octavo; 8vo (paper)
八方	BA¹ FANG¹	the eight points of the compass; all directions
九 (M10.3)	JIU₃	nine
九月	JIU³ YUE⁴	September
千 (M10.3)	QIAN₁	thousand
千萬	QIAN¹ WAN⁴	ten million; millions upon millions
千言萬語	QIAN¹ YAN² WAN⁴ YU³	thousands and thousands of words
千萬小心	QIAN¹ WAN⁴ XIAO³ XIN¹	do be careful

只 (M11.1)	ZHI₃	only
只是	ZHI³ SHI⁴	merely; only
只有	ZHI³ YOU³	only; alone
只要	ZHI³ YAO⁴	as long as; provided that
只得	ZHI³ DE²	obligated to
只好	ZHI³ HAO³	no choice but to
只等	ZHI³ DENG³	only waiting for
只不過	ZHI³ BU⁴ GUO⁴	nothing more than; only
四 (M11.1)	SI₄	four
四成	SI⁴ CHENG²	forty percent
四月	SI⁴ YUE⁴	April
四方	SI⁴ FANG¹	square; four directions
四面	SI⁴ MIAN⁴	four sides
四邊	SI⁴ BIAN¹	four sides (edges)
四起	SI⁴ QI³	from all directions
四出	SI⁴ CHU¹	in all directions
四面八方	SI⁴ MIAN⁴ BA¹ FANG¹	all directions
	(Literally: 4 sides and 8 directions.)	
成 (M11.1)	CHENG₂	accomplish; succeed; one tenth / 10%
成功	CHENG² GONG¹	succeed; success
成績	CHENG² JI¹	accomplishment; results
成家	CHENG² JIA¹	get married (and form a family)

成人	CHÉNG RÉN (2,2)	adult
成見	CHÉNG JIÀN (2,4)	prejudice
成天	CHÉNG TIAN (2,1)	all day long
成交	CHÉNG JIAO (2,1)	transaction; close a deal
成功在即	CHÉNG GONG ZAI JI (2,1,4,2)	Success is in sight. (Success is around the corner.)

把 (M11.1)	BA₃	hold; grasp; handle
把手	BA SHOU (3,3)	knob; person in charge
把握	BA WO (3,4)	grasp; certainty

握 (M11.1)	WO₄	hold; grasp
握手	WO SHOU (4,3)	shake hands; handshake
握別	WO BIE (4,2)	shake hands and part
握力	WO LI (4,4)	grip

分 (M11.2)	FEN₁	separate; score
分開	FEN KAI (1,1)	separate; divide
分別	FEN BIE (1,2)	differentiate; respectively
分明	FEN MING (1,2)	clearly; sharply demarcated
分家	FEN JIA (1,1)	break up the family and live apart
分作	FEN ZUO (1,4)	divide into
分成	FEN CHENG (1,2)	divide into
分等	FEN DENG (1,3)	grade; grading

分管	FEN¹ GUAN³	be put in charge of
分行	FEN¹ HANG²	branch office (of a bank, company)
分會	FEN¹ HUI⁴	chapter of an association
分力	FEN¹ LI⁴	component (of force)
分手	FEN¹ SHOU³	part company; say goodbye
分心	FEN¹ XIN¹	distract one's attention; divert
分項	FEN¹ XIANG⁴	sub-category
分相	FEN¹ XIANG⁴	split phase (electrical)
分工合作	FEN¹ GONG¹ HE² ZUO⁴	share the work and cooperate
分路前進	FEN¹ LU⁴ QIAN² JIN⁴	advance along separate routes

別 (M11.2)	BIE₂	part; other; differentiate
別人	BIE² REN²	other people

(別 is used as an adjective here.)

別字	BIE² ZI⁴	wrongly written or misspelled character

(NOTE: 別字 = 白字 BAI₂ ZI₄ (M7.2))

別說	BIE² SHUO¹	not to say; not to mention

(NOTE: "別+Verb" == '不要 + Verb' == 'don't + verb')

別看	BIE² KAN⁴	don't think
別忙	BIE² MANG²	wait a minute; don't hurry
別有用心	BIE² YOU³ YONG⁴ XIN¹	have an axe to grind; with ulterior motives

別開生面	BIÉ KĀI SHĒNG MIÀN	entirely new (and somewhat surprising)
別有天地	BIÉ YǑU TIĀN DÌ	a place with unique beauty or feature

記 (M11.2)	JÌ	remember; record
記得	JÌ DE	remember; be sure to
記分	JÌ FĒN	record the score
記工	JÌ GŌNG	record work point; time-card record
記功	JÌ GŌNG	record a merit
記過	JÌ GUÒ	record a demerit
記事	JÌ SHÌ	record events
記者	JÌ ZHĚ	reporter

辦 (M11.2)	BÀN	do; handle; establish
辦法	BÀN FǍ	way; means; measure
辦到	BÀN DÀO	accomplish; get it done
辦理	BÀN LǏ	handle; conduct (verb)
辦公	BÀN GŌNG	handle office tasks; office work
辦報	BÀN BÀO	run a newspaper business
辦學	BÀN XUÉ	run a school; manage education

法 (M11.2)	FǍ	law; standard
法國	FǍ GUÓ	France

法國人	FA³ GUO² REN²	French (people)
法文	FA³ WEN²	French (language)
法語	FA³ YU³	French (language)
法人	FA³ REN²	legal person
法學	FA³ XUE²	the science of law
法辦	FA³ BAN⁴	bring to justice; punish by law
法子	FA³ ZI	way; method (oral)

(NOTE: 法子 = 辦法 BAN₄ FA₃)

應 (M11.3)	YING₁	should; respond
應該	YING¹ GAI¹	should; ought to
應當	YING¹ DANG¹	should; ought to
應得	YING¹ DE²	deserve
應有	YING¹ YOU³	deserve; proper
應分	YING¹ FEN⁴	obliged; within duties

該 (M11.3)	GAI₁	should; ought to
該有多好！	GAI¹ YOU³ DUO¹ HAO³!	How nice if only …
該還就還	GAI¹ HUAN² JIU⁴ HUAN²	return whatever ought to be returned

該…(verb)就…(verb): e.g.該說/做/寫就說/做/寫

| 合 (M11.3) | HE₂ | combine; close |
| 合作 | HE² ZUO⁴ | cooperate; cooperation |

合理	HÉ LǏ	rational; reasonable
合同	HÉ TÓNG	contract
合約	HÉ YUĒ	contract (Southern usage)
合力	HÉ LÌ	pool effort; joint force
合法	HÉ FǍ	legal; lawful
合心意	HÉ XĪN YÌ	to one's satisfaction
合情合理	HÉ QÍNG HÉ LǏ	fair and reasonable; fair and sensible
合資公司	HÉ ZĪ GŌNG SĪ	joint venture company
商 (M11.3)	SHĀNG₁	discuss; commerce; business
商量	SHĀNG LIÁNG	discuss; negotiate
商人	SHĀNG RÉN	merchant; businessman
商定	SHĀNG DÌNG	decide through consultation
	(Note: 商定 = 商量決定 SHĀNG₁ LIÁNG₂ JUÉ₂ DÌNG₄)	
商行	SHĀNG HÁNG	business firm; trading company
商情	SHĀNG QÍNG	market information; market move
商會	SHĀNG HUÌ	trade association
量 (M11.3)	LIÁNG₂	measure
	LIÀNG₄	quantity; capacity
量地	LIÁNG DÌ	measure land
量入而出	LIÀNG RÙ ÉR CHŪ	spend within income limit

(Or: 量入爲出 LIANG4 RU4 WEI2 CHU1)		live within one's means)
量力而爲	LIANG4 LI4 ER2 WEI2	act within one's capability
(Or: 量力而行 LIANG4 LI4 ER2 XING2)		
兩 (M12.1)	LIANG3	couple; both; two
兩天	LIANG3 TIAN1	two days
兩年	LIANG3 NIAN2	two years (not 兩個年)
兩個月	LIANG3 GE4 YUE4	two months (not 兩月)
兩人	LIANG3 REN2	two persons (兩個人 OK)
兩全其美	LIANG3 QUAN2 QI2 MEI3	satisfy both sides
朋 (M12.1)	PENG2	friend
朋友	PENG2 YOU3	friend
友 (M12.1)	YOU3	friend
友人	YOU3 REN2	friend
友情	YOU3 QING2	friendly sentiments; friendship
友好	YOU3 HAO3	friendly
之 (M12.1)	ZHI1	of
之前	ZHI1 QIAN2	before; prior to
之後	ZHI1 HOU4	after; after that; afterwards
之間	ZHI1 JIAN1	between; among
之所以	ZHI1 SUO3 YI3	the reason why

間 (M12.1)	JIAN₁	between; among (e.g. 之間 ZHI₁ JIAN₁ (MI2.1))
	JIAN₄	opening; space in between
間或	JIAN₄ HUO₄	occasionally
間開	JIAN₄ KAI₄	alternate; separate
談 (M12.2)	TAN₂	talk
談話	TAN₂ HUA₄	conversation
談天	TAN₂ TIAN₁	hat
談心	TAN₂ XIN₂	heart-to-heart talk
談到	TAN₂ DAO₄	mention in conversation
談不上	TAN₂ BU₄ SHANG₄	out of the question
談天說地	TAN₂ TIAN₁ SHUO₁ DI₄	open end chatting
話 (M12.2)	HUA₄	words; talk
話題	HUA₄ TI₂	subject of conversation
話別	HUA₄ BIE₄	say parting words and good-bye
話中有話	HUA₄ ZHONG₁ YOU₃ HUA₄	words said contain second meaning
題 (M12.2)	TI₂	topic; subject
題目	TI₂ MU₄	topic; subject
題外	TI₂ WAI₄	away from the topic
題字	TI₂ ZI₄	inscription; autograph

也 (M12.2)	YE₃	also; as well; too
也好	YE₃ HAO₃	might as well; it may not be a bad idea
也就完了	YE₃ JIU₄ WAN₂ LE	and everything is over
廣 (M12.2)	GUANG₃	broad; wide; extensive
廣大	GUANG₃ DA₄	vast; extensive
廣告	GUANG₃ GAO₄	advertisement; commercial
廣東	GUANG₃ DONG₁	Guangdong (a province in southern China)
廣西	GUANG₃ XI₁	Guangxi (an autonomous region (equivalent to a province) west of Guangdong Province)
廣而言之	GUANG₃ ER₂ YAN₂ ZHI₁	in a general sense
廣開言路	GUANG₃ KAI₁ YAN₂ LU₄	encourage free airing of views
廣開才路	GUANG₃ KAI₁ CAI₂ LU₄	open all avenues for talented people
當 (M12.3)	DANG₁	when; equal
	DANG₄	assume; treat as
當然	DANG₁ RAN₂	certainly; as it should be
當時	DANG₁ SHI₂	at that time; then
當天	DANG₁ TIAN₁	the same day
當年	DANG₁ NIAN₂	in those days; in the past years
當今	DANG₁ JIN₁	nowadays; at present

當面	DĀNG MIÀN (1,4)	in person; face to face
當即	DĀNG JÍ (1,2)	at once; right away
當初	DĀNG CHŪ (1,1)	originally; in the first place
當前	DĀNG QIÁN (1,2)	present; now; facing
當中	DĀNG ZHŌNG (1,1)	among; in the middle
當家	DĀNG JIĀ (1,1)	household management
當事人	DĀNG SHÌ RÉN (1,4,2)	the person or party directly involved
當真	DÀNG ZHĒN (4,1)	take it seriously; really
當作	DÀNG ZUÒ (4,4)	treat as; assume

然 (M12.3)	RAN2	correct; but
然後	RÁN HÒU (2,4)	afterwards; and then
然而	RÁN ÉR (2,2)	yet; however
然則	RÁN ZÉ (2,2)	then; in that case (written)

高 (M12.3)	GAO1	tall; high
高興	GĀO XÌNG (XING4) (1,4)	glad; happy; cheerful
高大	GĀO DÀ (1,4)	tall and big
高等	GĀO DĚNG (1,3)	higher (e.g. education)
高明	GĀO MÍNG (1,2)	brilliant; wise
高地	GĀO DÌ (1,4)	highland; elevation
高原	GĀO YUÁN (1,2)	plateau
高手	GĀO SHǑU (1,3)	master-hand; ace
高才生	GĀO CÁI SHĒNG (1,2,1)	outstanding student

高高在上	GAO¹ GAO¹ ZAI⁴ SHANG⁴	assume oneself high above others
高人一等	GAO¹ REN² YI¹ DENG³	a cut above other people
高大無比	GAO¹ DA⁴ WU² BI³	extremely tall and huge
興 (M12.3)	XING₁	prosper; rise; popular
興辦	XING¹ BAN⁴	initiate; set up
興起	XING¹ QI³	spring up; getting popular
講 (M12.3)	JIANG₃	talk; speak; say
講話	JIANG³ HUA⁴	speech; presentation
講明	JIANG³ MING²	state explicitly
講理	JIANG³ LI³	reason with somebody
講學	JIANG³ XUE²	lecture
講習	JIANG³ XI²	lecture and study (such as a seminar)
由 (M13.1)	YOU₂	from; cause
由於	YOU² YU²	since; as a result of
由不得	YOU² BU DE	beyond the control of
由此可見	YOU² CI³ KE³ JIAN⁴	thus it can be seen; that proves
於 (M13.1)	YU₂	at
於是	YU² SHI⁴	then; as a result

決 (M13.1)	JUE₂	decide; determine
決定	JUE² DING⁴	decide; decision
決心	JUE² XIN¹	determined; resolution
決然	JUE² RAN²	definitely; decisively
定 (M13.1)	DING₄	calm; stable; fixed
定理	DING⁴ LI³	theorem
定論	DING⁴ LUN⁴	final conclusion
定量	DING⁴ LIANG⁴	ration; fixed quantity
定向	DING⁴ XIANG⁴	directional
定做	DING⁴ ZUO⁴	custom order
定了	DING⁴ LE	decision made already
遲 (M13.1)	CHI₂	late; slow
遲到	CHI² DAO⁴	being late
遲誤	CHI² WU⁴	delay
遲慢	CHI² MAN⁴	slowly; tardy
遲早	CHI² ZAO³	sooner or later
需 (M13.2)	XU₁	need; require
需要	XU¹ YAO⁴	need; require
需求	XU¹ QIU²	demand; require
立 (M13.2)	LI₄	stand; set
立即	LI⁴ JI²	immediate; immediately

VOCABULARY: 1,800+

立時	LI⁴ SHI²	immediately; instantly
立功	LI⁴ GONG¹	render meritorious service
立方	LI⁴ FANG¹	cubic; cube
即 (M13.2)	JI²	reach; that is
即日	JI² RI⁴	the very day
即時	JI² SHI²	immediately; instantly
即便	JI² BIAN⁴	even if; even
即使	JI² SHI³	even; even if
幫 (M13.2)	BANG¹	help; assist
幫助	BANG¹ ZHU⁴	help; assist (formal)
幫忙	BANG¹ MANG²	help; assist (casual)
幫手	BANG¹ SHOU³	help; assist (casual)
幫工	BANG¹ GONG¹	helper
幫辦	BANG¹ BAN⁴	assist in management
助 (M13.2)	ZHU⁴	help; assist
助手	ZHU⁴ SHOU³	assistant; aid
助理	ZHU⁴ LI³	aid; deputy
助人爲樂	ZHU⁴ REN² WEI² LE⁴	pleasure to help others; enjoy helping others
靠 (M13.3)	KAO⁴	depend on; lean against
靠邊	KAO⁴ BIAN¹	keep to the side

靠手	KAO⁴ SHOU³	armrest
靠人	KAO⁴ REN²	depend on other people
(靠人=靠別人 KAO4 BIE2 REN2)		
及 (M13.3)	JI2	and; reach
及時	JI² SHI²	on time; timely
及早	JI² ZAO³	early on; before it is too late
及至	JI² ZHI⁴	up to; until
及時報告	JI² SHI² BAO⁴ GAO⁴	report on a timely basis
時 (M13.3)	SHI2	time
時間	SHI² JIAN¹	time; o'clock
時候	SHI² HOU⁴	time; at a point in time
時事	SHI² SHI⁴	news; current affairs
時時	SHI² SHI²	often; frequent
時常	SHI² CHANG²	often; frequent
(時時=時常=常常 (M5.1)=經常 (M7.1))		
(時時、時常 more often used in Cantonese)		
時工	SHI² GONG¹	hourly worker/work
時至今日	SHI² ZHI⁴ JIN¹ RI⁴	as of today; until now
管 (M13.3)	GUAN3	control; pipe; tube
管理	GUAN³ LI³	manage; management

管人事	GUAN³ REN² SHI¹	manage personnel
(管人事 = 管理人事)		
管道	GUAN³ DAO⁴	pipeline; channel
管路	GUAN³ LU⁴	pipeline route
管子	GUAN³ ZI	pipe; tube
管用	GUAN³ YONG⁴	helpful; effective
管理不當	GUAN³ LI³ BU⁴ DANG⁴	inappropriate management
理 (M13.3)	LI³	manage; reason
理想	LI³ XIANG³	ideal
理由	LI³ YOU²	reason; cause
理論	LI³ LUN⁴	theory
理應	LI³ YING¹	should; ought to
理會	LI³ HUI⁴	pay attention to
理事	LI³ SHI⁴	panel; member of council
理事會	LI³ SHI⁴ HUI⁴	council
理所當然	LI³ SUO³ DANG¹ RAN²	of course; certainly
意 (M14.1)	YI⁴	idea; meaning
意思	YI⁴ SI	meaning; idea
意見	YI⁴ JIAN⁴	opinion; view; objection; complaint
意向	YI⁴ XIANG⁴	intention; intent
意氣	YI⁴ QI⁴	will and spirit
意氣相投	YI⁴ QI⁴ XIANG¹ TOU²	alike in temperament

意向不明	YI⁴ XIANG⁴ BU⁴ MING²	intention not clear
意外相見	YI⁴ WAI⁴ XIANG¹ JIAN⁴	meet unexpectedly
意想不到	YI⁴ XIANG³ BU⁴ DAO⁴	unexpected; caught by surprise
意見不一	YI⁴ JIAN⁴ BU⁴ YI¹	different views and voices
意見多多	YI⁴ JIAN⁴ DUO¹ DUO¹	full of complaints and objection
意在言外	YI⁴ ZAI⁴ YAN² WAI⁴	with implied meaning; meaning is implied

(cf. 言外之意 YAN₂ WAI₄ ZHI₁ YI₄ (M19.3))

思 (M14.1) SI₁ — think; consider
思想	SI¹ XIANG³	thought; thinking
思路	SI¹ LU⁴	train of thought; thinking
思前想後	SI¹ QIAN² XIANG³ HOU⁴	think repeatedly and cautiously

等 (M14.1) DENG₃ — wait; grade; class
等候	DENG³ HOU⁴	wait; expect
等等	DENG³ DENG³	etc; and so on
等一等	DENG³ YI¹ DENG³	wait; wait a minute
等量	DENG³ LIANG³	equal quantity
等邊	DENG³ BIAN¹	equilateral (triangle)

候 (M14.1) HOU₄ — wait; await; time

VOCABULARY: 1,800+

信 (M14.1)	XIN$_4$	letter; believe
信件	XIN$_4$ JIAN$_3$	letter; mail
信使	XIN$_4$ SHI$_4$	courier
信心	XIN$_4$ XIN$_1$	confidence
信用	XIN$_4$ YONG$_4$	trustworthiness; credit
信不信由你	XIN$_4$ BU$_4$ XIN$_4$ YOU$_2$ NI$_3$	Believe it or not, it's up to you.

情 (M14.2)	QING$_2$	situation; sentiment
情況	QING$_2$ KUANG$_4$	situation; circumstances
情報	QING$_2$ BAO$_4$	intelligence; information
情理	QING$_2$ LI$_3$	reason; sense
情由	QING$_2$ YOU$_2$	the hows and whys; the circumstances
情面	QING$_2$ MIAN$_4$	feelings; sensibility
情人	QING$_2$ REN$_2$	lover; sweetheart
情信	QING$_2$ XIN$_2$	love letter
情話	QING$_2$ HUA$_4$	lovers' prattle
情意	QING$_2$ YI$_4$	tender regards; affection
情投意合	QING$_2$ TOU$_2$ YI$_4$ HE$_2$	find each other congenial; hit it off perfectly
情有可原	QING$_2$ YOU$_3$ KE$_3$ YUAN$_2$	excusable; pardonable

況 (M14.2)	KUANG$_4$	condition; situation
況且	KUANG$_4$ QIE$_3$	moreover; besides; in addition

VOCABULARY: 1,800+

寫 (M14.2)	XIE₃	write
寫字	XIE₃ ZI₄	write a word / character
寫信	XIE₃ XIN₄	write a letter
寫作	XIE₃ ZUO₄	writing
寫真	XIE₃ ZHEN₁	draw a portrait
寫生	XIE₃ SHENG₁	paint from live

清 (M14.2)	QING₁	clear
清楚	QING₁ CHU₃	clear; distinct
清白	QING₁ BAI₂	clean; innocent
清理	QING₁ LI₃	sort out; clear up
清明	QING₁ MING₂	clear and bright; a Chinese festival in memory of ancestors and the deceased
清早	QING₁ ZAO₃	early morning
清真	QING₁ ZHEN₁	Muslim (Mosque)
清清楚楚	QING₁ QING₁ CHU₃ CHU₃	clear and distinct

楚 (M14.2)	CHU₃	clear; neat; attractive
楚楚可人	CHU₃ CHU₃ KE₃ REN₂	attractive look (in describing a young lady)

其 (M14.3)	QI₂	(relative pronoun in general form)
其他	QI₂ TA₁	others
其次	QI₂ CI₄	next; secondly

Mastering Mandarin: Your Path to Proficiency

VOCABULARY: 1,800+

其餘	QI² YU²	the rest; the balance
其中	QI² ZHONG¹	among which; in which
其人其事	QI² REN² QI² SHI⁴	the person and his/her affairs

餘 (M14.3)	YU²	remaining; extra; surplus; spare
餘年	YU⁰ NIAN⁰	the remaining years/life
餘生	YU² SHENG¹	one's remaining life
餘地	YU² DI⁴	leeway; room
餘下	YU² XIA⁴	remaining

交 (M14.3)	JIAO¹	hand over; cross; reach
交通	JIAO¹ TONG¹	transportation
交出	JIAO¹ CHU¹	submit; surrender
交錯	JIAO¹ CUO⁴	interlocked
交點	JIAO¹ DIAN³	point of intersection
交會	JIAO¹ HUI⁴	intersect
交公	JIAO¹ GONG¹	turn over to (group, company,...)
交情	JIAO¹ QING²	friendly relationship; rapport
交心	JIAO¹ XIN¹	open one's heart to
交錢	JIAO¹ QIAN²	pay; make payment
交朋友	JIAO¹ PENG² YOU³	make friends
交通安全	JIAO¹ TONG¹ AN¹ QUAN²	traffic safety

開 (M14.3)	KAI₁	open
開會	KAI¹ HUI⁴	meeting; attend a meeting
開工	KAI¹ GONG¹	go to work; start production operation
開辦	KAI¹ BAN⁴	set up; establish
開心	KAI¹ XIN¹	feel happy
開明	KAI¹ MING²	enlightened
開通	KAI¹ TONG¹	remove obstacles from
開路	KAI¹ LU⁴	clear the way; open a way
會 (M14.3)	HUI₄	meeting; get together; can; understand
會見	HUI⁴ JIAN⁴	meet with (especially foreign visitor)
會面	HUI⁴ MIAN⁴	meet
會談	HUI⁴ TAN²	talks (e.g. political)
會客	HUI⁴ KE⁴	receive a visitor/guest
會合	HUI⁴ HE²	join; converge
會同	HUI⁴ TONG²	join with
會話	HUI⁴ HUA⁴	conversation (as in a language course); colloquial
會心	HUI⁴ XIN¹	understanding
會意	HUI⁴ YI⁴	understanding
會不會	HUI⁴ BU⁴ HUI⁴	could it be ...

向 (M15.1)	XIANG⁴	direction; face; to
向前	XIANG⁴ QIAN²	forward; ahead
向後	XIANG⁴ HOU⁴	backward; towards the back
向來	XIANG⁴ LAI²	all along; always
向上	XIANG⁴ SHANG⁴	upward
向下	XIANG⁴ XIA⁴	downward
向左	XIANG⁴ ZUO³	to the left
向右	XIANG⁴ YOU⁴	to the right
向內	XIANG⁴ NEI⁴	inward
向外	XIANG⁴ WAI⁴	outward
向上報告	XIANG⁴ SHANG⁴ BAO⁴ GAO⁴	report to the higher authority

公 (M15.1)	GONG¹	public; metric; fair
公司	GONG¹ SI¹	company
公事	GONG¹ SHI¹	official business; official duties
公文	GONG¹ WEN²	official document; official letter
公開	GONG¹ KAI¹	open; make public
公用	GONG¹ YONG⁴	for public use
公有	GONG¹ YOU³	publicly owned
公共	GONG¹ GONG⁴	public; common
公家	GONG¹ JIA¹	(belong to) government, company or organization
公報	GONG¹ BAO⁴	communique; bulletin

公告	GŌNG GÀO	announcement
公元	GŌNG YUÁN	the Christian era; A.D.
公道	GŌNG DÀO	fair; just
公平	GŌNG PÍNG	fair; just
公法	GŌNG FǍ	public law
公理	GŌNG LǏ	generally accepted truth
公安	GŌNG ĀN	public security (公共安全)
公立	GŌNG LÌ	government owned
公分	GŌNG FĒN	centimeter (cm)
公路	GŌNG LÙ	highway; freeway
公因子	GŌNG YĪN ZǏ	common factor (maths)
公共安全	GŌNG GÒNG ĀN QUÁN	public safety
公共交通	GŌNG GÒNG JIĀO TŌNG	public transportation
司 (M15.1)	SĪ	take charge of; a department under ministry
司法	SĪ FǍ	administration of justice
報 (M15.1)	BÀO	report; newspaper
報告	BÀO GÀO	report; to report
報時	BÀO SHÍ	give the correct time
報到	BÀO DÀO	report for duty; check in; register
報表	BÀO BIǍO	registration forms
報應	BÀO YÌNG	retribution; judgement
報喜	BÀO XǏ	report success; announce good news

告 (M15.1)	GAO₄	tell; notify; announce
告別	GAO₄ BIE	leave; bid farewell to
告知	GAO₄ ZHI₁	tell; inform
而 (M15.2)	ER₂	(and, but)
而且	ER₂ QIE₃	also
而已	ER₂ YI₃	that's all; nothing more
而今	ER₂ JIN₁	and now
而後	ER₂ HOU₄	after that
且 (M15.2)	QIE₃	just; for the time being
且慢	QIE₃ MAN₄	wait a minute
且談且走	QIE₃ TAN₂ QIE₃ ZOU₃	all the way (they) talk as (they) walk

(NOTE: 且談且走 = 邊走邊談 BIAN₁ ZOU₃ BIAN₁ TAN₂ M6.1)

打 (M15.2)	DA₃	hit; strike; dial; open
打電話	DA₃ DIAN₄ HUA₄	dial telephone
打電報	DA₃ DIAN₄ BAO₄	send telegram
打傳真	DA₃ CHUAN₂ ZHEN₁	send FAX (facsimile)
打電腦	DA₃ DIAN₄ NAO₃	use the computer
打交道	DA₃ JIAO₁ DAO₄	encounter; deal with
打字	DA₃ ZI₄	type; typing
打人	DA₃ REN₂	hit; strike; battery
打工	DA₃ GONG₁	work as an employee; being employed

VOCABULARY: 1,800+

打量	DA³ LIANG⁴	look closely; look at somebody up and down
打通	DA³ TONG¹	make it through
打開	DA³ KAI¹	open
打氣	DA³ QI⁴	pump up; boost morale
打通思想	DA³ TONG¹ SI⁴ XIANG⁴	straighten thinking; convince
打通電話	DA³ TONG¹ DIAN¹ HUA¹	phone connected
打個比方	DA³ GE⁴ BI³ FANG¹	say, for instance

傳 (M15.2) CHUAN₂ pass; pass on

(cf. 自傳 ZI₄ ZHUAN₄ (M2.3))

傳眞	CHUAN² ZHEN¹	fax; facsimile
傳說	CHUAN² SHUO¹	it is said; hearsay
傳言	CHUAN² YAN²	it is said; hearsay
傳到	CHUAN² DAO⁴	pass on to
傳道	CHUAN² DAO⁴	preach (religion)

眞 (M15.3) ZHEN₁ true; real

眞心	ZHEN¹ XIN¹	heartfelt; wholehearted
眞相	ZHEN¹ XIANG⁴	real situation; facts
眞情	ZHEN¹ QING²	true feelings; the real situation
眞假	ZHEN¹ JIA³	true or false; genuine or fake
眞是	ZHEN¹ SHI¹	goodness
眞人眞事	ZHEN¹ REN² ZHEN¹ SHI⁴	real person and event
眞心眞意	ZHEN¹ XIN¹ ZHEN¹ YI⁴	sincere

VOCABULARY: 1,800+

電 (M15.3)	DIAN₄	electricity; electric
電話	DIAN⁴ HUA⁴	telephone
電腦	DIAN⁴ NAO³	computer
電力	DIAN⁴ LI⁴	electric power
電傳	DIAN⁴ CHUAN²	telex
電氣	DIAN⁴ QI⁴	electric
電學	DIAN⁴ XUE²	electricity (science)
電工	DIAN⁴ GONG¹	electrician
電子	DIAN⁴ ZI³	electron

腦 (M15.3)	NAO₃	brain
腦子	NAO³ ZI	brain

內 (M15.3)	NEI₄	inner; inside
內部	NEI⁴ BU⁴	internal
內地	NEI⁴ DI⁴	interior; inland
內功	NEI⁴ GONG¹	exercises to benefit internal organs
內力	NEI⁴ LI⁴	internal force
內行	NEI⁴ HANG²	expert in a trade
內情	NEI⁴ QING²	insider news; situation inside
內在	NEI⁴ ZAI⁴	inherent; internal
內向	NEI⁴ XIANG⁴	introversion
內心	NEI⁴ XIN¹	in mind; in heart
內外	NEI⁴ WAI⁴	inside and outside; domestic and foreign

外 (M15.3)	WAI₄	outer; outside; foreign
外國	WAI₄ GUO₂	foreign country
外文	WAI₄ WEN₂	foreign language
外語	WAI₄ YU₃	foreign language
外來語	WAI₄ LAI₂ YU₃	word of foreign origin
外事	WAI₄ SHI₄	foreign affairs
外交	WAI₄ JIAO₁	diplomacy
外交部	WAI₄ JIAO₁ BU₄	foreign ministry
外商	WAI₄ SHANG₁	foreign businessman
外資	WAI₄ ZI₁	foreign capital
外地	WAI₄ DI₄	outside the local area
外邊	WAI₄ BIAN₁	outside
外面	WAI₄ MIAN₄	outside
外部	WAI₄ BU₄	external
外表	WAI₄ BIAO₃	appearance; external look
外來	WAI₄ LAI₂	of foreign origin
外快	WAI₄ KUAI₄	extra income
外向	WAI₄ XIANG₄	extroversion; outgoing
外行	WAI₄ HANG₂	layman; non-professional
(外行 = 外行人)		
外人	WAI₄ REN₂	outsider
外國人	WAI₄ GUO₂ REN₂	foreigner
通 (M15.3)	TONG₁	through; open
通知	TONG₁ ZHI₁	notice

通報	TONG¹ BAO⁴	bulletin; circulate
通告	TONG¹ GAO⁴	public notice
通常	TONG¹ CHANG²	usual; generally
通過	TONG¹ GUO⁴	via; by means of; pass through
通話	TONG¹ HUA⁴	phone connected; on the phone
通商	TONG¹ SHANG¹	trade relations
通年	TONG¹ NIAN²	year round
通路	TONG¹ LU⁴	passageway
通順	TONG¹ SHUN⁴	clear and coherent (writing style)
通信	TONG¹ XIN⁴	correspondence
通行	TONG¹ XING²	pass through
通用	TONG¹ YONG⁴	universally applicable; general-purpose
通則	TONG¹ ZE²	general rules
通電	TONG¹ DIAN⁴	electrically connected
通通	TONG¹ TONG¹	entirely; completely
通天	TONG¹ TIAN¹	access to top authority
通力合作	TONG¹ LI⁴ HE² ZUO⁴	cooperate with full effort

(Note: 通力合作 = 全力合作 QUAN² LI⁴ HE² ZUO⁴)

(全力合作 tends to be Southern usage, Cantonese)

但 (M16.1)	DAN⁴	but; yet; only
但是	DAN⁴ SHI⁴	but; yet

VOCABULARY: 1,800+

但求	DAN⁴ QIU²	if only; wish
但求無過, 不求有功。	DAN⁴ QIU² WU² GUO⁴, BU⁴ QIU² YOU³ GONG¹.	Hope to get by without making mistakes; don't expect to have meritorious contribution. (a drift-along attitude to work)

求 (M16.1)	QIU₂	beg; request
求人	QIU² REN²	ask for help
求學	QIU² XUE²	pursue one's studies
求知	QIU² ZHI²	seek knowledge
求助	QIU² ZHU⁴	seek help
求情	QIU² QING²	plead; ask for a favor
求之不得	QIU² ZHI¹ BU⁴ DE²	all that one could wish for; most welcome

從 (M16.1)	CONG₂	from
從此	CONG² CI³	from now on; from then on; henceforth
從來	CONG² LAI²	always; all along
從不	CONG² BU⁴	(=從來不…)never; never ever
從前	CONG² QIAN²	once upon a time
從中	CONG² ZHONG¹	out of; from which
從而	CONG² ER²	thus; thereby
從事	CONG² SHI⁴	engaged in; in the business of
從今以後	CONG² JIN¹ YI³ HOU⁴	from now on

從小到大	CONG₂ XIAO₃ DAO₄ DA₄	from small to big; from young to grown up
從東到西	CONG₂ DONG₁ DAO₄ XI₁	from east to west

此 (M16.1)　　CI₃　　this

此事	CI₃ SHI₄	this matter; the issue

(Note: 此事 = 這件事 ZHE₁ JIAN₄ SI II₄, 此事 is in classical style writing.)

此後	CI₃ HOU₄	hereafter

(Note: 此後 = 從此以後 CONG₂ CI₃ YI₃ HOU₄)

此人	CI₃ REN₂	this guy; this fellow (sometimes derogatory)
此地	CI₃ DI₄	here; this place
此外	CI₃ WAI₄	in addition; furthermore
此時此地	CI₃ SHI₂ CI₃ DI₄	here and now; here at this point in time
此路不通	CI₃ LU₄ BU₄ TONG₁	not a through road; not feasible

忙 (M16.1)　　MANG₂　　busy

忙人	MANG₂ REN₂	busy person
忙不過來	MANG₂ BU₄ GUO₄ LAI₂	too busy and falling behind schedule

早 (M16.2)　　ZAO₃　　early

早安	ZAO₃ AN₁	good morning
早點	ZAO₃ DIAN₃	breakfast
早一點	ZAO₃ YI₁ DIAN₃	earlier

早上	ZAO³ SHANG⁴	morning hours
早晚	ZAO³ WAN³	morning to evening; sooner or later

(cf. 遲早 CHI² ZAO³ (M13.1) sooner or later; 早晚 tends to be northern China oral usage)

早日	ZAO³ RI⁴	soon; at an early date
早年	ZAO³ NIAN³	the early years
早已	ZAO³ YI³	long ago; for a long time
至 (M16.2)	ZHI⁴	to; until; extremely
至此	ZHI⁴ CI³	up to this point
至於	ZHI⁴ YU²	as to
至今	ZHI⁴ JIN¹	until now; so far
至多	ZHI⁴ DUO¹	at the most
至少	ZHI⁴ SHAO³	at least
至上	ZHI⁴ SHANG⁴	supreme; the highest
至高無上	ZHI⁴ GAO¹ WU² SHANG⁴	supreme; paramount
至為重要	ZHI⁴ WEI² ZHONG⁴ YAO⁴	most important
晚 (M16.2)	WAN³	late; evening
晚上	WAN³ SHANG⁴	in the evening
晚間	WAN³ JIAN¹	in the evening
晚安	WAN³ AN¹	good night
晚報	WAN³ BAO⁴	evening newspaper
晚年	WAN³ NIAN²	old age; remaining years

晚會	WAN³ HUI⁴	evening party; evening entertainment
晚點	WAN³ DIAN³	late; behind schedule (bus, train, plane)
晚了	WAN³ LE	too late; belated

(cf. 遲 CHI2 (M13.1); 晚了 = 遲了)

晚一點	WAN³ YI¹ DIAN³	a little later
晚了一點	WAN³ LE YI¹ DIAN³	a little too late

(In the above last 3 expressions, 晚=遲, interchangeable; 晚 is northern China oral usage.)

平 (M16.2)	PING₂	flat; level; smooth
平安	PING² AN¹	safe and sound
平白	PING² BAI²	for no reason
平常	PING² CHANG²	ordinary; normal
平時	PING² SHI²	at ordinary times
平等	PING² DENG³	equality
平地	PING² DI⁴	level ground
平分	PING² FEN¹	equally shared/split
平定	PING² DING⁴	calm down; put down (a riot, rebellion)
平手	PING² SHOU³	draw (tie in a match)
平平	PING² PING²	mediocre; so so
平方	PING² FANG¹	square (maths)
平面	PING² MIAN⁴	plane (geometry)
平行	PING² XING²	parallel; of equal rank

VOCABULARY: 1,800+

安 (M16.2)	AN₁	peaceful; calm
安心	AN¹ XIN¹	feel at ease; relieved
安樂	AN¹ LE⁴	happy and peaceful
安定	AN¹ DING⁴	stable; settled
安好	AN¹ HAO³	safe and sound
安家	AN¹ JIA¹	settle down the family
安全	AN¹ QUAN²	safe; secure
安安樂樂過晚年	AN¹ AN¹ LE⁴ LE⁴ GUO⁴ WAN³ NIAN²	Pass the remaining old age in happiness and peace.
使 (M16.3)	SHI₃	send; cause
使得	SHI³ DE²	cause; usable
使到	SHI³ DAO⁴	cause
使用	SHI³ YONG⁴	use
使出	SHI³ CHU¹	exert
使人放心	SHI³ REN² FANG⁴ XIN¹	make people feel at ease
初 (M16.3)	CHU₁	beginning; preliminary
初步	CHU¹ BU⁴	preliminary
初次	CHU¹ CI⁴	first time
初等	CHU¹ DENG³	elementary
初交	CHU¹ JIAO¹	new acquaintance
初學	CHU¹ XUE²	begin to learn
初中	CHU¹ ZHONG¹	junior high school

Mastering Mandarin: Your Path to Proficiency

步 (M16.3)	BU₄	step
步子	BU₄ ZI	step
步法	BU₄ FA₃	footwork (e.g. dancing)
步行	BU₄ XING₂	on foot; walk
比 (M16.3)	BI₃	compare
比較	BI₃ JIAO₄	compare
比方	BI₃ FANG₁	for instance (= 比方說)
比分	BI₃ FEN₁	score (in a game match)
比重	BI₃ ZHONG₄	specific gravity (relative density)
較 (M16.3)	JIAO₄	compare
較量	JIAO₄ LIANG₄	have a contest; square off
較爲	JIAO₄ WEI₂	more / less (comparatively: stronger, weaker, ...)
必 (M17.1)	BI₄	certainly; necessarily
必須	BI₄ XU₁	must
必需	BI₄ XU₁	necessity
必然	BI₄ RAN₂	inevitable
必定	BI₄ DING₄	bound to
必不可少	BI₄ BU₄ KE₃ SHAO₃	indispensable; necessity
必由之路	BI₄ YOU₂ ZHI₁ LU₄	the only way

須 (M17.1)	XU₁	must
須要	XŪ YÀO	must; have to
須知	XŪ ZHĪ	must understand; one should know

視 (M17.1)	SHI₄	look (視 = 看 KAN₄ (cf. M3.1))
視力	SHÌ LÌ	eye sight
視覺	SHÌ JUÉ	visual sense
視而不見	SHÌ ÉR BÙ JIÀN	look but see not; turn a blind eye to
視同路人	SHÌ TÓNG LÙ RÉN	regard as a stranger

表 (M17.1)	BIAO₃	surface; external
表現	BIĂO XIÀN	perform; do; behave
表面	BIĂO MIÀN	surface; appearance
表決	BIĂO JUÉ	decide by vote; vote
表明	BIĂO MÍNG	demonstrate; show
表白	BIĂO BÁI	vindicate
表報	BIĂO BÀO	forms; statistics
表語	BIĂO YŬ	predicate (grammar)
表裡不一	BIĂO LĬ BÙ YĪ	say one thing and behave another
表現不錯	BIĂO XIÀN BÙ CUÒ	pretty good performance or behavior
表意文字	BIĂO YÌ WÉN ZÌ	ideograph

VOCABULARY: 1,800+

現 (M17.1)	XIAN₄	show; now
現在	XIAN⁴ ZAI⁴	now; present time
現時	XIAN⁴ SHI²	present; currently
現年	XIAN⁴ NIAN²	aged; present age
現今	XIAN⁴ JIN¹	nowadays
現有	XIAN⁴ YOU³	currently available
現成	XIAN⁴ CHENG²	readily available; ready made
現行	XIAN⁴ XING²	currently in force (laws, rules, codes ...)

注 (M17.2)	ZHU₄	pour
注重	ZHU⁴ ZHONG⁴	pay attention to
注意	ZHU⁴ YI⁴	attention
注音	ZHU⁴ YIN¹	phonetic notation
注視	ZHU⁴ SHI⁴	observe closely
注明	ZHU⁴ MING²	indicate in writing
注目	ZHU⁴ MU⁴	gaze at; eyes on
注定	ZHU⁴ DING⁴	be doomed; bound to

重 (M17.3)	ZHONG₄	heavy; important;
	CHONG₂	repeat; duplicate
重視	ZHONG⁴ SHI⁴	value; take something seriously
重要	ZHONG⁴ YAO⁴	important; significant
重大	ZHONG⁴ DA⁴	major

重點	ZHÒNG DIǍN	focus
重用	ZHÒNG YÒNG	put somebody in an important position
重辦	ZHÒNG BÀN	punish heavily (e.g. criminal offense)
重音	ZHÒNG YĪN	accent (on a certain syllable)
重量	ZHÒNG LIÀNG	weight
重力	ZHÒNG LÌ	gravity
重心	ZHÒNG XĪN	center of gravity; core
重點所在	ZHÒNG DIǍN SUǑ ZÀI	where the focus is
重現	CHÓNG XIÀN	reappear
重合	CHÓNG HÉ	coincide (math)
重見天日	CHÓNG JIÀN TIĀ RÌ	out of persecution, oppression or suffering

(Literally: Get to see the sun and the sky again.)

字 (M17.2)	ZÌ₄	word; character
字裡行間	ZÌ LǏ HÁNG JIĀN	between the lines of words

拼 (M17.2)	PĪN₁	put together
拼音	PĪN YĪN	phoneticize
拼寫	PĪN XIĚ	spelling

音 (M17.2)	YĪN₁	sound
音樂	YĪN YUÈ	music
音量	YĪN LIÀNG	sound volume
音信	YĪN XÌN	mail; information

錯 (M17.3)	CUO₄	wrong; interlocked
錯誤	CUO₄ WU₄	wrong; mistake
錯過	CUO₄ GUO₄	miss; let slip
錯開	CUO₄ KAI₁	stagger
錯字	CUO₄ ZI₄	wrongly written character; misprint
錯別字	CUO₄ BIE₂ ZI₄	wrongly written character; mis-spelled word
錯誤百出	CUO₄ WU₄ BAI₃ CHU₁	mistakes all over; full of errors

(Literally: Mistakes occur hundreds of times.)

誤 (M17.3)	WU₄	mistake; error; miss
誤會	WU₄ HUI₄	misunderstand
誤點	WU₄ DIAN₃	late; behind schedule

(cf. 晚點 WAN₃ DIAN₃ (M16.2))

誤時	WU₄ SHI₂	late; behind schedule
誤事	WU₄ SHI₄	cause delay or loss to business or work
誤工	WU₄ GONG₁	late at work; loss of time at work

未 (M17.3)	WEI₄	not yet; not
未完	WEI₄ WAN₂	unfinished; not yet completed
未了	WEI₄ LIAO₃	unfinished; not yet ended
未知	WEI₄ ZHI₁	unknown

VOCABULARY: 1,800+

未定	WEI⁴ DING⁴	not yet decided; to be determined
未必	WEI⁴ BI⁴	not necessarily; may not
未能	WEI⁴ NENG²	cannot; not being able to
未來	WEI⁴ LAI²	future; coming
未便	WEI⁴ BIAN⁴	hard to; not in the position to (written)

(未便 is a gentle expression, more often in writing, for 不便 BU₄ BIAN₄ 。不便 = 不方便 BU₄ FANG₁ BIAN₄)(cf. M1.3)

除 (M17.3)	CHU₂	eliminate; divide
除了	CHU² LE	in addition to; except
除外	CHU² WAI⁴	except
除非	CHU² FEI¹	unless
除光	CHU² GUANG¹	totally eliminate

(Note: 除光 = 清除光 QING₁ CHU₂ GUANG₁ (Mandarin); ==除清光 CHU₂ QING₁ GUANG₁ (Cantonese))

除法	CHU² FA³	division (maths)
除此以外	CHU² CI³ YI³ WAI⁴	in addition; furthermore

(除此以外 = 除此之外(CHU₂ CI₃ ZHI₁ WAI₄) = 此外 CI₃ WAI₄ (cf. M16.1))

光 (M17.3)	GUANG₁	light; bright; only
光明	GUANG¹ MING²	bright
光年	GUANG¹ NIAN²	light year (astronomy)
光電	GUANG¹ DIAN⁴	photoelectricity
光子	GUANG¹ ZI³	photon

Mastering Mandarin: Your Path to Proficiency

光合作用	GUANG¹ HE² ZUO⁴ YONG⁴	photosynthesis
光天白日	GUANG¹ TIAN¹ BAI² RI⁴	in bright day light (e.g. describe an evil act)

假 (M18.1)	JIA₃	false; fake; artificial
假如	JIA³ RU²	if; suppose
假使	JIA³ SHI³	if; in case
假定	JIA³ DING⁴	suppose; hypothetical
假說	JIA³ SHUO¹	hypothesis
假想	JIA³ XIANG³	hypothesis; imagination
假話	JIA³ HUA⁴	lie
假手	JIA³ SHOU³	make a cat's paw of somebody
假和平	JIA³ HE² PING²	phony peace

如 (M18.1)	RU₂	if; such as
如此	RU² CI³	so; such; this way
如常	RU² CHANG²	as usual
如上	RU² SHANG⁴	as above
如下	RU² XIA⁴	as follows
如今	RU² JIN¹	nowadays; and now ...
如意	RU² YI⁴	as one wishes
如此而已	RU² CI³ ER² YI³	that's all it is; nothing more than that
如日中天	RU² RI⁴ ZHONG¹ TIAN¹	like the sun at high noon; at the apex of one's career, power,...; heyday

VOCABULARY: 1,800+

怕 (M18.1)	PA₄	fear; afraid of
怕事	PA⁴ SHI⁴	afraid of getting into trouble
怕麻煩	PA⁴ MA² FAN²	don't want to take the trouble
怕這怕那	PA⁴ ZHE⁴ PA⁴ NA⁴	afraid of everything
(Literally: afraid of this and that)		

麻 (M18.1)	MA₂	jute
麻煩	MA² FAN²	troublesome; inconvenience
麻子	MA² ZI	pockmarks; person with a pockmarked face

煩 (M18.1)	FAN₂	trouble; annoy
煩請	FAN² QING³	could you, please (written expression)

樣 (M18.2)	YANG₄	appearance; shape; look
樣子	YANG⁴ ZI	appearance
樣樣	YANG⁴ YANG⁴	everything

子 (M18.2)	ZI₃	son
子女	ZI³ NÜ (NYU)	sons and daughters
子音	ZI³ YIN¹	consonant

無 (M18.2)	WU₂	nothing; nil; regardless
無謂	WU² WEI⁴	senseless
無所謂	WU² SUO³ WEI⁴	take it easy; wouldn't bother

無不	WÚ BÙ (2,4)	all without exception
無情	WÚ QÍNG (2,2)	merciless; no pity
無視	WÚ SHÌ (2,4)	ignore; disregard
無從	WÚ CÓNG (2,2)	not in the position to; no way of
無從下手	WÚ CÓNG XIÀ SHŎU (2,2,4,3)	no way to start
無法無天	WÚ FĂ WÚ TIĀN (2,3,2,1)	defy all laws; run wild
無心向學	WÚ XĪN XIÀNG XUÉ (2,1,4,2)	no desire to learn
無師自通	WÚ SHĪ ZÌ TŌNG (2,1,4,1)	self-taught without a teacher
無能爲力	WÚ NÉNG WÈI LÌ (2,2,2,4)	helpless
無事生非	WÚ SHÌ SHĒNG FĒI (2,1,1,1)	make trouble out of nothing
無中生有	WÚ ZHŌNG SHĒNG YŎU (2,1,1,3)	fabricated
無話可說	WÚ HUÀ KĔ SHUŌ (2,4,3,1)	have nothing to explain
無言以對	WÚ YÁN YĬ DUÌ (2,2,3,4)	have nothing to respond
無所不爲	WÚ SUŎ BÙ WÉI (2,3,4,2)	stop at nothing; do all evil
無所不能	WÚ SUŎ BÙ NÉNG (2,3,4,2)	omnipotent; nothing incapable
無所不知	WÚ SUŎ BÙ ZHĪ (2,3,4,1)	omniscient
無所不在	WÚ SUŎ BÙ ZÀI (2,3,4,4)	omnipresent; present everywhere
無所不至	WÚ SUŎ BÙ ZHÌ (2,3,4,4)	occurs everywhere
無所事事	WÚ SUŎ SHÌ SHÌ (2,3,4,4)	killing time; nothing get done
無所用心	WÚ SUŎ YÒNG XĪN (2,3,4,1)	mind without drive
無所作爲	WÚ SUŎ ZUÒ WÉI (2,3,4,2)	without accomplishment

無出其右	WÚ CHŪ QÍ YÒU	second to none
所 (M18.2)	SUŎ	place
所以	SUŎ YĬ	so; therefore
所以然	SUŎ YĬ RÁN	the whys and wherefores
所謂	SUŎ WÈI	so called
所有	SUŎ YŎU	all; in possession
所在	SUŎ ZÀI	where; place
所在地	SUŎ ZÀI DÌ	location; place
所得無幾	SUŎ DÉ WÚ JĬ	end up very little
謂 (M18.2)	WÈI	say
謂之	WÈI ZHĪ	known as; called
謂語	WÈI YŬ	predicate (grammar)
怎 (M18.3)	ZĚN	how; why
怎能	ZĚN NÉNG	how can
怎樣	ZĚN YÀNG	how
怎麼	ZĚN ME	why
怎麼樣	ZĚN ME YÀNG	how is it; how about
怎麼得了	ZĚN ME DÉ LIĂO	what a mess
能 (M18.3)	NÉNG	ability; energy
能夠	NÉNG GÒU	able to; capable of
能力	NÉNG LÌ	ability; capability

能量	NÉNG LIÀNG	energy
能人	NÉNG RÉN	capable person
能手	NÉNG SHŎU	dab; expert
能說會道	NÉNG SHUŌ HUÌ DÀO	have a glib tongue
能者爲師	NÉNG ZHĚ WÉI SHĪ	let those who know teach

(Literally: Whoever is capable can be the teacher.)

建 (M19.3)	JIAN₄	establish; build
建立	JIÀN LÌ	set up; build; establish
建成	JIÀN CHÉNG	establish
建交	JIÀN JIĀO	establish diplomatic relation

(Note: 建交 = 建立外交 JIAN₄ LI₄ WAI₄ JIAO₁)

建國	JIÀN GUÓ	founding of a Nation

(Note: 建國 = 建立國家 JIAN₄ LI₄ GUO₂ JIA₁)

功 (M18.3)	GONG₁	merit
功能	GŌNG NÉNG	function; feature
功用	GŌNG YÒNG	function; use
功績	GŌNG JÌ	merits and accomplishment
功到自然成	GŌNG DÀO ZÌ RÁN CHÉNG	Constant effort yields sure success.

績 (M18.3)	JI₁	accomplishment

買 (M19.1)	MAI₃	buy; purchase

買方	MAI³ FANG¹	buyer; purchasing party (legal form)
買家	MAI³ JIA¹	buyer, person or party (respectful address)
買賣	MAI³ MAI⁴	buy and sell; business
買通	MAI³ TONG¹	bribe; buy over
買好	MAI³ HAO³	try to win favor; play up to
買賣公平	MAI³ MAI⁴ GONG¹ PING²	fair buy and sell

東 (M19.1)	DONG₁	east
東方	DONG¹ FANG¹	east; eastern
東邊	DONG¹ BIAN¹	east side
東面	DONG¹ MIAN⁴	east side
東北	DONG¹ BEI³	northeast
東南	DONG¹ NAN²	southeast
東西	DONG¹ XI¹	east west; thing, object
東經	DONG¹ JING¹	Longitude east
東方人	DONG¹ FANG¹ REN²	Easterner
東方語言	DONG¹ FANG¹ YU³ YAN²	Eastern Languages

西 (M19.1)	XI₁	west
西方	XI¹ FANG¹	west; western
西邊	XI¹ BIAN¹	west side
西面	XI¹ MIAN⁴	west side
西北	XI¹ BEI³	northwest
西南	XI¹ NAN²	southwest

西安	XI¹ AN¹	XI-AN (city, ancient capitol of China)
西經	XI¹ JING¹	Longitude west
西西	XI¹ XI¹	c.c. (cubic centimeter)
西樂	XI¹ YUE⁴	Western music
西方語言	XI¹ FANG¹ YU³ YAN²	Western Languages
帶 (M19.1)	DAI₄	carry; bring; belt
帶電	DAI⁴ DIAN⁴	electrified; charged
帶人	DAI⁴ REN²	guide (such as a tour); accompany
帶工	DAI⁴ GONG¹	lead a team of workers
帶路	DAI⁴ LU⁴	show the road; as a guide
帶錢	DAI⁴ QIAN²	bring money
帶子	DAI⁴ ZI⁴	belt; (in Cantonese; fresh scallop)
錢 (M19.1)	QIAN₂	money
賣 (M19.2)	MAI₄	sell
賣方	MAI⁴ FANG¹	seller; selling party
賣力	MAI⁴ LI⁴	work hard; spare no effort (at work, job)
賣力氣	MAI⁴ LI⁴ QI⁴	work hard; spare no effort (at work, job)
賣國	MAI⁴ GUO²	betray one's country; turn traitor

則 (M19.2)	ZE₂	(then)
走 (M19.2)	ZOU₃	walk; go
走路	ZOU³ LU⁴	walk; go on foot
走向	ZOU³ XIANG⁴	run; trend
走樣	ZOU³ YANG⁴	lose shape; out of form; distorted
南 (M19.2)	NAN₂	south
南方	NAN² FANG¹	south; the south
南邊	NAN² BIAN¹	southern part
南面	NAN² MIAN¹	south side
南極	NAN² JI²	south Pole
南北	NAN² BEI³	north and south; from north to south
北 (M19.2)	BEI₃	north
北方	BEI³ FANG¹	north; northern
北邊	BEI³ BIAN¹	northern part
北面	BEI³ MIAN⁴	north side
北極	BEI³ JI²	north Pole
言 (M19.3)	YAN₂	speech; word
言語	YAN² YU³	talk; words
言談	YAN² TAN²	the manner of speaking

言論	YAN² LUN³	opinion on public affairs
言路	YAN² LU⁴	channels for criticism and comments
言外之意	YAN² WAI⁴ ZHI¹ YI⁴	implication; what the words really mean

(cf. 意在言外 YI⁴ ZAI⁴ YAN² WAI⁴ (M14.2))

言之過早	YAN² ZHI¹ GUO⁴ ZAO³	too early to talk about it; premature
言之有理	YAN² ZHI¹ YOU³ LI³	(what one says is) reasonable and convincing
言必有中	YAN² BI⁴ YOU³ ZHONG¹	right to the point in speaking
言而無信	YAN² ER² WU² XIN⁴	fail to keep one's words
言行不一	YAN² XING² BU⁴ YI¹	one's deeds do not match with one's words

(cf. 表裡不一 BIAO³ LI³ BU⁴ YI¹ (M17.1))

言論自由	YAN² LUN⁴ ZI⁴ YOU²	freedom of speech
語 (M19.3)	YU³	language; words
語言	YU³ YAN²	language
語氣	YU³ QI⁴	tone; manner of speaking
語文	YU³ WEN²	language (a course)
語法	YU³ FA³	grammar
語音	YU³ YIN¹	speech sound; pronunciation
語言文字	YU³ YAN² WEN² ZI⁴	spoken and written language
極 (M19.3)	JI²	utmost; extreme

VOCABULARY: 1,800+

極點	JI₂ DIAN₃	the limit; the extreme
極地	JI₂ DI₄	Polar region
極光	JI₂ GUANG₁	aurora; Polar lights
極之順利	JI₂ ZHI₁ SHUN₄ LI₄	extremely smooth and successful
極其快樂	JI₂ QI₂ KUAI₄ LE₄	extremely happy
極力做好	JI₂ LI₄ ZUO₄ HAO₃	try very hard to do well

客 (M19.3)	KE₄	guest; visitor; customer
客氣	KE₄ QI₄	polite; courteous
客人	KE₄ REN₂	guest; visitor
客商	KE₄ SHANG₁	visiting business counterpart
客家話	KE₄ JIA₁ HUA₄	Karkah (based on that dialect); Hakka (based on Cantonese)

氣 (M19.3)	QI₄	gas; air; weather; outraged
氣候	QI₄ HOU₄	climate
氣人	QI₄ REN₂	annoying; outraged
氣量	QI₄ LIANG₄	tolerance towards others
氣量大	QI₄ LIANG₄ DA₄	large-minded
氣量小	QI₄ LIANG₄ XIAO₃	narrow-minded
氣力	QI₄ LI₄	physical strength
(氣力=力氣 LI₄ QI₄ (M2.2))		
氣管	QI₄ GUAN₃	windpipe; trachea
氣道	QI₄ DAO₄	air duct

VOCABULARY: 1,800+

男 (M20.1)	NAN₂	male; man
男子	NAN₂ ZI₃	man; male (courteous)
男人	NAN₂ REN₂	man; male (casual)
男方	NAN₂ FANG₁	male side
男家	NAN₂ JIA₁	bridegroom's/husband's family
男高音	NAN₂ GAO₁ YIN₁	tenor
男中音	NAN₂ ZHONG₁ YIN₁	baritone
男朋友	NAN₂ PENG₂ YOU₃	boyfriend
男男女女	NAN₂ NAN₂ NÜ₃ NÜ₃	men and women
男女老少	NAN₂ NÜ₃ LAO₃ SHAO₄	men and women, old and young; all ages

女 (M20.1)	NÜ₃ (NYU₃)	woman; female

(NOTE: The original notation is NÜ with two dots on U, tone 3 ; for simplicity, some computer programs modify it to NV or NYU for input.)

女子	NÜ ZI₃	girl; woman (courteous)
女人	NÜ REN₃	woman; female (casual)
女方	NÜ FANG₁	female side
女家	NÜ JIA₁	bride's or wife's family
女高音	NÜ GAO₁ YIN₁	soprano
女中音	NÜ ZHONG₁ YIN₁	mezzo-soprano

老 (M20.1)	LAO₃	old; aged
老師	LAO₃ SHI₁	teacher (respectful salutation/expression)

VOCABULARY: 1,800+

老人	LAO³ REN²	elderly; senior citizen
老年	LAO³ NIAN²	old age
老年人	LAO³ NIAN² REN²	elderly; senior citizen
老家	LAO³ JIA¹	hometown; native place
老大	LAO³ DA⁴	head of a crew; oldest brother
老子	LAO³ ZI¹	father (casual use); I (disrespect to the party spoken to/about)
老手	LAO³ SHOU³	old hand
老成	LAO³ CHENG²	old head on young shoulders
老話	LAO³ HUA⁴	old saying
老千	LAO³ QIAN¹	crook
老公	LAO³ GONG¹	husband (orally, casual)
老公公	LAO³ GONG¹ GONG¹	grandpa (respectful salutation)
老太太	LAO³ TAI⁴ TAI⁴	old lady (respectful salutation)
老交情	LAO³ JIAO¹ QING²	long time friendship; long time rapport
老朋友	LAO³ PENG² YOU³	old friend
師 (M20.1)	SHI₁	teacher; master
師資	SHI¹ ZI¹	teacher resource
樂 (M20.1)	LE₄	happy
	YUE₄	music (cf. M17.2 音樂 YINYUE)

樂意	LE⁴ YI⁴	willing to; happy to
樂事	LE⁴ SHI⁴	pleasure
樂得	LE⁴ DE²	be only too glad to
樂於	LE⁴ YU²	be delighted to
樂意幫忙	LE⁴ YI⁴ BANG¹ MANG²	willing to help
樂在其中	LE⁴ ZAI⁴ QI² ZHONG¹	there is joy in it; enjoy doing it

先 (M20.2)	XIAN₁	first; earlier; in advance
先生	XIAN¹ SHENG¹	mister (Mr.); teacher; husband
先後	XIAN¹ HOU⁴	orderly; in order
先前	XIAN¹ QIAN²	before; previously; prior
先人	XIAN¹ REN²	ancestors (cf. 前人 QIAN₂ REN₂ M8.2)
先天	XIAN¹ TIAN¹	congenital; inborn
先行	XIAN¹ XING²	start off first
先行者	XIAN¹ XING² ZHE³	pioneer; forerunner
先見之明	XIAN¹ JIAN⁴ ZHI¹ MING²	foresight; vision
先入為主	XIAN¹ RU⁴ WEI² ZHU³	first impression
先來後到	XIAN¹ LAI² HOU⁴ DAO⁴	in the order of arrival
先到先得	XIAN¹ DAO⁴ XIAN¹ DE²	first come first served
先知先覺	XIAN¹ ZHI¹ XIAN¹ JUE²	having foresight; a person with foresight
先人後己	XIAN¹ REN² HOU⁴ JI³	put oneself behind others

VOCABULARY: 1,800+

生 (M20.2)	SHENG₁	grow; raw; active
生日	SHENG¹ RI⁴	birthday
生意	SHENG¹ YI⁴	business
生理	SHENG¹ LI³	physiology
生路	SHENG¹ LU⁴	way out; given a chance
生前	SHENG¹ QIAN²	before one's death
生人	SHENG¹ REN²	stranger
生手	SHENG¹ SHOU³	new hand (at work, job)
生氣	SHENG¹ QI⁴	angry; outraged; vital
生字	SHENG¹ ZI⁴	new word; new character

特 (M20.2)	TE⁴	special; particular
特別	TE⁴ BIE²	special; particular
特地	TE⁴ DI⁴	specially; on purpose
特意	TE⁴ YI⁴	specially; purposely
特為	TE⁴ WEI⁴	specially for
特定	TE⁴ DING⁴	specified; specific
特有	TE⁴ YOU²	unique
特出	TE⁴ CHU⁴	extraordinary
特等	TE⁴ DENG³	special grade/class
特大	TE⁴ DA⁴	extra large
特快	TE⁴ KUAI⁴	express
特使	TE⁴ SHI³	special envoy
特工	TE⁴ GONG¹	secret service
特此通知	TE⁴ CI³ TONG¹ ZHI¹	Notice is hereby given; It is hereby notified

喜 (M20.2)	XI₃	happy; delighted
喜歡	XI₃ HUAN₁	like; love; fond of
喜好	XI₃ HAO₄	love (music, sports,..)
喜事	XI₃ SHI₄	happy occasion (wedding, new born baby,..)
喜事重重	XI₃ SHI₄ CHONG₂ CHONG₂	full of happy occasions

(Note: The character 重 ZHONG₁ (M17.2) is here pronounced CHONG₂.)

NOTE: 囍 written as one character is often seen on the wall panel in a Chinese restaurant. It is known as 雙喜 SHUANG₁ XI₃ which means double happiness. It is for wedding banquet decoration.

歡 (M20.2)	HUAN₁	joyous
歡喜	HUAN₁ XI₃	like; love
(歡喜 = 喜歡 (M20.2))		
歡樂	HUAN₁ LE₄	joyous; jubilant
歡天喜地	HUAN₁ TIAN₁ XI₃ DI₄	overjoyed; overwhelmingly cheerful

祝 (M20.3)	ZHU₄	wish somebody (express good wishes)
祝您成功	ZHU₄ NIN₂ CHENG₂ GONG₁	wish you success

路 (M20.3)	LU₄	road; way
路途	LU₄ TU₂	road; journey
路上	LU₄ SHANG₄	on the way
路過	LU₄ GUO₄	pass by; pass through

路面	LU⁴ MIAN⁴	road surface
路人	LU⁴ REN²	passerby; stranger
途 (M20.3)	TU²	road; way
途中	TU² ZHONG¹	on the way (中途 M4.1)
順 (M20.3)	SHUN⁴	smooth; with the direction
順利	SHUN⁴ LI⁴	smoothly; successfully; without a hitch
順手	SHUN⁴ SHOU³	conveniently; without special effort
順便	SHUN⁴ BIAN⁴	conveniently; in passing
順帶	SHUN⁴ DAI⁴	conveniently; in passing
順心	SHUN⁴ XIN¹	as one wishes; as anticipated
順應	SHUN⁴ YING⁴	comply with
順從	SHUN⁴ CONG²	being obedient to
順其自然	SHUN⁴ QI² ZI⁴ RAN²	let it take its course
利 (M20.3)	LI⁴	benefit; profit; sharp (knife, cutter)
利用	LI⁴ YONG⁴	use; utilize; take advantage of
利錢	LI⁴ QIAN²	profit; profit margin (casual)
利己利人	LI⁴ JI³ LI⁴ REN²	benefit other people as well as oneself
利之所在	LI⁴ ZHI¹ SUO³ ZAI⁴	where the interest lies; where the bottom line is

APPENDICES

A. Table of 300 Chinese Characters: Traditional Print

B. Table of 300 Chinese Characters: Simplified Print

C. Table of 84 Characters: Traditional vs. Simplified

APPENDIX A

TRADITIONAL PRINT OF THE 300 CHINESE CHARACTERS

一二三十人　　日月大小天　　不是很好嗎
上下午工作　　左右手用力　　肯自己出入
我請你來看　　他和她們問　　說你還在家
學習中英文　　美國都去了　　叫謝又再見
常做慣就行　　今年並沒有　　要多少才夠
這裡非那邊　　哪些相同的　　為甚麼難懂
已經過各地　　心完全明白　　知道或者對
每次前面快　　後半放慢點　　原因太方便
想起幾件事　　覺得可以搞　　討論給提到
五六個項目　　共七百萬元　　投資八九千
只四成把握　　分別記辦法　　應該合商量
兩朋友之間　　談話題也廣　　當然高興講
由於決定遲　　需立即幫助　　靠及時管理
意思等候信　　情況寫清楚　　其餘交開會
向公司報告　　而且打傳真　　電腦內外通
但求從此忙　　早至晚平安　　使初步比較
必須視表現　　注重字拼音　　錯誤未除光
假如怕麻煩　　樣子無所謂　　怎能建功績
買東西帶錢　　賣則走南北　　言語極客氣
男女老師樂　　先生特喜歡　　祝路途順利

APPENDIX B
SIMPLIFIED PRINT OF THE 300 CHINESE CHARACTERS

一二三十人　　日月大小天　　不是很好吗
上下午工作　　左右手用力　　肯自己出入
我请你来看　　他和她们问　　说您还在家
学习中英文　　美国都去了　　叫谢又再见
常做惯就行　　今年并没有　　要多少才够
这里非那边　　哪些相同的　　为甚么难懂
已经过各地　　心完全明白　　知道或者对
每次前面快　　后半放慢点　　原因太方便
想起几件事　　觉得可以搞　　讨论给提到
五六个项目　　共七百万元　　投资八九千
只四成把握　　分别记办法　　应该合商量
两朋友之间　　谈话题也广　　当然高兴讲
由於决定迟　　需立即帮助　　靠及时管理
意思等候信　　情况写清楚　　其余交开会
向公司报告　　而且打传真　　电脑内外通
但求从此忙　　早至晚平安　　使初步比较
必须视表现　　注重字拼音　　错误未除光
假如怕麻烦　　样子无所谓　　怎能建功绩
买东西带钱　　卖则走南北　　言语极客气
男女老师乐　　先生特喜欢　　祝路途顺利

吗请来们问说还学习国谢见惯并这边为什么难经过对后点几觉讨论给个项万资记办应该两间谈话题广当兴讲迟帮时写余开会报传电脑从较须视现错误烦样无谓绩买东带钱卖则语极气师乐欢顺 (Simplified characters: 84)

APPENDIX C
COMPARISON: Traditional vs. Simplified Print

L -- Left portion simplified: (22)

請 說 謝 討 記 談 話 語 誤 該 謂 師 難
请 说 谢 讨 记 谈 话 语 误 该 谓 师 难

對 歡 報 則 較 錯 給 點 餘
对 欢 报 则 较 错 给 点 余

R -- Right portion simplified: (15)

傳 們 現 視 順 須 煩 項 慣 嗎 時 樣 極
传 们 现 视 顺 须 烦 项 惯 吗 时 样 极

腦 題
脑 题

T -- Top portion simplified: (15)

這 邊 還 過 遲 麼 電 帶 幫 學 興 問 間
这 边 还 过 迟 么 电 带 帮 学 兴 问 间

開 眞
开 真

B -- Bottom portion simplified: (8)

資 當 氣 會 廣 見 習 兩
资 当 气 会 广 见 习 两

W -- Whole character simplified: (24)

應 買 賣 錢 經 講 論 績 覺 樂 東 來 國
应 买 卖 钱 经 讲 论 绩 觉 乐 东 来 国

辦 從 寫 爲 無 幾 萬 個 並 後 甚
办 从 写 为 无 几 万 个 并 后 什

Notice the general look and the similarities. (84)

ABOUT THE AUTHOR

Allen S.C. Choi cultivated expert knowledge of linguistic education throughout his international career. With a deep understanding of both the art and science of language and critical cultural earmarks that distinguish populations worldwide, he became a sought-after translator and instructor. While many language-learning resources provide broad, spartan translations, Allen's in-depth approach reaches the heart of communication, addressing the importance of cultural understanding and regional nuance.

Fluent in English and four Chinese dialects, Allen has worked extensively throughout Asia and the United States, managing international legal, business, and governmental communication where there is little room for error. In these roles, he would go beyond simple translation to identifying strategies for comprehension across cultural divides. Bringing this learning-focused approach to English-speaking audiences, he has helped students worldwide Master written and spoken Chinese.

"*Mastering Mandarin: Your Path to Proficiency*" is the culmination of a lifetime of experience in translation and education. Born in Hong Kong, where he received a bi-lingual education, Allen would later come to the United States, where he earned his Master's degree at Oregon State University and became a member of the American Translators Association. Leveraging this foundation, Allen proudly presents this book to help others along the language learning path to lay the groundwork for greater global understanding and success.

Allen S.C. Choi

INDEX

THE 300 CHINESE CHARACTERS IN ALPHABETICAL ORDER

INDEX

THE 300 CHINESE CHARACTERS
IN ALPHABETICAL ORDER

(Simplified characters are added in parenthesis)

SPELLING	CHARACTER	MODULE	PRONUNCIATION	MEANING
A				
AN	安	M 16.2	AN_1	peaceful; calm
B				
BA	八	M 10.3	BA_1	eight
BA	把	M 11.1	BA_3	handle (noun)
BAI	白	M 7.2	BAI_2	white
BAI	百	M 10.2	BAI_3	hundred
BAN	半	M 8.2	BAN_4	half
BAN	辦 (办)	M 11.2	BAN_4	handle (verb)
BANG	幫 (帮)	M 13.2	$BANG_1$	help
BAO	報 (报)	M 5.1	BAO_4	newspaper; report
BEI	北	M 19.2	BEI_3	North
BI	比	M 16.3	BI_3	compare
BI	必	M 17.1	BI_4	must; certain
BIAN	邊 (边)	M 6.1	$BIAN_1$	edge; side
BIAN	便	M 8.3	$BIAN_4$	convenient
BIAO	表	M 17.1	$BIAO_3$	appearance; surface

Mastering Mandarin: Your Path to Proficiency

INDEX

BIE	別	M 11.2	BIE$_2$	different; don't
BING	並 (并)	M 5.2	BING$_4$	and; with
BU	不	M 1.3	BU$_4$	no; not
BU	步	M 16.3	BU$_4$	step

C

CAI	才	M 5.3	CAI$_2$	talent
CHANG	常	M 5.1	CHANG$_2$	often
CHENG	成	M 11.1	CHENG$_2$	become
CHI	遲 (迟)	M 13.1	CHI$_2$	being late
CHONG	(重) (cf. 重 ZHONG$_4$)	M 17.2	CHONG$_4$	repeat
CHU	出	M 2.3	CHU$_1$	out
CHU	初	M 16.3	CHU$_1$	preliminary
CHU	除	M 17.3	CHU$_2$	eliminate; divide
CHU	楚	M 14.2	CHU$_3$	neat
CHUAN	傳 (传)	M 15.2	CHUAN$_2$	pass
CI	此	M 16.1	CI$_3$	this; now
CI	次	M 8.1	CI$_4$	time
CONG	從 (从)	M 16.1	CONG$_2$	from
CUO	錯 (错)	M 17.3	CUO$_4$	wrong

D

DA	打	M 15.2	DA$_3$	strike; dozen
DA	大	M 1.2	DA$_4$	big; large
DAI	帶 (带)	M 19.1	DAI$_4$	bring; carry

DAN	但	M 16.1	DAN$_4$		but
DANG	當 (当)	M 12.3	DANG$_1$		when
DANG	(當)	M 12.3	DANG$_4$		treated as
DAO	到	M 9.3	DAO$_4$		arrive
DAO	道	M 7.3	DAO$_4$		doctrine
DE	得	M 9.2	DE$_2$		obtain
DE	的	M 6.2	DE, DE$_5$		of
DENG	等	M 14.1	DENG$_3$		wait
DI	地	M 7.1	DI$_4$		place
DIAN	點 (点)	M 8.2	DIAN$_3$		dot; bit
DIAN	電 (电)	M 15.3	DIAN$_4$		electricity
DING	定	M 13.1	DING$_4$		fixed; determine
DONG	東 (东)	M 19.1	DONG$_1$		East
DONG	懂	M 6.3	DONG$_3$		understand
DOU	都	M 4.2	DOU$_1$		also
DU	(都)	M 4.2	DU$_1$		capitol
DUI	對 (对)	M 7.3	DUI$_4$		correct; pair
DUO	多	M 5.3	DUO$_1$		many; a lot

E

ER	而	M 15.2	ER$_2$		but; also
ER	二	M 1.1	ER$_4$		two

F

FA	法	M 11.2	FA$_3$		method; law

FAN	煩 (烦)	M 18.1	FAN$_2$		trouble
FANG	方	M 8.3	FANG$_1$		square; direction
FANG	放	M 8.2	FANG$_4$		put
FEI	非	M 6.1	FEI$_1$		not
FEN	分	M 11.2	FEN$_1$		separate; distribute

G

GAI	該 (该)	M 11.3	GAI$_1$		should; which
GAO	高	M 12.3	GAO$_1$		tall; high
GAO	搞	M 9.2	GAO$_3$		do
GAO	告	M 15.1	GAO$_4$		tell; notify
GE	各	M 7.1	GE$_4$		each
GE	個 (个)	M 10.1	GE$_4$		piece; count
GEI	給	M 9.3	GEI$_3$		give
GONG	工	M 2.1	GONG$_1$		work
GONG	功	M 18.3	GONG$_1$		merit
GONG	公	M 15.1	GONG$_1$		official; public
GONG	共	M 10.2	GONG$_4$		total
GOU	夠	M 5.3	GOU$_4$		enough
GUAN	管	M 13.3	GUAN$_3$		manage; control
GUAN	慣 (惯)	M 5.1	GUAN$_4$		get used to
GUANG	光	M 17.3	GUANG$_1$		bright
GUANG	廣 (广)	M 12.2	GUANG$_3$		broad
GUO	國 (国)	M 4.2	GUO$_2$		nation; country

GUO	過 (过)	M 7.1	GUO₄		pass
H					
HAI	還 (还)	M 3.3	HAI₂		still
HANG	(行) (cf. XING 行 (M5.1))	M 11.2	HANG₂		branch office
HAO	好	M 1.3	HAO₃		good
HAO	(好)	M 1.3	HAO₄		like; fond of
HE	合	M 11.3	HE₂		together
HE	和	M 3.2	HE₂		and
HEN	很	M 1.3	HEN₃		very
HOU	候	M 14.1	HOU₄		wait
HOU	後 (后)	M 8.2	HOU₄		rear; after
HUA	話 (话)	M 12.2	HUA₄		words (said)
HUAN	歡 (欢)	M 20.2	HUAN₁		cheerful
HUAN	(還) (还)	M 3.3	HUAN₂		return
HUI	會 (会)	M 14.3	HUI₄		meeting
HUO	或	M 7.3	HUO₄		or
J					
JI	績 (绩)	M 18.3	JI₁		accomplishment
JI	及	M 13.3	JI₂		and
JI	即	M 13.2	JI₂		at is (i.e.)
JI	極 (极)	M 19.3	JI₂		extremely
JI	己	M 2.3	JI₃		self
JI	幾 (几)	M 9.1	JI₃		several

INDEX

JI	記 (记)	M 11.2	JI₄		record; remember
JIA	家	M 3.3	JIA₁		home
JIA	假	M 18.1	JIA₃		fake; false
JIA	(假)	M 18.1	JIA₄		holiday; vacation
JIAN	間 (间)	M 12.1	JIAN₁		between
JIAN	見 (见)	M 4.3	JIAN₄		see
JIAN	件	M 9.1	JIAN₄		piece
JIAN	建	M 18.3	JIAN₄		establish
JIANG	講 (讲)	M 12.3	JIANG₃		talk; speak
JIAO	交	M 14.3	JIAO₁		hand over
JIAO	較 (较)	M 16.3	JIAO₄		compare
JIAO	叫	M 4.3	JIAO₄		call
JIN	今	M 5.2	JIN₁		now; present
JING	經 (经)	M 7.1	JING₁		pass by
JIU	九	M 10.3	JIU₃		nine
JIU	就	M 5.1	JIU₄		toward
JUE	覺 (觉)	M 9.2	JUE₂		feel
JUE	決	M 13.1	JUE₂		decide

K

KAI	開 (开)	M 14.3	KAI₁		open
KAN	看	M 3.1	KAN₄		see
KAO	靠	M 13.3	KAO₄		rely; depend
KE	可	M 9.2	KE₃		may; can
KE	客	M 19.3	KE₄		guest; visitor

INDEX

KEN	肯	M 2.3	KEN₃	willing
KUAI	快	M 8.1	KUAI₄	fast; quick
KUANG	況	M 14.2	KUANG₄	condition; situation

L

LAI	來	M 3.1	LAI₂	come
LAO	老	M 20.1	LAO₃	old
LE	樂 (乐)	M 20.1	LE₄	joy (cf. YUE)
LI	理	M 13.3	LI₃	reason; logic
LI	裡	M 6.1	LI₃	location; inside
LI	立	M 13.2	LI₄	stand
LI	力	M 2.2	LI₄	strength; force
LI	利	M 20.3	LI₄	profit; benefit
LIANG	兩 (两)	M 12.1	LIANG₃	two; couple
LIANG	量	M 11.3	LIANG₂ LIANG₄	measure quantity
LIAO	了	M 4.2	LIAO₃ LE (LE₅)	end (indicates past / perfect tense)
LIU	六	M 10.1	LIU₄	six
LU	路	M 20.3	LU₄	road
LUN	論 (论)	M 9.3	LUN₄	discuss

M

MA	嗎 (吗)	M 1.3	MA(MA₅)	(question)
MA	麻	M 18.1	MA₂	jute
MAI	買 (买)	M 19.1	MAI₃	buy

INDEX

MAI	賣 (卖)	M 19.2	MAI$_4$	sell
MAN	慢	M 8.2	MAN$_4$	slow
MANG	忙	M 16.1	MANG$_2$	busy
ME	麼 (么)	M 6.3	ME(ME$_5$)	(question)
MEI	沒	M 5.2	MEI$_2$	not; without
MEI	每	M 8.1	MEI$_3$	each; every
MEI	美	M 4.1	MEI$_3$	pretty; beauty
MEN	們 (们)	M 3.2	MEN$_2$	(plural form of pronouns)
MIAN	面	M 8.1	MIAN$_4$	face; side
MING	明	M 7.2	MING$_2$	understand; clear
MU	目	M 10.1	MU$_4$	eye

N

NA	哪	M 6.2	NA$_3$	which; where
NA	那	M 6.1	NA$_4$	that
NAN	南	M 19.2	NAN$_2$	South
NAN	難 (难)	M 6.3	NAN$_2$ NAN$_4$	difficult disaster
NAN	男	M 20.1	NAN$_2$	male
NAO	腦 (脑)	M 15.3	NAO$_3$	brain
NEI	內	M 15.3	NEI$_4$	inside
NENG	能	M 18.3	NENG$_2$	able; can
NI	你	M 3.1	NI$_3$	you
NIN	您	M 3.3	NIN$_2$	you (respect)
NIAN	年	M 5.2	NIAN$_2$	year

NÜ (NYU)	女	M 20.1	NÜ₃		female

P

PA	怕	M 18.1	PA₄		afraid of; fear
PENG	朋	M 12.1	PENG₂		friend
PIN	拼	M 17.2	PIN₁		put together
PING	平	M 16.2	PING₂		flat

Q

QI	七	M 10.2	QI₁		seven
QI	其	M 14.3	QI₂		which; whose
QI	起	M 9.1	QI₃		up; raise
QI	氣 (气)	M 19.3	QI₄		gas; air
QIAN	千	M 10.3	QIAN₁		thousand
QIAN	前	M 8.1	QIAN₂		front
QIAN	錢 (钱)	M 19.1	QIAN₂		money
QIE	且	M 15.2	QIE₃		just; for the time being
QING	清	M 14.2	QING₁		clear
QING	情	M 14.2	QING₂		feeling; affection
QING	請 (请)	M 3.1	QING₃		invite; invite
QIU	求	M 16.1	QIU₂		request; beg
QU	去	M 4.2	QU₄		go
QUAN	全	M 7.2	QUAN₂		entire; whole

INDEX

R

RAN	然	M 12.3	RAN$_2$	however
REN	人	M 1.1	REN$_2$	person; human
RI	日	M 1.2	RI$_4$	day
RU	如	M 18.1	RU$_2$	such as; if
RU	入	M 2.3	RU$_4$	in

S

SAN	三	M 1.1	SAN$_1$	three
SHANG	商	M 11.3	SHANG$_1$	commerce
SHAO	少	M 5.3	SHAO$_3$ SHAO$_4$	less; little young
SHEN	甚 (什)	M 6.3	SHEN$_4$	very
SHENG	生	M 20.2	SHENG$_1$	live; alive
SHI	師 (师)	M 20.1	SHI$_1$	teacher
SHI	十	M 1.1	SHI$_2$	ten
SHI	時 (时)	M 13.3	SHI$_2$	time
SHI	使	M 16.3	SHI$_3$	send; make
SHI	事	M 9.1	SHI$_4$	matter; affair
SHI	是	M 1.3	SHI$_4$	yes; is
SHI	視 (视)	M 17.1	SHI$_4$	view; look
SHANG	上	M 2.1	SHANG$_4$	up
SHOU	手	M 2.2	SHOU$_3$	hand
SHUN	順 (顺)	M 20.3	SHUN$_4$	smooth in alignment
SHUO	說 (说)	M 3.3	SHUO$_1$	say

SI	司	M 15.1	SI$_1$		take charge
SI	思	M 14.2	SI$_1$		think
SI	四	M 11.1	SI$_4$		four
SUO	所	M 18.2	SUO$_3$		place

T

TA	他	M 3.2	TA$_1$	he, him
TA	她	M 3.2	TA$_1$	she, her
TAI	太	M 8.3	TAI$_4$	too; excessively
TAN	談 (谈)	M 12.2	TAN$_2$	talk; speak
TAO	討 (讨)	M 9.3	TAO$_3$	ask for; demand
TE	特	M 20.2	TE$_4$	specially
TI	提	M 9.3	TI$_2$	lift; mention
TI	題 (题)	M 12.2	TI$_2$	topic; subject
TIAN	天	M 1.2	TIAN$_1$	sky
TONG	通	M 15.3	TONG$_1$	through
TONG	同	M 6.2	TONG$_2$	same
TOU	投	M 10.3	TOU$_2$	throw
TU	途	M 20.3	TU$_2$	way; trip

W

WAI	外	M 15.3	WAI$_4$	outside
WAN	完	M 7.2	WAN$_2$	end; finish
WAN	晚	M 16.2	WAN$_3$	evening; late
WAN	萬 (万)	M 10.2	WAN$_4$	ten thousand

INDEX

WEI	未	M 17.3	WEI$_4$	not yet
WEI	謂 (谓)	M 18.2	WEI$_4$	say; call
WEI	爲 (为)	M 6.3	WEI$_4$ WEI$_2$	for do; is
WEN	文	M 4.1	WEN$_2$	language
WEN	問 (问)	M 3.2	WEN$_4$	ask
WO	我	M 3.1	WO$_3$	I; me
WO	握	M 11.1	WO$_4$	grasp; hold
WU	無 (无)	M 18.2	WU$_2$	no; without
WU	五	M 10.1	WU$_3$	five
WU	午	M 2.1	WU$_3$	noon
WU	誤 (误)	M 17.3	WU$_4$	error

X

XI	西	M 19.1	XI$_1$	West
XI	習 (习)	M 4.1	XI$_2$	practice
XI	喜	M 20.2	XI$_3$	happy; joy
XIA	下	M 2.1	XIA$_4$	down
XIAN	先	M 20.2	XIAN$_1$	first
XIAN	現 (现)	M 17.1	XIAN$_4$	now
XIANG	相	M 6.2	XIANG$_1$	one another; each other
XIANG	想	M 9.1	XIANG$_3$	think
XIANG	項 (项)	M 10.1	XIANG$_4$	item
XIANG	向	M 15.1	XIANG$_4$	face; direction
XIAO	小	M 1.2	XIAO$_3$	little; small

INDEX

XIE	些	M 6.2	XIE$_1$	some
XIE	寫 (写)	M 14.2	XIE$_3$	write
XIE	謝 (谢)	M 4.3	XIE$_4$	thank
XIN	心	M 7.2	XIN$_1$	heart; mind
XIN	信	M 14.1	XIN$_4$	letter
XING	行 (cf. HANG 行 M11.2))	M 5.1	XING$_2$	fine; walk
XING	(興)	M 12.3	XING$_1$	rise
XING	興 (兴)	M 12.3	XING$_4$	excitement
XU	需	M 13.2	XU$_1$	need
XU	須 (须)	M 17.1	XU$_1$	must
XUE	學 (学)	M 4.1	XUE$_2$	learn; study

Y

YAN	言	M 19.3	YAN$_2$	word; speech
YANG	樣 (样)	M 18.2	YANG$_4$	appearance
YAO	要	M 5.3	YAO$_4$	want
YE	也	M 12.2	YE$_3$	also
YI	一	M 1.1	YI$_1$	one
YI	以	M 9.2	YI$_3$	use; with
YI	已	M 7.1	YI$_3$	already
YI	意	M 14.1	YI$_4$	opinion; idea
YIN	因	M 8.3	YIN$_1$	because
YIN	音	M 17.2	YIN$_1$	sound
YING	應 (应)	M 11.3	YING$_1$	ought to

YING	英	M 4.1	YING₁		English
YONG	用	M 2.2	YONG₄		use
YOU	由	M 13.1	YOU₂		from; since
YOU	有	M 5.2	YOU₃		have; possess
YOU	友	M 12.1	YOU₃		friend
YOU	右	M 2.2	YOU₄		right side
YOU	又	M 4.3	YOU₄		again
YU	於	M 13.1	YU₂		at
YU	餘 (余)	M 14.3	YU₂		extra
YU	語 (语)	M 19.3	YU₃		language
YUAN	元	M 10.2	YUAN₂		dollar; first
YUAN	原	M 8.3	YUAN₂		original
YUE	月	M 1.2	YUE₄		month
YUE	(樂) (乐) (cf. LE₄ 樂 (乐) (M20.1))	M 20.1	YUE₄		music

Z

ZAI	再	M 4.3	ZAI₄		again
ZAI	在	M 3.3	ZAI₄		at
ZAO	早	M 16.2	ZAO₃		morning; early
ZE	則 (则)	M 19.2	ZE₂		then; rule
ZEN	怎	M 18.3	ZEN₃		why; how
ZHE	者	M 7.3	ZHE₃		that; which
ZHE	這 (这)	M 6.1	ZHE₄		this
ZHEN	眞 (真)	M 15.2	ZHEN₁		real; true

INDEX

ZHI	之	M 12.1	ZHI₁	that; which
ZHI	知	M 7.3	ZHI₁	know
ZHI	只	M 11.1	ZHI₃	only
ZHI	至	M 16.2	ZHI₄	to
ZHONG	中	M 4.1	ZHONG₁	central; China
ZHONG	重 (cf. (重) CHONG₂)	M 17.2	ZHONG₄	heavy
ZHU	注	M 17.2	ZHU₄	note
ZHU	祝	M 20.3	ZHU₄	wish congratulate
ZHU	助	M 13.2	ZHU₄	help; assist
ZI	資 (资)	M 10.3	ZI₁	capital
ZI	子	M 18.2	ZI₃, ZI	son
ZI	字	M 17.2	ZI₄	character; word
ZI	自	M 2.3	ZI₄	self; from
ZOU	走	M 19.2	ZOU₃	go; walk
ZUO	左	M 2.2	ZUO₃	left side
ZUO	作	M 2.1	ZUO₄	do
ZUO	做	M 5.1	ZUO₄	do; make

www.ingramcontent.com/pod-product-compliance
Lightning Source LLC
Chambersburg PA
CBHW070603170426
43200CB00012B/2581